SEWING
MADE SIMPLE

SEWING
MADE SIMPLE

THE DEFINITIVE GUIDE TO
HAND AND MACHINE SEWING

TESSA EVELEGH

with photography by Michael Wicks

CHRONICLE BOOKS

SAN FRANCISCO

First published in the United States in 2012
by Chronicle Books LLC.

First published in 2012 by Jacqui Small LLP,
an imprint of Aurum Press Ltd.
7 Greenland Street
London NW1 0ND

Library of Congress Cataloging-in-Publication Data available.
ISBN: 978-1-4521-0630-4

Manufactured in Singapore

10 9 8 7 6 5 4 3 2 1

Chronicle Books LLC
680 Second Street
San Francisco, California 94107
www.chroniclebooks.com

contents

6 INTRODUCTION
8 for the love of sewing

12 THE SEWING BOX
14 tools of the trade
21 notions: putting it together
25 notions: fastening it
30 notions: trimming it

36 THE SECRETS OF SEWING-MACHINE SUCCESS
38 sewing-machine anatomy
42 starting off

44 STITCH CRAFT
46 essential stitches

50 THE PAPER PATTERN
52 the envelope inside and out
54 taking measurements
56 using the pattern
62 pattern marking

64 FABRIC CHOICES
66 a buyer's guide
70 fabric weave
72 patterned fabric
74 cotton
76 linen
78 silk
80 wool
82 synthetic fibers and mixed-fiber fabrics
84 fabric glossary

88 BASIC SEWING SKILLS
90 getting started
91 seams
95 seam finishes
98 pressing
100 swedish shade
104 tote bag
107 enclosed seams
110 pajama pants
113 shaping and contouring: darts
116 camisole
120 gathering and easing
123 sweetest sundress
126 classic drapes
129 fastenings
134 travel kit
140 tailored pillow
149 drawstring bag
152 trimmings
156 bolster
163 customized T-shirt
164 vintage apron
169 pretty pillow
172 embellishments
175 evening purse
177 appliqué
179 child's craft apron
184 the perfect finish
188 bias-cut skirt
192 box cushion
196 mitered corners
198 tablecloth and napkins
200 place mats
203 quilting
208 baby quilt

212 PATTERNS AND TEMPLATES
222 INDEX
224 SUPPLIERS
224 ACKNOWLEDGMENTS

INTRODUCTION

From sewing basic seams, to mastering appliqué methods and inserting zippers, this is the book that gives you all the information you need, in plain and simple terms, for ultimate sewing success. Even if you start out thinking you can't sew, once you have learned the basic skills and are armed with the sewing-machine know-how contained in these pages, you could be surprised at how quickly you will be able to whip up something that looks very professional, from simple skirts and dresses to pillows and drapes.

for the love of sewing

I always get a frisson of satisfaction when I see my chosen fabrics and trimmings folded up together on the shop counter and ready to go. This is the point when I can really visualize what I am going to make and it is totally unique, totally me.

There is also great satisfaction that, by this stage, all the major design decisions have been made and I just can't wait to get on with the making. It is the same thrill I had as a little girl, making clothes for my dolls, usually cut from my mother's old broderie anglaise petticoats and retro skirts and trimmed with something pretty from her button box. Nowadays, the project is more likely to be a shade, drapes, or cute pillow covers to perk up the home; bridesmaids' dresses, costumes for a school production, or something gorgeous to wear.

GETTING STARTED

Sewing is immensely satisfying, doesn't have to be difficult, and, certainly when it comes to home furnishings, can save you money. Yet so many people nowadays don't believe they can do it. Even if you have never threaded a needle and don't know one end of a machine from another, between these pages you will find all you need to know to make almost anything. The mysteries of the workings of sewing machines will be unlocked, you will have a roadmap to help you make the best use of paper patterns, and you will have all the basic sewing skills at your fingertips. These are not clogged up with how to insert every kind of sleeve or attach every cuff, because too much information can be daunting. But to do all of these things, you will need to know how to match seams, how to gather, how to ease,

left Almost any box with compartments can be used to house all your sewing equipment. This old mini trunk, with a removable top tray, is both pretty and practical. A not-quite-so-pretty, but undeniably practical, alternative would be a regular toolbox.

opposite, clockwise from top left Ribbons offer plenty of scope when it comes to pretty trimmings. **Thimbles** make for more comfortable and speedy hand-sewing. **Stripy thread** can be used to hand-stitch decorative borders. **Pretty vintage buttons** can be reused again and again to bring an individual feel to simple garments. **Pins** come in several sizes—dressmaker's pins are the most useful; bridal or lace pins are the finest.

left Pearl-headed pins are easier on the fingertips, are often longer than regular pins, and can be more easily seen in your work.

below The turned-up tips of some embroidery scissors make it much easier to snip threads in awkward corners.

opposite Old buttons look so pretty stored in glass jars, they can be used as a decorative detail on the sewing room shelf.

above Don't forget to add thread in the right shades to your shopping basket when you are buying fabric. Make sure it is the right type of thread for the job and check the length on the spool.

right Many dressmaker's tapes are marked with imperial calibrations on one side and metric on the other.

and how to fit. These are the skills that are explained here. Then, if you can use a commercial paper pattern, you should be able to create almost any design.

The key to early success is not to be too ambitious. Sewing, like any skill, improves with experience. If you feel confident only sewing straight seams, choose to make something that only requires straight seams. This isn't as limiting as it seems. Most drapes, shades, and pillows can be made entirely using straight seams.

SMART, EASY-TO-STITCH PROJECTS

To give you hands-on experience, "Basic Sewing Skills" (pages 88–211) is interspersed with 20 easy-to-stitch projects. You will be able to make lined drapes using gathering tape, simple shades, and several kinds of pillows. Then there is a simple quilt to give you a primer on basic patchwork and quiltmaking skills.

I've included several garments, not only to showcase various techniques, but to give an idea of what constitutes a simple-to-sew design. A bias-cut drawstring skirt, for example, is an excellent beginner's project, as it is made stitching only straight seams and there are no fussy bits like zippers or darts. Bias-cut skirts are a classic design, but this one is updated by the choice of fabric and detailing; the grosgrain braid trimming also makes for a simpler hemline than applying bias binding. Sleeves can be a challenge, so the only project with sleeves is the child's craft apron, which features super-simple raglan sleeves.

Even if you don't want to sew a garment from scratch, you may want to adapt one—for example, by cutting a different neckline or adding a new detail. The customized T-shirt shows how a few frills and a vat of dye can be be used to reinvent your clothes.

KEEP IT CLEAN

The secret to achieving a professional finish is to cut and match the pieces accurately, and keep your work neat at all times. Dangling threads are likely to get caught up and less-than-flat fabric on the flat bed is just waiting to get stitched up in the seam. Aim to make the inside as neat as the outside and you will get a much better finished result.

Clever fabric choices make a design stand out. Some fabric stores stock remnant rolls from designers, so you can make really classy garments at a fraction of the cost. Always assess the weight and drape of fabric as well as its pattern and color, then choose buttons and trims that you love to make your creation unique.

THE
SEWING
BOX

Well-stocked sewing boxes hold huge appeal with their rainbow rows of threads, ranks of needles, boxes of pins and buttons, curls of ribbon and braid, scissors for snipping, and endless other delights. Best of all, with the right tools at hand, it is so much easier to efficiently get on with any job. But which tools to choose? Good notions and craft stores offer a dizzying range of choices. This chapter unravels what you really need for the projects you want to tackle.

tools of the trade

NEEDLES AND PINS

However similar all the different needles and pins might look, choosing the right one for the job really does make a difference for the ease, speed, and quality of your work. It might be obvious that you wouldn't be able to thread a beading needle with darning yarn, but most choices are far more subtle. Keep pins in a pincushion and needles in a needlecase. Not only will they be more ordered and easy to find, but rattling around together in a box, they can become blunted and less efficient. Here are the types of needles and pins that you are likely to find most useful and why.

1. Beading needles have small eyes and are fine enough to ensure that both needle and thread can pass easily though the hole in the bead. Use short, easy-to-manage beading needles for sewing on little beads, such as rocailles (seed beads), sequins, and bugles. For larger beads and for bead weaving, you will need very long, fine needles. Beading needles are very bendy and delicate, so they should be kept separately from other needles, preferably wrapped in tissue paper. By contrast, upholstery requires the sturdiest of needles, many of which are straight and some of which, such as mattress needles, are very long, so that they can pass through a mattress or upholstery for button-backing. This **sturdy curved needle** is also for upholstery, designed to be able to work through the corners and hard-to-reach areas of stuffed cushions and tightly covered upholstery. **2. Pins** with pearl heads are easy to see in your work, longer than regular pins, and easy on the fingertips. The even longer white-headed pins are quilter's pins, designed to work through multiple layers of fabrics. Regular pins come next, but even they come with a choice. These are dressmaker's pins: extra-fine and easy to use, they are the professional's favorite. There are other pins that look much the same

as these, such as sturdier household pins, which are more robust, and lace or bridal pins, which are the finest, designed for use with delicate fabrics. Tiny sequin (or craft) pins are about half the length of regular pins and are used for pinning sequins or beads into polystyrene shapes to make decorations and ornaments. Safety pins are available in a variety of sizes and are useful for turning narrow ties through to the right side. **3. Darning needles** are sturdy with large, easy-to-thread eyes. They are long with sharp points to make fast work of the weaving action of darning over a hole. Tapestry needles are similar to darning needles, but have blunt ends. **4. Sharps** are general-purpose needles: robust with round, easy-to-thread eyes. Available in sizes 1–12, you will be able to tackle most jobs with sizes 6–9. **5. Betweens** are short and fine needles with small, round eyes; they are favored by quilters as they make easy work of small, neat hand-stitches. **6. Ballpoint needles** have a tiny ballpoint tip and are ideal for working with fabrics such as tulle, where a sharp point is not needed. They are easier on the fingertips, so you can work faster. **7. Crewel or embroidery needles** are long and have oval eyes for the easy threading of stranded threads (floss).

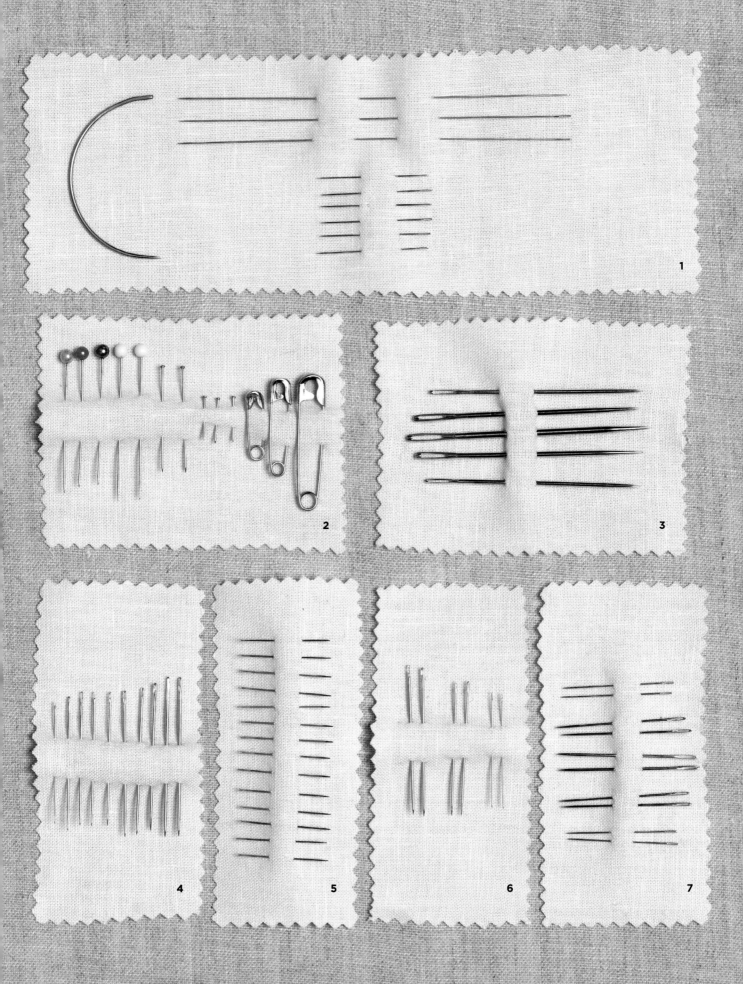

CUTTING AND SNIPPING

When it comes to cutting, invest in the best. It is not only irritating struggling with blunt scissors to induce them to make clean cuts, but it also makes a difference to the finished work: fabric pieces that have been cut out neatly are the easiest to seam together accurately. Top-quality scissors should feel comfortable in your hand—try them out to check that you can open the blades fully in order to make clean cuts. Feel their weight and balance. If they are properly and ergonomically designed, you won't struggle to find a comfortable angle for cutting.

1. Dressmaker's shears should have handles that bend upward so that the blades can sit flat along the surface as you cut. This steadies the blades and keeps your hands clear of the surface for better control. The top handle has room for just your thumb, and a stop to take the pressure off the closing blades, while the bottom handle provides comfortable space for the rest of your hand. Good-quality shears can be resharpened, will last for decades, and can become a dressmaker's most treasured tool. Guard them jealously from the rest of the family and keep them only for cutting fabric to save them from blunting. Keep a pair of general household scissors alongside them for cutting out the paper pattern pieces. **2. Spring-loaded scissors** take the strain from cutting out, operating in the opposite way to most scissors. The spring opens the blade: you just squeeze to cut and then relax to release. The little orange button on these is a lock—for safety, always slide it shut when the scissors are not in use. Spring-loaded scissors may seem to be the answer for a weary dressmaker at the cutting-out stage, but in reality they are not as robust as the classic shears: drop them on the floor too many times and the spring gets damaged.

3. Thread snippers are another spring-loaded tool. They are ergonomically designed so that when you slip your thumb in the thumbhole, your hand automatically wraps around them, almost making the scissor blades part of your hand. Just because threads are small, don't underestimate the comfort of using a properly weighted tool, such as this one. The weight aids the cutting action. **4. Pinking shears** have zigzag blades that cut an attractive edge with reduced fraying. This is the quickest way to finish seams. They can also be used to make a decorative edge on fray-free fabrics, such as felt. However, they are heavy and quite stiff to use, so take a rest part of the way through the job, if you need to, to avoid hand-strain. **5. Embroidery scissors** are small and light for precision cutting of even the smallest threads. Some, like these, have curved blades that can get close to the fabric surface even in tight corners. Try them out before you buy. They should open and close very easily with no stiffness. **6. Rotary cutter:** This is designed to be used in conjunction with a self-healing mat and a straight edge for the precise cutting of patchwork pieces. A rotary cutter is also invaluable for cutting bias strips.

MEASURING AND MARKING

Every dressmaker benefits from the carpenter's mantra: measure twice, cut once. The more precise you are with measurements and marking, the better the pieces will fit together and the better the final finish will be. At its most basic, you could limit yourself to a kit of the tailor's classic trio: a roll-up measuring tape, which you can hang around your neck, a needle and thread for marking the pattern pieces with tailor's tacks, and some tailor's chalk for marking adjustments. But there is some more up-to-date equipment to help speed up the job. Dressmaker's dot-and-cross pattern-making paper, marked with regular dots and crosses, is also useful if you want to cut your own patterns or templates.

1. Retractable tape neatly stores itself away, so there is no irritating tangling up in the sewing box. However, for accuracy, you will also need the classic roll-up dressmaker's measuring tape, which is made of a coated closely woven cloth to prevent any stretching. **2. Fabric pencil** for fine marking onto fabric. The markings from this pencil can be gently rubbed off or laundered. **3. Water- or air-soluble pen** can be used lightly to mark fabric. The marks will either vanish as it dries, or dissolve when sprayed with water. Not suitable for fabrics that are easily watermarked, such as silk.

4. Rotary marker is used in conjunction with dressmaker's carbon (see 6) to transfer markings from paper pattern pieces onto layers of fabric. Run the wheel over the pattern lines and markings and its spikes will make an impression on the carbon papers slid between the layers of fabric, marking the fabric beneath with dotted lines. **5. Sewing gauge,** with its slider marker, is invaluable for accurate details. Use it to measure up hemlines and casing positions and to check seam allowances. The pointed end is brilliant for pushing out sharp corners once you have turned your work through to the right side. **6. Dressmaker's carbon paper**

is used with the rotary marker (see 4). Test it on a scrap of fabric first, as it doesn't remove easily from all fabrics, then choose a color that provides a faint contrast to the fabric and use it on the wrong side of the fabric. **7. Tailor's chalk** easily marks and easily brushes off most fabrics. The sharpener both keeps the chalk clean and retains its fine edge. **8. Gridded ruler:** This is translucent, wider than average, and marked with parallel lines to make light work of marking and cutting straight edges and accurate corners. Diagonal lines at different angles make for precise mitering and bias cutting. Designed for quilters, it is nevertheless an invaluable tool for cutting bias, marking hem turnings, and endless other sewing projects. **9. Self-healing cutting mat**, which is marked out in inch or centimeter increments, is primarily a protective surface for rotary cutting or for using a craft knife. **10. Triangular tailor's chalk** has slightly curved sides for ease of use and more accurate marking. Available in a variety of colors, yellow is a handy hue in that it shows well against both dark and pale fabrics. **11. Tailor's tacks** are also known as thread marking. All you need to make them are a needle, thread, and a little know-how (see page 63).

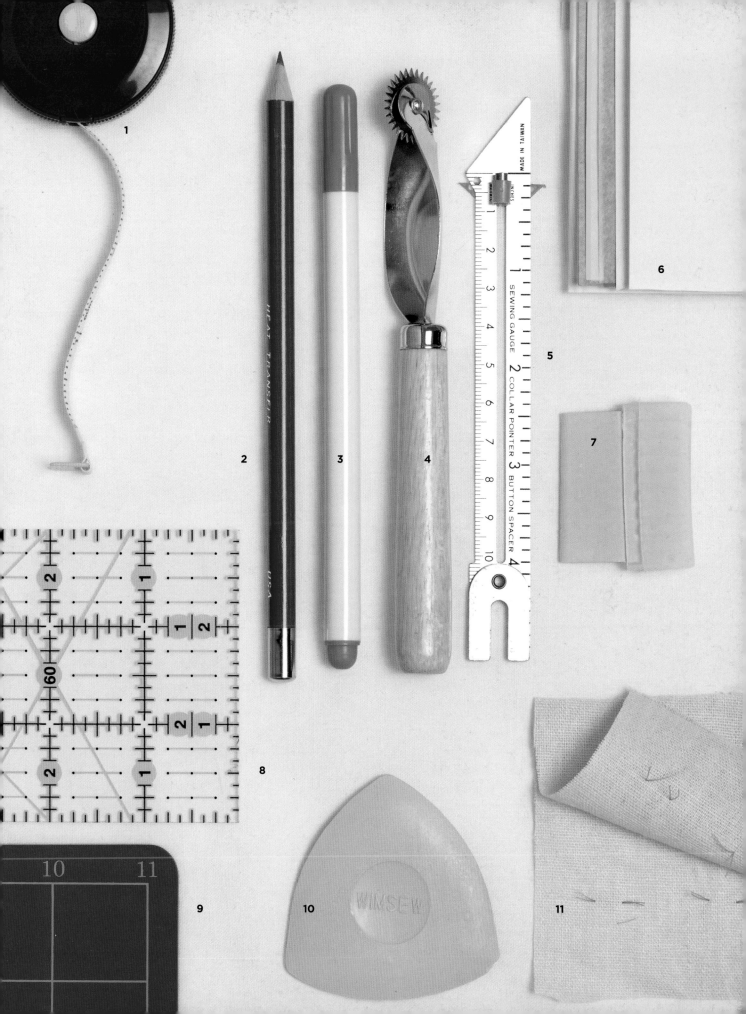

1

2

HEAT TRANSFER

USA

3

4

SEWING GAUGE

COLLAR POINTER

BUTTON SPACER

MADE IN TAIWAN

INCHES

5

6

7

8

9

10

WINSEW

11

notions: putting it together

THREAD

Sewing boxes used to be filled mainly with wooden cotton spools wound with a rainbow of tempting colors. Things are a little more complicated now, with the introduction of synthetic fibers as well as different machines, such as interlockers, which require different threads on different spools. We still have cotton, but there are also threads designed specifically for sewing synthetics, jeans, upholstery, linens, and for machine embroidery. The choice can be dizzying. These four are the types you will find most useful.

Topstitch This is a strong, thick thread that adds to the decorative appeal of topstitching. It can be made of any fiber, such as cotton or linen, but nowadays, it is often made from polyester for ease of use and durability. Use it with the stitch set to long on the sewing machine for best effect.

Viscose This silky, shiny thread is used for machine embroidery to great effect. Use it with a loose top tension of 2.5 or 3 and stabilize the fabric by using interfacing on the wrong side. Highly decorative, it is also remarkably strong and prone to few breakages, resulting in faster and neater work.

Polyester This is the most useful all-purpose thread for machine- and hand-sewing, combining the fine sewing qualities of silk with the extra "give" and strength of polyester. It is less likely to tangle than other threads and can be used on natural and synthetic fabrics. It can be washed and ironed at a hot temperature, but it won't absorb dye.

Cotton Traditional cotton is the all-purpose thread loved by generations. Fine yet strong, it withstands hot washing and ironing temperatures. Cotton absorbs dye well, so if you plan to dye your project, this is the thread to use. The best cotton threads are mercerized to give them added strength and luster.

SECRET FASTENINGS AND ELASTICS

There are many hidden secrets to sewing success, including some fastenings, which don't shout about the part they play. The elegance of a particular design may rely upon the absence of embellishment that some fastenings, such as buttons, contribute. Or, sometimes, the "fastening," such as elastic, isn't so much a fastening as a stretchy means of getting in and out of the garment. There is a wide range of available elastics, some of which like to put themselves on show.

1. Hook-and-loop tape (or Velcro) can be used as a fastening, generally replacing a zipper, or as a way to fix shades to battens at the window. Whereas zippers are sometimes exposed as part of the design, hook-and-loop tape is invariably hidden. It is available in three forms: sew and sew, where both parts can be stitched to fabric—for all sewing projects; stick and sew, where one part can be stuck to wood and the other part stitched to fabric—the best choice for putting up shades; and stick and stick, which is more of a do-it-yourself product. All types are available in black or white in a variety of widths. Hooks and loops are extraordinarily strong: they won't lose grip due to strain, as long as you keep the hook section clean and free from fluff. **2. Hook-and-eye tape** was originally developed for corsetry, as tiny hooks give discreet strength. As with a zipper, it may also be revealed, rather than concealed. **3. Hook-and-loop dots** are available in the same variety as the tape (see 1) and work in the same way, but in some cases the smaller dots are easier to use than long strips.

4. Wide elastic is not usually inserted into a casing. It is more likely to be stitched directly onto the fabric while it is fully stretched, and then, when it springs back, it will naturally gather the piece. **5. Narrow elastic** is usually threaded into a casing, which is a channel made in the item specifically for this purpose. **6. General-purpose elastic** comes in a limited range of colors. **7. Sequin-embellished elastic** is a pretty, sparkly show-off, designed to be surface-stitched to party garments. **8. Button elastic** is a lifesaver for those of us with expanding waistlines; it is especially useful during pregnancy. Stitch it in place of a waistband buttonhole. **9 and 10. Revealed elastic** in pretty colors and with pretty edgings looks good when surface-stitched. **11. Extra strength** in the black core could make this elastic uncomfortable without the support of the wider white sections.

below This pretty frill-edged elastic is designed to be surface-stitched to the garment for delightful detailing that is also practical.

notions: fastening it

BUTTONS

An easy and practical form of fastening, buttons can also be an integral part of the design—even a major feature. As well as the material they are made from, decisions need to be made as to their color, size, shape, how many to use, and even how they are positioned on a garment.

OPPOSITE 1. Tiny shell buttons reflect light and look delightful arranged in lines on a cuff or dress. **2. Toggles** were originally made of horn, hence their shape. Associated with heavy outerwear, they can also be used to make a statement on smarter items. **3. Small shell buttons** have great charm, even in their packaging. Imagine these from neck to waist on an evening dress, buttoned into rouleaux loops. **4. Special shapes** are appealing for children. The Scottie dog, daisy, and tiny square are made from shell, while the delicate butterfly has been carved from wood. **5. Printing** adds an extra element to buttons of many materials. This printed shell button has a floral design. **6. White-painted metal** with an irregular outline gives a subtle contemporary edge. **7. Faux horn**, such as this plastic version, lends a traditional utility feel to any garment. **8. Big buttons** don't have to be confined to coats. This shiny purple shell button would make a statement on any item. **9. A "specimen" button**, such as this irregular two-layer metal one, can be positioned off-center as a feature. Try buttons near the top of a placket, to the left or the right. **10. Mismatched buttons** make a charming alternative to a peas-in-a-pod arrangement. The trick is to choose the same size but be flexible with shape and color. **11. Off-white round shell buttons** are the traditional choice for

smart shirts and look delightful on most garments. **12. Self-cover buttons** are available in kits from craft or notions stores and enable you to make the perfect match. **13. Brightly colored buttons** bring life to more subdued garments.

BELOW 1. Translucent acrylic can be molded into bold designs, like this vintage example. **2. Covered buttons** are easy to make using the fabric of the garment. **3. Ceramic buttons** can be glazed with intense colors. **4. Faux horn** gives this toggle a traditional look. **5. Plastic** offers ultimate flexibility in color and texture. This ikat-style design is a classy example. **6. Fabric buttons** often incorporate a coiled braid design, such as this classic coat button. **7. Metal jeans buttons** are attached using a riveter for workwear styling. **8. Glass** is expensive, but adds sparkle to eveningwear. **9. Horn** has a translucency that is difficult to match in plastic. **10. Leather** is a classic choice for men's outerwear. **11. Brass buttons** inspire a military feel. **12. Metal**, with its light-reflecting neutral tones, looks great on any garment. **13. Wood** can be carved into interesting shapes, such as this leaf. **14. Shell** and more expensive mother-of-pearl give a classy finish. **15. Plastic** comes in unlimited colors and shapes. **16. Dyed wood** combines color and pattern with the appeal of a natural material.

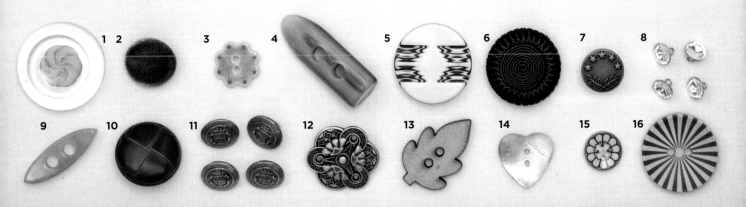

ZIPPERS

Long openings in garments of all kinds—indoor or outdoor, for children or adults—can be fastened with zippers. They are also used for bags, seat cushions, luggage, even tents. Some zippers are designed to be hidden or disguised within the garment; others prefer to be shown off as one of the design features. Originally, all zippers were made up of two rows of teeth with a slider that opened them up and locked them together. Nowadays, some have "coils" instead of teeth, which work in a similar way on a finer basis.

1. Robust zippers with nylon teeth are designed to be showy and part of the overall design of an item. This one was used for the travel kit (see page 134), both contributing to the design and because the large nylon teeth are easy to open and deal happily with any dampness. **2. "Nylon" zippers** nowadays are made of polyester, although they are still referred to as "nylon." They have fine coils that interlock instead of teeth. Smaller and neater than metal teeth, they can also be made in any color, and so "disappear" against the tapes. **3. Metal zippers** have showy teeth and are often used for a design statement, where an exposed zipper is required. **4. Invisible zippers** have coils that are tucked behind, rather than between, the tapes. When sewn in position, typically on skirts and dresses, they sit behind the seam with only the pull on view. Invisible zippers are also used widely for home furnishings,

such as on cushion or bolster covers. Once inserted, all you can see is the seam, giving an incredibly neat finish. However, they can be fussy to fit and you need a special invisible-zipper foot to enable you to do so easily and efficiently. All makes of sewing machine do their own version, which is well worth the investment. **5, 6 and 7. Nylon zippers** are available in a rainbow of colors. With neat matching coils instead of teeth, these have replaced metal zippers as the dressmaker's most popular choice.
8. Open-ended zippers are used for coats, jackets, cardigans, and, commercially, for some outdoor items such as camping equipment. The two pieces can be parted or slotted together ready for closing. Being able to part the two sides along their full length makes these the easiest zippers to fit.

below Zippers by the yard can be bought to any length with one slider per yard. They are useful when you need long zipper lengths, such as for upholstery projects like sofa or seat covers.

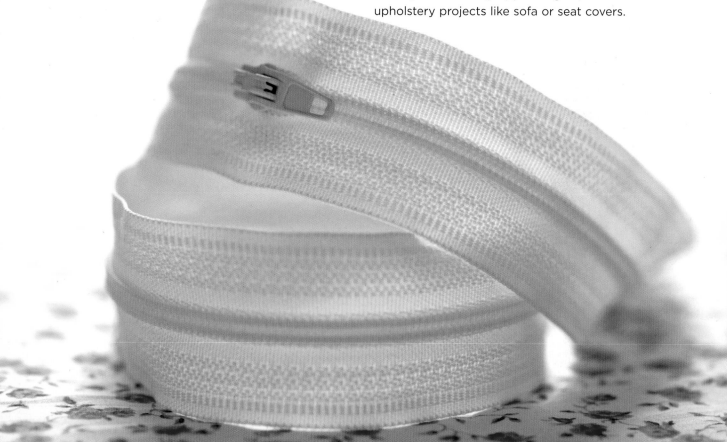

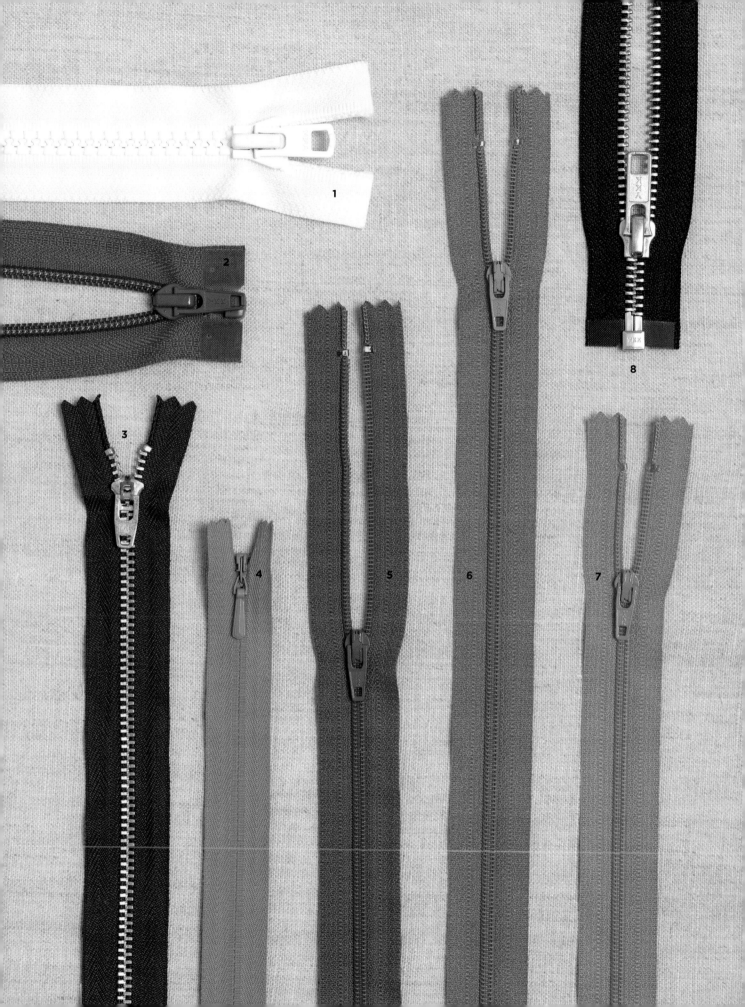

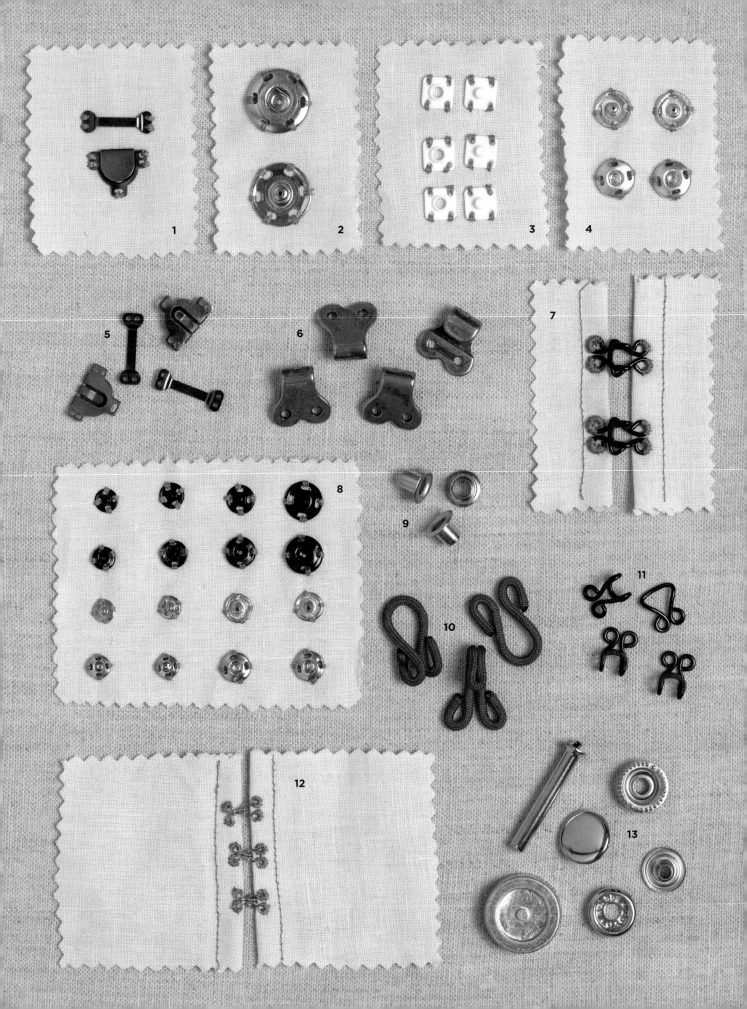

SNAPS, STUDS, AND HOOKS AND EYES

Generally designed to be discreet closures, snaps, studs, and hooks and eyes are mainly used to secure and add strength to the top of a closure where it takes most of the strain. Hooks and eyes can take more strain than these other types of fastenings, so they are generally used for waistbands on skirts and pants. Smaller snaps are used to fix the corner of a garment in position, for example, to stop it flapping about. Scaled up in size, both hooks and eyes and snaps can be promoted to take on the role of design statement, as a front fastening, for instance.

1. Pant and skirt hooks are designed to be flat, both to keep them discreet and for comfort. They have to be robust as even the slimmest of waistlines take plenty of strain with bending and stretching (see also 5). **2. Large snaps** such as this one are used for robust outdoor garments. They are designed to be discreet, so you need to ensure that the stitching does not show on the front of the garment. For this reason, this type of fastening is often used where there is a flap in front of the placket to give a neat, embellishment-free finish. **3. Flat plastic snaps** make neat closures. This is the type normally chosen for bedding: to close comforter covers, for example. They are quick to pull open when changing the sheets and will not be damaged by frequent machine-washing. **4. Brass snaps** are a good choice for garments made of fabrics that include gold-colored metallic fibers. **5. Pant and skirt hooks** are designed to securely hook into the bars, yet be easy to unhook. This is the underside view of the hooks above (see 1), showing the mechanism whereby this is made possible. **6. Beautiful metal hooks** with a polished finish are designed to make a statement. Try them down the full closure of a robust garment. **7. Pretty black hooks** can either be used discreetly or revealed corset-style where two edges meet. These are slightly bigger than regular hooks and so can make more of a statement (see also 11). **8. Snaps** come in a wide variety of sizes, suitable for use with every kind of fabric from the finest bridal silk to the heaviest canvas. Metal is the most common material for snaps and they are generally available in a nickel or a black finish. **9. Eyelets** are needed for garments that are fastened by lacing. They are inserted using special pliers, piercing the fabric as they go in. Buy both pliers and eyelets at a notions store. **10. Fur hooks and eyes** are for use with fur coats or knitwear. They are bound in braid to prevent damage and to tone with the garment. **11. Decorative hooks and eyes** have a delightful handmade quality (see 7). **12. Tiny hooks** have remarkable strength and are often used at the top of dress zippers. **13. No-sew press studs** are supplied with simple tools so that they can be riveted into place. Shown here is the two-part tool alongside the four elements that make up the two parts of a riveted press stud. They are a striking choice for all-weather outdoor garments.

notions: trimming it

FRINGES, FRILLS, AND BRAIDS

Trimmings are to fabric what seasoning, spices, and herbs are to food. They add the flavor and detail that make your project special. Fringes, frills, and piping are designed to be stitched between two pieces of fabric, so that they peek out from the seam. Braids, on the other hand, should be surface-mounted. Because trimmings are relatively small, you can afford to be brave with the color and that will define the personality of your project. Keep the colors tonal and it will look elegant, discreet. Add a strong contrast hue, and you will have an altogether more extrovert result.

1. Beaded fringing, especially in a metallic tone such as this coppery look, evokes the Roaring Twenties and flapper-style dresses. **2. Golden-toned braid** lends an opulent Victorian feel, bringing a richness to any project. **3. Pom-pom trim** is fun and flirty. The braid part of the trim should be stitched into the seam, leaving only the pom-poms peeking out. **4. Fringes** don't have to be flashy. This one, in tones of taupe and white cotton, has a smart, natural, country feel. **5. Narrow braid** can have a surprising influence on the look of a project because the smaller the accent, the stronger the colors can afford to be. This one, in bright fuchsia with a turquoise picot edge, will add zing to many color schemes.

6. Big pom-pom trim adds extrovert personality to pillows and other furnishings. **7. Beaded trims** come in a wide choice of colors and styles. The satin ribbon base allows it to be surface-mounted or stitched into a seam. **8. Feather trims** add a natural soft touch. **9. Rickrack** brings a lively vintage feel to any project. Apply just one row or layer up several colors. You can even mix sizes, perhaps using a wider rickrack between two narrower pieces. **10. Spotty chiffon roses** make a flamboyant yet elegant trim. Mounted on net, they can be stitched into a seam.

below Cotton lace braid can be used both for surface decoration and as an edging.

1

2

3

4

5

6

7

8

9

10

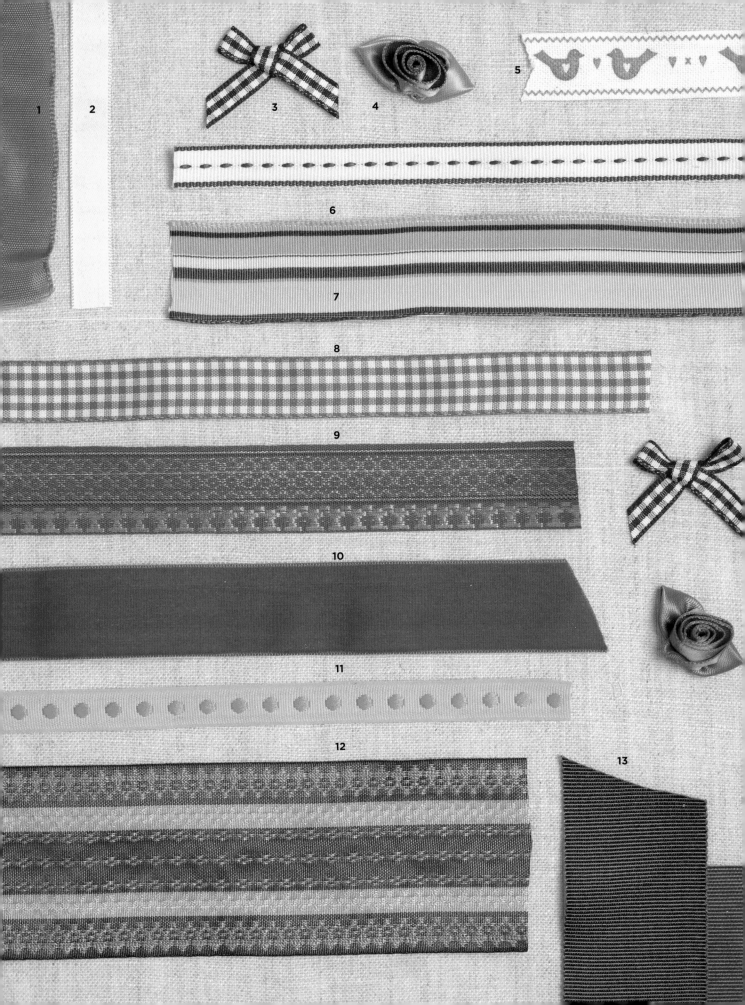

RIBBONS AND BOWS

Ribbons come in a wide variety of fabrics, from fine chiffon to chunky grosgrain and luxurious velvet, and in widths that range from a tiny ⅛ in/3 mm to a chunky 3 in/76 mm. They are designed to be surface-stitched, but if they are wide enough, they can also be stitched into a seam to make a smart edging. Even used discreetly, such as a toning velvet or satin down the button band of a cardigan, ribbon can add a sense of luxury. Bows can be bought ready-made to add extra embellishment, or you can make them yourself in matching or contrasting ribbon.

1. Taffeta ribbon can be dyed to a range of rich colors, such as this bright fuchsia. This one is wire edged. **2. Narrow cream grosgrain ribbon** makes a smart trimming on its own or in conjunction with other grosgrain ribbons of different colors and widths. **3. Gingham bows** are available ready-made from notions stores. Use them to trim lingerie or children's dresses. **4. Satin roses** are also available ready-made for trimming lingerie and bridal wear. **5. Printed cotton ribbon** has a vintage charm. **6. Subtle details**, such as the red edging and stitching on this cream ribbon, give a classy finish. **7. Stripy grosgrain** can be used to introduce a bright color accent to even the most neutral of fabrics. This ribbon is made from rayon. **8. Gingham polyester** is a popular ribbon, used to lend vintage style to both furnishings and fashion projects.

9. Sari braid is jacquard-woven in a wonderful array of widths and colors, often enriched with metal threads. Look for it in Asian stores. **10. Velvet ribbon** is available in a range of widths, from shoe-lace narrow to 1 in/2.5 cm and more. **11. Jacquard ribbon**, which has the design incorporated into the weave, can come in simple repeat designs such as this spot. Even a basic pattern adds a fun accent if it is in a strong color combination like this pink on lime. **12. Wide jacquard ribbon** can incorporate many colors and intricate designs. **13. Grosgrain ribbon** is made of rayon (or, somewhat more expensively, silk) woven into a coarse grain. It comes in a wide variety of widths and colors, either plain or in stripes.

below Sheer ribbon made of chiffon or organza has a delightful diaphanous appearance.

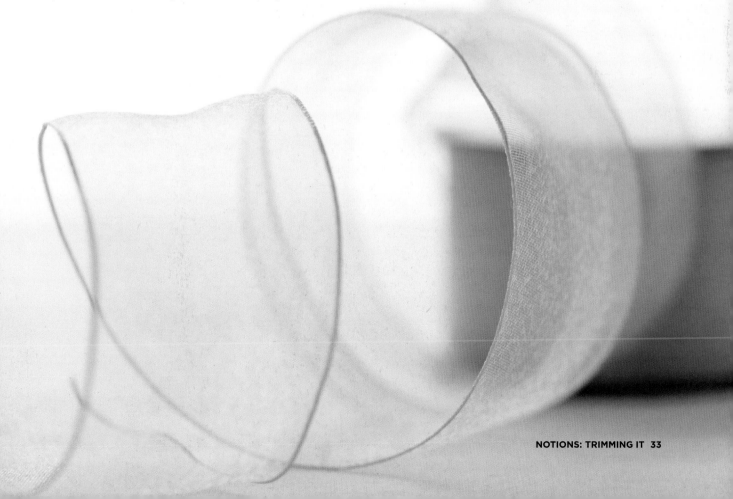

BEADS, BUCKLES, AND SEQUINS

There are endless ways to embellish garments and home furnishings: in addition to the many types of braids, ribbons, and trimmings, you can add a touch of glamorous sparkle and texture with beads and sequins, or the integral accessory of a pretty broochlike buckle, which can be attached to pillows and bags as well as clothing. Beads from all over the world come in an astounding range of materials, shapes, sizes, and colors, but for the purposes of bead embroidery on garments and furnishings, the most useful are small glass beads. These, and sequins, can be sewn on in discreet rows—around hemlines, necklines, or front openings, for example—used to embellish a detail, such as a collar or cuff, or they can be used as intricate all-over embroidery. Large beads can also be used in place of buttons.

1. Pretty vintage buckles, such as this delicate rounded one, bring an individual touch to any garment. Incorporate one into a special project, or make up a belt for a favorite dress. Search them out in markets, vintage stores and antique shops. **2. Rose-colored seed beads**, or rocailles, as they are otherwise known, add sparkling texture and a feminine touch when embroidered onto garments. They would be perfect for embellishing a floral design on a printed cotton fabric, for instance, using them to highlight some of the detail. They could also be used in combination with the pale pink seed beads, which would add delicate highlights (see 7). **3. Bugles**, or small tubelike beads, are classically used with rocailles for making up designs. You will need a long, fine beading needle to stitch these in place. **4. Indigo blue seed beads**, reminiscent of the semiprecious stone lapis lazuli, add richness to any garment. Imagine them around the hem or neckline of a dress or silk camisole, or embellishing a silk-velvet pillow. **5. Little square beads** could be used for a modern touch. Either use them on their own, or team them with smaller seed beads or bugles for a more richly textured look. **6. Indian glass beads** are inexpensive and come in a wide variety of shapes and sizes that can make pretty edgings for summer skirts or home furnishings. Some are lined with foil for extra luster. This is particularly noticeable on the oblong blue bead here. **7. Pale pink rocailles** look good when interspersed with a few stronger rose-toned versions (see 2). Experiment with mixing your favorite colors to create a lustrous effect. **8. Sequins** come in a huge range of sparkly colors. Less obviously, they also come in a variety of sizes and types. These green ones are faceted for extra light-reflection, but flat sequins are also widely available. **9. Iridescent glass beads** can be used in conjunction with rocailles. **10, 11, and 13. Antique buckles**, such as these beauties, can be found in specialist antique markets and shops. It is worth trawling thrift stores, too, for buckles, beads, and buttons that can be reinvented. **12. Sequin strips** are a quick option when you need to sew on lines of sequins. These are flat sequins, in contrast to the faceted ones above (see 8).

1

2

3

4

5

6

7

8

9

10

11

12

13

THE SECRETS OF SEWING-MACHINE SUCCESS

You can't begin to take sewing seriously until you have a sewing machine and you know how to use it. Take time to find one that suits the kinds of projects you are likely to take on. You need to try before you buy, so go to a specialist shop where the staff will give you a mini tutorial and let you try it out. As you use your sewing machine, you will get to understand its idiosyncrasies and know how to sort out any problems. Here is a sewing machine primer.

sewing-machine anatomy

It is advisable to choose one of the best-known makes and models of sewing machine, so that parts are readily available. Spend time familiarizing yourself with your machine so that you can really get the most from it.

Don't be beguiled by a top-of-the-range computerized embroidery machine if you are new to sewing and, like many household sewers, you will probably use only straight and zigzag stitch. A basic all-purpose machine is likely to give you all you need and will also be easy to master. For a wider choice of embroidery stitches and a start/stop button instead of foot-pedal control, you may want to consider a basic computerized machine. More sophisticated computerized embroidery machines (often combined with general sewing) can be used to create multicolored embroidery designs, copying, for example, hand-drawn alphabets and illustrations.

Overlockers are used by professionals in addition to general sewing machines to finish and trim seams in one action. They are expensive and not completely necessary, as you can finish seams in many other ways. As they trim and sew the fabric in one action, you need to be adept at handling them, otherwise you could be at risk of damaging the garment you are stitching. If you decide to invest in an overlocker, it is best to finish the seams before you stitch them to avoid this problem.

Basic theory behind the working of sewing machines has not changed hugely since Isaac Singer first went into production with his machines in the 1850s and, in essence, they are still threaded up the same way. The thread on the top spool is threaded down through levers, channels, and hooks on the machine and into the eye of the needle. A smaller bobbin of thread is kept in a compartment under the throat plate and threaded so that it can be picked up by the top loop to create an interlocking stitch. However, modern machines have made the job of threading up much simpler, with the stages numbered on the machine and hooks, rather than eyes, for easy threading.

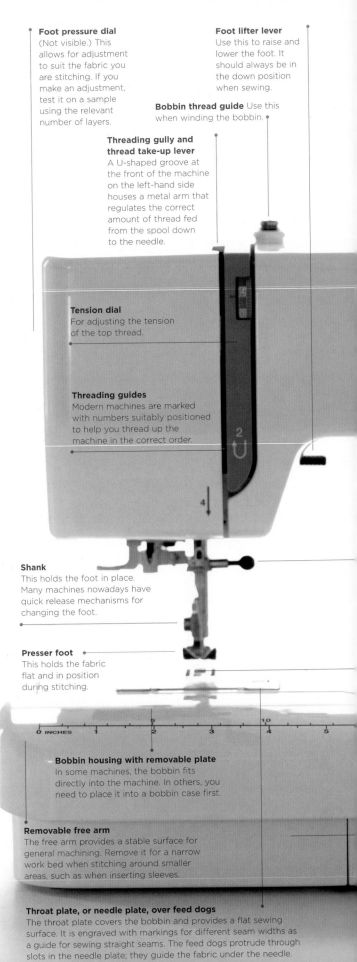

Foot pressure dial
(Not visible.) This allows for adjustment to suit the fabric you are stitching. If you make an adjustment, test it on a sample using the relevant number of layers.

Foot lifter lever
Use this to raise and lower the foot. It should always be in the down position when sewing.

Bobbin thread guide Use this when winding the bobbin.

Threading gully and thread take-up lever
A U-shaped groove at the front of the machine on the left-hand side houses a metal arm that regulates the correct amount of thread fed from the spool down to the needle.

Tension dial
For adjusting the tension of the top thread.

Threading guides
Modern machines are marked with numbers suitably positioned to help you thread up the machine in the correct order.

Shank
This holds the foot in place. Many machines nowadays have quick release mechanisms for changing the foot.

Presser foot
This holds the fabric flat and in position during stitching.

Bobbin housing with removable plate
In some machines, the bobbin fits directly into the machine. In others, you need to place it into a bobbin case first.

Removable free arm
The free arm provides a stable surface for general machining. Remove it for a narrow work bed when stitching around smaller areas, such as when inserting sleeves.

Throat plate, or needle plate, over feed dogs
The throat plate covers the bobbin and provides a flat sewing surface. It is engraved with markings for different seam widths as a guide for sewing straight seams. The feed dogs protrude through slots in the needle plate; they guide the fabric under the needle.

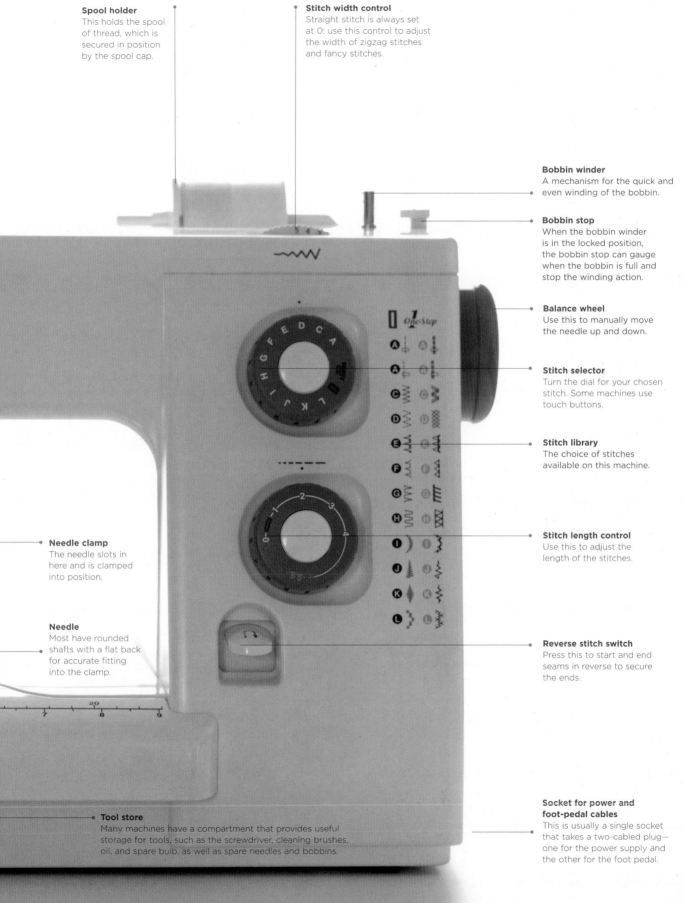

Spool holder
This holds the spool of thread, which is secured in position by the spool cap.

Stitch width control
Straight stitch is always set at 0: use this control to adjust the width of zigzag stitches and fancy stitches.

Bobbin winder
A mechanism for the quick and even winding of the bobbin.

Bobbin stop
When the bobbin winder is in the locked position, the bobbin stop can gauge when the bobbin is full and stop the winding action.

Balance wheel
Use this to manually move the needle up and down.

Stitch selector
Turn the dial for your chosen stitch. Some machines use touch buttons.

Stitch library
The choice of stitches available on this machine.

Stitch length control
Use this to adjust the length of the stitches.

Needle clamp
The needle slots in here and is clamped into position.

Needle
Most have rounded shafts with a flat back for accurate fitting into the clamp.

Reverse stitch switch
Press this to start and end seams in reverse to secure the ends.

Tool store
Many machines have a compartment that provides useful storage for tools, such as the screwdriver, cleaning brushes, oil, and spare bulb, as well as spare needles and bobbins.

Socket for power and foot-pedal cables
This is usually a single socket that takes a two-cabled plug— one for the power supply and the other for the foot pedal.

MACHINE ACCESSORIES

Every sewing machine comes with a pack of basic accessories, which is stored in the compartment under the throat plate. These should be enough for all your basic needs. Once you progress to more complicated projects, it may be worth investing in more elaborate feet. The feet, and even the bobbins, are designed to fit particular makes and models of machines, so make sure you buy the right brand.

1. Screwdriver to tighten foot fixings and release the bulb chamber, depending on the machine. **2. Stitch unpicker:** A handy tool that combines a cutting edge with a spike to get into the seam. **3. Cleaning tool**, incorporating a little brush with a pick. **4. Needle threader:** This is actually a hand-needle threader, but it works just as well with a machine needle. Push the wire through the eye of the needle, pass the thread through the wire and pull it through the eye of the needle. **5. Quilting foot**, designed to be used when the feed dogs on the machine are lowered so that the fabric can be maneuvered around 360 degrees. **6 & 12. Spare machine needles:** Always keep a spare set because needles always break at inconvenient moments. Two useful types of standby needles are regular sharps for most fabrics and ballpoints for knit fabrics. **7. Overlock foot**, to finish and trim seams in one action. **8. Zipper foot:** This has a central presser and can be fitted to the machine so that the needle is on its left or on its right, enabling you to stitch very close to the teeth on both sides of the zipper. **9. Button-sewing foot**, which stitches buttons into position. **10. Blind hem foot**, for neatly machined hems that are barely visible from the right side. **11. Disk/screwdriver:** This is used for some machines and would be included in the accessory pack. **13. Large spool cap**, designed to hold larger bobbins in place on the spool. **14. Medium spool cap and spindle** for slimmer bobbins. **15. Plastic bobbin** for the lower thread. **16. Metal bobbin:** This is not interchangeable with the plastic bobbin—each machine uses a different type and they can be slightly different sizes. Make sure you get the correct bobbin for your machine. Otherwise you may not be able to wind the bobbin or it may cause stitch problems. **17. Spare single needles**, supplied with the machine. **18. Twin needle**, designed to sew close parallel lines. **19. Buttonhole foot**, for a neatly machined finish.

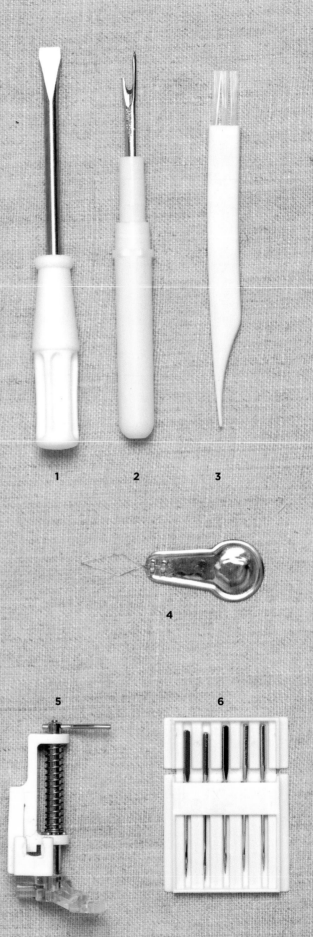

1

2

3

4

5

6

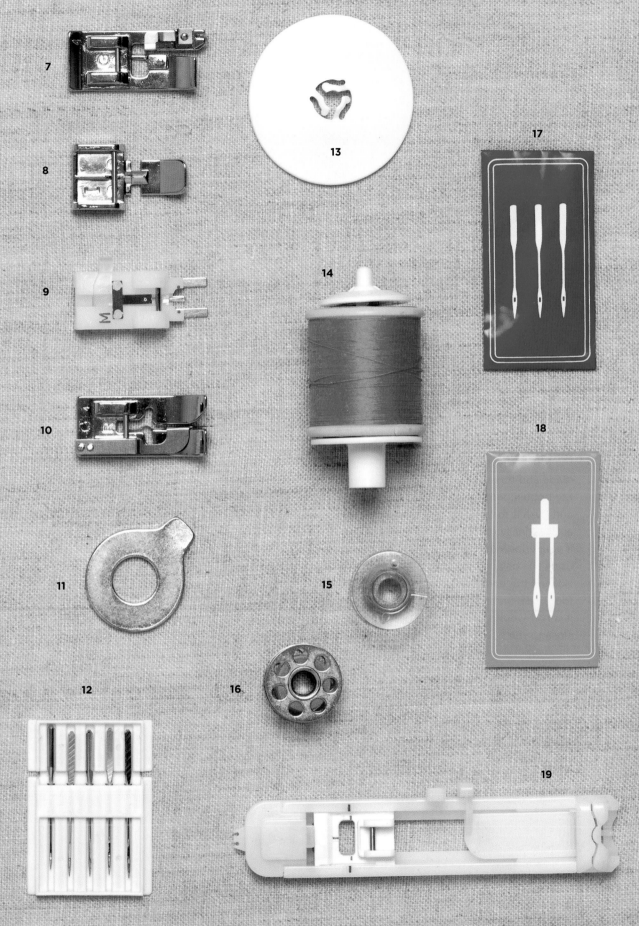

starting off

THREADING UP

Modern sewing-machine manufacturers mark their machines with numbers, cueing the order of loops, levers, gulley, and eyelets through which the thread needs to pass. All are slightly different, but the principle has changed little since the days of hand-operated machines. Stitches are created by two threads: one fed from a spool on top of the machine and one fed from a bobbin underneath. The top thread loops around the bobbin thread as you sew.

1. Prepare Raise the needle to the highest position by turning the balance wheel toward you. Raise the presser foot.

2. Wind the bobbin Pass thread from the spool on the top of the machine around the bobbin thread guide and thread it through one of the holes in the bobbin. Put the bobbin on the bobbin winder and push it to the right to lock it. Some machines automatically disengage the needle at this stage. If yours doesn't, you will need to disengage it using the balance wheel (check the manual). Holding the end of the thread loosely, press the foot pedal and the bobbin will start to wind. When it is half-wound, stop, trim the spare thread very close to the bobbin, then continue to wind. When the bobbin is full, it will automatically stop winding.

3. Insert the bobbin Some bobbins can be put straight in position under the throat plate; others need to be put into a bobbin case. Whichever, put the bobbin in so that the thread would unwind in an counterclockwise direction. You can then take the thread back through the spring in a clockwise direction: this provides tension. Once in position, bring about 4 in/10 cm of thread up to the flatbed surface and close the throat plate.

4. Thread up the top thread Take the thread from the top spool and pass it through the thread guide at the top of the sewing machine. Following the numbers, take the thread down through the tension mechanism, which is usually made up of two metal disks and a spring. It then goes down through a "gulley" and up to the take-up lever, then down through the threading guides to the needle.

5. Thread the needle Lower the presser foot, then pass the thread through the eye of the needle from front to back. Pull 6 in/15 cm of thread through.

6. Pick up the bobbin thread Raise the presser foot. Holding the end of the bobbin thread, turn the balance wheel toward you. The needle will go down into the machine. As it comes up again, it will bring a loop of bobbin thread with it. Pull on the top thread to pull out the loop. Pass the two threads toward the back of the machine.

TENSION

The tension and stitch length will be correctly set when you buy the machine, but you may need to make adjustments according to the type of fabric and thickness you are stitching. Always test the length and tension on a sample of the fabric you will be using. Stitch through a double thickness of fabric on the bias.

When the tension is correct, the stitches interlock in the middle of the fabric and look the same on both sides. The bobbin tension is set automatically, so you should only ever need to adjust the top tension. If the top stitches look loopy, the top tension is too loose and you need to turn the tension dial to a higher number. If the stitches are loopy underneath, the top tension is too tight and you will need to turn the dial to a lower number. The average tension is 4, so for most fabrics the dial should be set on 4. If you find that you generally need it to be too far in one direction, the bobbin tension may need to be adjusted by a specialist.

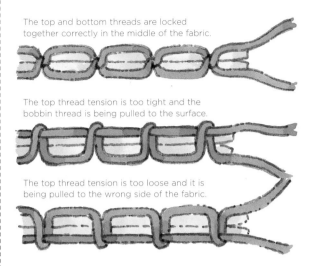

The top and bottom threads are locked together correctly in the middle of the fabric.

The top thread tension is too tight and the bobbin thread is being pulled to the surface.

The top thread tension is too loose and it is being pulled to the wrong side of the fabric.

STITCH LENGTH

Stitch length is measured in millimeters or stitches per inch and needs to be adjusted depending on the weight of the fabric. If the stitches are too long, they won't hold; if they are too short, they could pucker the fabric as you sew. If the stitches look right to the eye when you sew your stitch sample, leave the setting alone. If not, adjust the length and stitch another sample. Here is a general guide:

Fine fabrics: 2 mm/13–20 stitches per inch
Mid-weight fabrics: 2.5–3 mm/10–12 stitches per inch
Heavy fabrics, basting, gathering, and topstitching: 4–5 mm/5–6 stitches per inch.

STITCH WIDTH

This applies only to zigzag and decorative stitches using a swing needle. Many machines have a maximum width of ¼ in/6 mm. Decide what width is best for your project by sewing a few samples.

TROUBLESHOOTING

There is nothing more irritating than a machine that won't stitch evenly, jams, or eats up your fabric. Once you understand what might have gone wrong and how to put it right, you can soon get your stitching back on track. Here are some common hiccups and how to resolve them:

The needle won't move Make sure that the bobbin winder is not in the winding position. On some sewing machines, the needle won't move if the presser foot has not been lowered or if the top thread has run out.

Stitches don't form Check that neither thread has run out, the needle hasn't become unthreaded, and that the spool cap is the correct size for the spool. Make sure the machine is properly threaded.

Uneven stitches Check the spool-cap holder is the correct size. If this doesn't help, make sure you are not pulling the fabric through the machine: all you need do is guide it and the feed dogs will move it under the needle at the correct speed for the stitch length. Finally, it might be a tension problem. If the stitches look uneven but aren't obviously loopy, pull the fabric of your stitch sample until the stitches break. If the top thread breaks, loosen the tension by turning the dial to a lower number. If the bottom thread breaks, tighten the tension. If this doesn't work, rewind the bobbin and rethread the machine. A worn needle or one the wrong size can also cause uneven stitches, so try changing the needle.

Top thread breaks Rethread the machine and change the needle, making sure that the needle and thread are compatible. If that doesn't work, adjust the tension.

Bottom thread breaks Check to see that the bobbin has been wound evenly. If not, rewind it and rethread the bobbin.

Skipped stitches The machine might not be properly threaded, the top tension may be too tight, or the needle might be the wrong size for the thread. Rethread the machine, try a different needle, and then try another stitch sample. If this doesn't work, adjust the tension.

Thread jams If the bobbin has not been wound evenly, the needle may go through several threads and jam. Carefully cut away the threads, take out the bobbin, and rewind and rethread it. Another reason for thread jams is if the presser foot has worked loose, so tighten the screw.

Needle breaks Either it has hit metal (pin or zipper) or it has been inserted incorrectly, so refit the needle.

Needle jams If the needle has worked loose in the shaft, it may be hitting the needle plate. Another reason could be that you are using the wrong foot for the job—for example, a zigzag stitch needs a zigzag foot to allow for the swinging needle.

STITCH CRAFT

Stitches are the basic building blocks of any sewing project, and whatever you tackle, you will need to use a combination of hand and machine stitches. As with any skill, you will get quicker and neater with practice, but if you take your time, you should be able to achieve a professional finish from your very first project.

essential stitches

The days of laborious hand dressmaking and tailoring are long gone, but even the deftest of machinists need to employ hand stitches at some stage of a project. There are two basic sorts of stitches you will need to master: temporary stitches, to hold seams together or "anchor" pieces while you machine stitch; and neat finishing stitches. Most hand stitches are worked from right to left if you are right-handed and from the left if you are left-handed.

THREADING THE NEEDLE AND TYING THE KNOT

1 Snip off the tip of the thread to give it an easy-to-thread blunt end and then feed it through the eye of the needle. Choose a general-purpose needle in a size that suits the fabric—finer for lightweight fabric. A sharps needle with its wide, easy-to-thread eye is a good choice. Pull about 2 in/5 cm of thread through the needle. Unwind and cut off a length of thread about the same measurement as the distance from your wrist to your elbow.

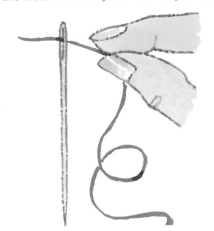

TYING THE KNOT

2 Wind the end of the thread around your forefinger.

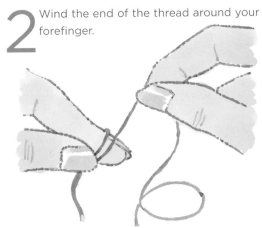

3 Then roll the thread between your thumb and forefinger until it rolls off the end of your finger.

4 Continue to roll the thread, then use your middle finger to tighten the knot while sliding it down to the end of the thread.

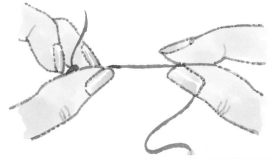

TEMPORARY STITCHES

These are used for basting (tacking), gathering, easing, or to hold newly stitched pleats in place while you press them.

EVEN BASTING

Also known as tacking, basting is used to hold layers of fabric together while it is being machine stitched. Straight seams in easy-to-handle fabric don't always need basting, but they will need pinning instead, with the pins inserted at right angles to the seam so that the machine can run over them. However, it is always best to hand-baste slippery, napped, or stretchy fabrics; or curved or small seams before machining.

Work stitches about $^3/_8$ in/1 cm long. If it is a long, straight seam, you could take longer stitches. The smaller or trickier the area, the smaller you should make your basting stitches.

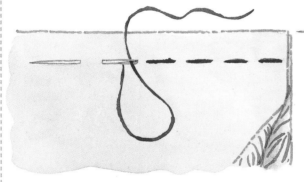

UNEVEN BASTING

A quick, stable way to baste long lengths is to make long stitches (up to 3 in/7.5 cm) with a little stitch between each one. As well as straight seams, this is a useful form of basting for keeping the layers of a quilt together while quilting.

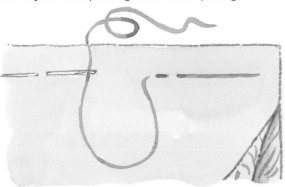

DIAGONAL BASTING

This type of basting is used to secure layers of fabrics together over larger areas while you stitch, such as the linings and interlinings on drapes or large lapels.

Make long, even, diagonal stitches by taking parallel horizontal stitches.

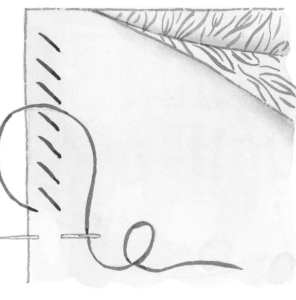

RUNNING STITCHES

Use simple running stitches for hand gathering and easing, or for fine seaming. It is similar to even basting, but the stitches are smaller and even, with even spaces between them.

For speed, slip your needle in and out of the fabric several times before pulling the thread through.

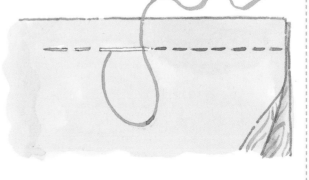

FINISHING STITCHES

Professionals use many different finishing stitches, but if you can master these essential ones, you will be able to finish off any home-sewing project with confidence. The key is to keep them neat and even. Start by concealing the knot at the end of the thread within the fold of a hem or seam allowance.

EVEN SLIPSTITCH

This stitch is useful for joining two folded edges, such as making a final closure where an item has been turned through. The idea is that most of the stitch is hidden. Start by passing the needle from the inside of the seam to the front. Bring the needle to the other side of the seam and run it behind the seam. When you bring it to the front, take a tiny stitch to the other side of the seam, and pass the needle behind that side of the seam. Finish by making several tiny stitches in a concealed place.

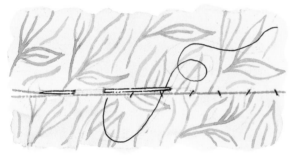

UNEVEN SLIPSTITCH

This is the most useful hand-hemming stitch. Pass the needle from the underside of the fold in the fabric. Take a tiny stitch (about two threads) in the main fabric, then pass the needle back to the top fold of the hem. Run the needle along the inside of the fold, then bring it up to take another tiny stitch. Finish by taking tiny stitches on top of each other.

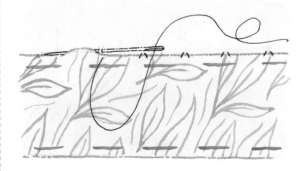

BACKSTITCH

This is useful for hand-stitching seams. Take two running stitches, then take the thread back to the end of the first stitch. The front side will look like machine stitching. The back will have a "double" row of overlapped stitches. Finish by taking two or more tiny stitches on top of each other.

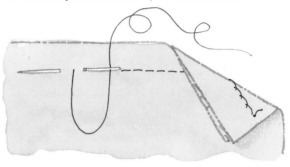

SADDLE STITCH

This is like a large running stitch, but designed to be decorative in the same way as machine topstitching. Make neat, even stitches about 1/4 in/6 mm long with gaps the same length.

BLANKET STITCH

Traditionally used for embroidery, especially as a decorative edging, blanket stitch also has a practical use in joining pieces of fabric. It works especially well on fray-free fabrics, such as felt, because there are no raw edges to turn under.

Using embroidery thread, work from left to right if you are right-handed and from right to left if you are left-handed. Fold the raw edge under, if there is one, and bring the needle to the front at the bottom edge of the hem. Now place the needle into the right side at the point where you would like the top of the stitch to be. Bring it out below the hem and loop the thread behind it. As you pull the thread through, you will have formed the first blanket stitch. Continue along the full length. To finish, after looping the thread behind the needle, secure by taking two tiny stitches on top of each other at the hem edge.

FINISHING OFF

Take a tiny stitch and pass the needle through the loop before pulling it tight. Repeat so you have two stitches on top of each other to secure well.

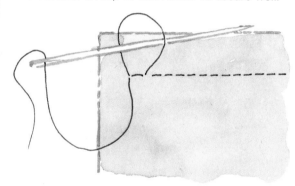

BASIC MACHINE STITCHES

Basic straight stitch, which creates an even line of stitches by interlocking the top and bottom threads, has changed little since Isaac Singer's first sewing machine, and it is still the most used and useful stitch. Sewing machines have come a long way, however, with simpler threading, refined engineering, and different stitch length and tension settings. The invention of the swing needle has increased stitch options considerably. At its most basic, the swing needle is used to create zigzag stitch. It is also indispensable for buttonholes, hemming, and various embroidery stitches. Here is a sample of the most elementary library of stitches. Each machine is different, so make a sampler of the stitches offered on yours. Try lengthening and widening the stitches so that you understand all the options.

BELOW 1. Straight stitch is the one to use for stitching seams. Set the length of the stitch to suit the fabric (shorter for finer fabrics; longer for heavier weights), and for purpose—choose the longest setting for basting. **2. Three-stitch zigzag:** This should be used for heavier weight, stretchy fabrics and for attaching elastic. It is also useful for mending tears. **3. Zigzag:** The machine swings the needle from side to side as it stitches, creating zigzag stitch. Some machines have a standard foot that accommodates both a fixed needle and the swing action; others require you to change the foot. Use zigzag stitch to finish seams quickly, to stitch around appliqué, to make buttonholes, and for embroidery. It is useful for stitching lighter weight and stretchy fabric, as it offers more give than straight stitch. Experiment with the length and width on spare fabric until you are happy with the effect. **4. Invisible hem stitch:** This is the machine version of uneven slipstitch, designed to create a hem that is almost invisible from the right side. **5. Satin stitch shapes:** There is usually a choice of these, which can be used to create pretty edges, or to contribute to larger embroidery designs. **6 and 7. Scallop edging:** This can be used for a prettily finished edge. **8. Satin stitch:** This is the same stitch as 5, but worked on a wider setting. **9. Stretch blind hem:** This is for use with stretchy fabrics.

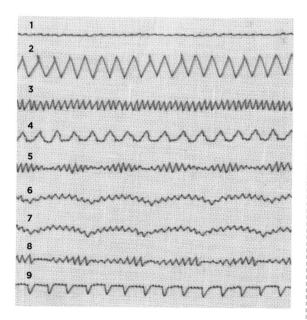

THE PAPER PATTERN

Printed paper patterns provide the recipes for successful dressmaking. The garments have been designed, sized, and tested by professionals. Each pattern lists exactly what materials you need to buy, provides the pieces, and gives clear instructions on how to create the garment. All the puzzling out has been done for you: you simply need to follow the directions. Here is the key to understanding how paper patterns work and how to make best use of them.

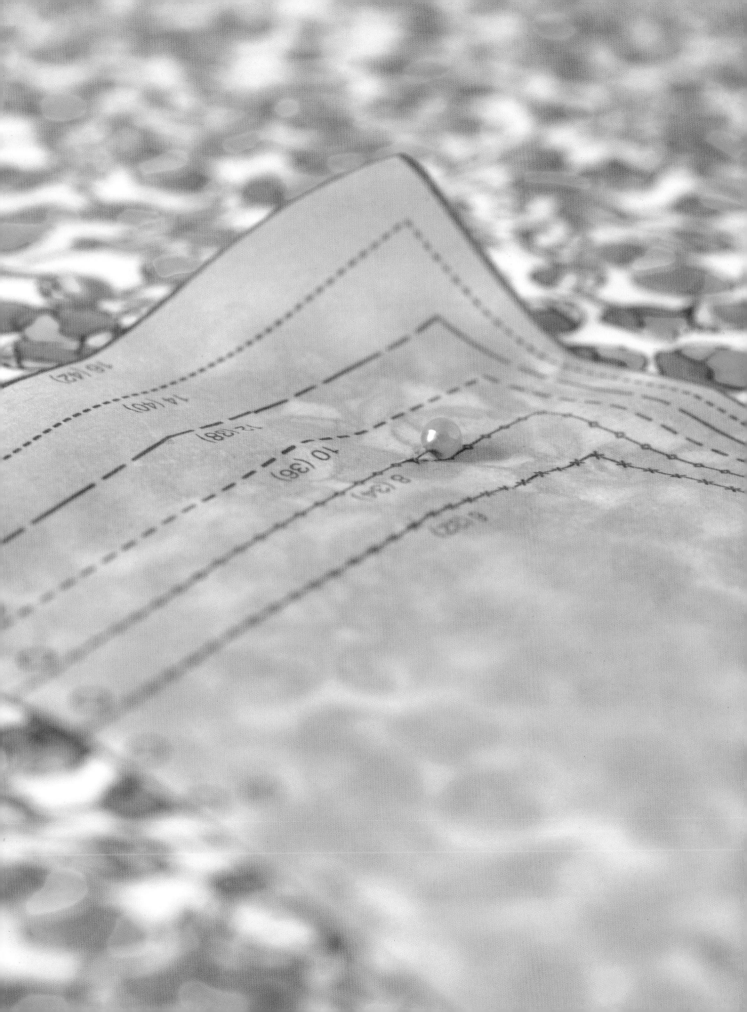

the envelope inside and out

There are three elements to the paper pattern. First, there is the envelope, which has important information on both the front and the back. Inside, you will find a sheet of instructions and, lastly, but most importantly, all the pattern pieces.

The front of the envelope shows illustrated (and sometimes photographed) designs. These are often variations on a theme, such as the same skirt in different lengths, or with different details and trimmings. On the front of some patterns, there is also an outline drawing of each of the garments, showing sewing details, such as the position of darts, gathers, and fastenings.

On the back, you will find information on sizes, measurements, and everything you need to buy. Inside, most patterns consist of the pattern pieces printed on tissue, although some are printed in color on more robust paper. You will also find a sheet of illustrated instructions that include how to lay out the pieces on different widths of fabric.

UNDERSTANDING THE SYMBOLS

There is an extensive set of pattern-marking symbols that are understood internationally (see right). To get the most out of the pattern and ensure a better finish for your project, it is worth understanding the symbols and taking the time to use them properly.

Note that sometimes grain lines have to follow the cross grain, but this will be stated on the pattern. Patterns that need to be cut on the cross will have a grain line running diagonally across the pattern piece. Seam lines do not always appear for every seam, especially on multisized patterns. In this case, the pattern will tell you what the seam allowance should be.

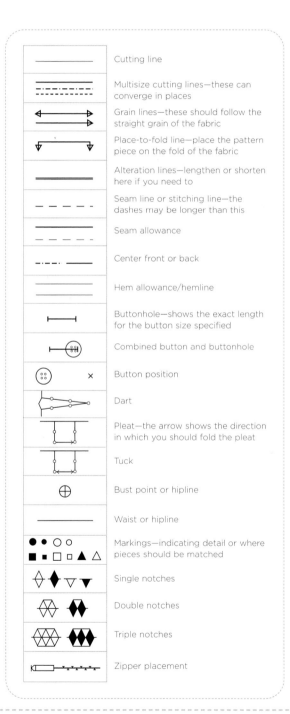

Cutting line

Multisize cutting lines—these can converge in places

Grain lines—these should follow the straight grain of the fabric

Place-to-fold line—place the pattern piece on the fold of the fabric

Alteration lines—lengthen or shorten here if you need to

Seam line or stitching line—the dashes may be longer than this

Seam allowance

Center front or back

Hem allowance/hemline

Buttonhole—shows the exact length for the button size specified

Combined button and buttonhole

Button position

Dart

Pleat—the arrow shows the direction in which you should fold the pleat

Tuck

Bust point or hipline

Waist or hipline

Markings—indicating detail or where pieces should be matched

Single notches

Double notches

Triple notches

Zipper placement

THE BACK OF THE PATTERN ENVELOPE

Each make of pattern differs slightly in the layout of information on the back of the envelope, but they all include the same basic elements. Below is an example.

Outline drawing of the back of each garment showing details such as darts, gathers, fastenings, collars, and frills. Some patterns also include a front view of each garment.

Imperial sizes included in the pattern plus the body measurements for each size.

Fabric requirement charts in imperial for each view. Check the width of your chosen fabric to work out the yardage you need.

Metric sizes included in the pattern plus the body measurements for each size.

Fabric requirement charts in metric for each view. Check the width of your chosen fabric to work out how much you need.

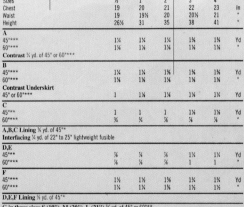

19 PIECES/PIEZAS

Métrages et instructions de couture en Français à l'intérieur de l'enveloppe.

6577 SIZE A 1/2-4

TODDLERS' FIVE SIZES IN ONE

	½	1	2	3	4	
Sizes	½	1	2	3	4	
Chest	19	20	21	22	23	In
Waist	19	19½	20	20½	21	"
Height	26½	31	35	38	41	"
A						
45"***	1¼	1¼	1¼	1⅜	1⅜	Yd
60"***	1⅛	1⅛	1⅛	1⅛	1⅛	"
Contrast ¾ yd. of 45" or 60"***						
B						
45"***	1¼	1¼	1⅜	1⅜	1⅜	Yd
60"***	1⅛	1⅛	1⅛	1⅛	1⅛	"
Contrast Underskirt						
45" or 60"***	1	1⅛	1⅛	1⅛	1¼	Yd
C						
45"**	1	1	1	1⅛	1⅛	Yd
60"***	¾	¾	⅞	⅞	⅞	"
A,B,C Lining ⅜ yd. of 45"*						
Interfacing ¼ yd. of 22" to 25" lightweight fusible						
D,E						
45"**	⅞	⅞	⅞	1¼	1¼	Yd
60"***	⅞	⅞	⅞	1	1	"
F						
45"***	1½	1½	1⅝	1¾	1¾	Yd
60"***	1¼	1¼	1⅜	1½	1½	"
D,E,F Lining ⅜ yd. of 45"*						

G in three sizes S (19"), M (20"), L (21") ⅝ yd. of 45" or 60"**
Lining ⅜ yd. of 45"*; **Interfacing** ½ yd. of 22" to 25" lightweight fusible

GARMENT MEASUREMENTS

Finished back length from base of neck:

A,B	21	22	23	24	25	In
C,D,E,F	17½	18½	19½	20½	21½	"

SUGGESTED FABRICS

Cotton and Cotton Blends, Gingham, Laundered Cottons, Baby Cord, Broadcloth, Calico, Chambray, Damask, Pique, Poplin, Seersucker, Sateen, Eyelet, Linen and Linen Blends, Embroidered Fabrics. Not suitable for sleepwear. Allow extra fabric for matching plaids or stripes.

REQUIREMENTS

One 12" zipper, hook and eye. A: 2½ yd. of ⅜" wide ribbon.
B: Two ⅜" buttons, 1⅞ yd. of ⅜" wide lace, five rosettes. one flower corsage.
C: Five ⅜" buttons, 5 yd. of ⅜" wide ribbon.
D: 1½ yd. of 1¼" wide ribbon, 1¼ yd. of ⅝" wide pregathered lace.
E: 1¼ yd. of 1¼" wide ribbon, one pkg. of medium rick rack.
G: ¾ yd. of ⅝" wide ribbon, ¾ yd. of 1¼" wide ribbon.

*without nap **with nap ***with or without nap

PETITE ENFANT: PATRON CINQ TAILLES
NIÑOS PEQUEÑOS: PATRON CINCO TALLAS

		½	1	2	3	4	
Tailles / Tallas		½	1	2	3	4	
Poitrine / Pecho		48	51	53	56	58	cm
Taille / Cintura		48	50	51	52	53	"
Hauteur / Altura		67.5	76.5	89	96.5	104	"
A	115cm***	1.10	1.20	1.20	1.20	1.30	m
	150cm***	1.00	1.00	1.00	1.00	1.00	"
Partie contrastante - 0.70m de 115cm ou 150cm*** / **Parte contrastante** - 0.70m de 115cm ó 150cm***							
B	115cm***	1.10	1.20	1.20	1.20	1.30	m
	150cm***	1.00	1.00	1.00	1.00	1.10	"
Jupon contrastant / Enagua contrastante							
	115cm / 150cm***	0.90	1.00	1.00	1.00	1.10	m
C	115cm**	0.90	0.90	1.00	1.00	1.10	m
	150cm***	0.70	0.70	0.70	0.80	0.80	"
A,B,C Doublure - 0.30m de 115cm*; **Entoilage**- 0.30m de 55cm à 64cm léger, thermocollant							
A,B,C Forro - 0.30m de 115cm*; **Entretela** - 0.30m de 55cm a 64cm ligera, adhesiva							
D,E	115cm**	0.80	0.80	0.80	1.10	1.10	m
	150cm***	0.80	0.80	0.80	0.90	0.90	"
F	115cm***	1.30	1.40	1.50	1.60	1.60	m
	150cm***	1.10	1.20	1.20	1.30	1.40	"
D,E,F Doublure - 0.40m de 115cm* / **D,E,F Forro** - 0.40m de 115cm*							

G en trois tailles P (48.5cm), M (51cm), G (53.5cm)- 0.60m de 115cm ou 150cm**; **Doublure** - 0.30m de 115cm*; **Entoilage**- 0.40m de 55cm à 64cm léger, thermocollant
G de tres tallas P (48.5cm), M (51cm), G (53.5cm)- 0.60m de 115cm ó 150cm**; **Forro** - 0.30m de 115cm*; **Entretela**- 0.40m de 55cm a 64cm ligera, adhesiva

TISSUS SUGGERES: Coton et Cotonnades, Vichy, Cotons prélavés, Piqué très fin, Popeline, Calicot, Chambray, Damas, Piqué, Popeline fine, Seersucker, Satinette, Broderie anglaise, Toile de lin et mélanges de lin, Tissus brodés. Ces modèles ne conviennent pas pour vêtements de nuit. Prévoyez davantage de tissu pour raccorder les écossais ou rayures.

MERCERIE: Une glissière de 30cm, une agrafe. A: 2.30m de ruban de 1cm de large. B: Deux boutons de 1cm, 1.70m de dentelle de 1cm de large, cinq rosettes, un petit bouquet de fleurs pour le corsage. C: Cinq boutons de 1cm, 4.50m de ruban de 1cm de large. D: 1.30m de ruban de 3.2cm de large, 1.20m de dentelle préfroncée de 1.5cm de large. E: 1.10m de ruban de 3.2cm de large, un paquet de croquet moyen. G: 0.70m de ruban de 1.5cm de large, 0.60m de ruban de 3.2cm de large.

TELAS SUGERIDAS: Algodón y mezclas de algodones, Guiguán, Algodones lavados, Piqué muy fino, Popelina, Calico, Chambray, Damasco, Piqué, Popelina fina, Seersucker, Satén de algodón, Encaje inglés, Lino y mezclas de lino, Telas bordadas. Estos modelos no convienen para ropa de dormir. Se necesita tela extra para casar cuadros o rayas.

MERCERIA: Una cremallera de 30cm, un corchete. A: 2.30m de cinta de 1cm de ancho. B: Dos botones de 1cm, 1.70m de encaje de 1cm de ancho, cinco rositas artificiales, un pequeño ramo de flores para el corpiño. C: Cinco botones de 1cm, 4.50m de cinta de 1cm de ancho. D: 1.30m de cinta de 3.2cm de ancho, 1.20m de encaje fruncido de 1.5cm de ancho. E: 1.10m de cinta de 3.2cm de ancho, un paquete de cinta de espiguilla mediana. G: 0.70m de cinta de 1.5cm de ancho, 0.60m de cinta de 3.2cm de ancho.

*sans sens **avec sens ***avec ou sans sens *sin pelusa **con pelusa ***con o sin pelusa

Actual measurements of the finished garments. This will be larger than the body measurements.

A list of suitable fabrics for these garments.

Notions needed for each garment.

Suggested fabrics and notions needed for each garment in French.

Suggested fabrics and notions needed for each garment in Spanish.

taking measurements

Learning how to take measurements correctly and accurately is well worth the time and effort, as it makes all the difference to the success of your finished garment. A piece of clothing that fits your shape correctly and skims your curves in the right places will hang better and be more flattering, as well as more comfortable to wear. All you need is a good-quality dressmaker's roll-up tape measure and a notepad. Bear in mind that you will always get the most accurate measurements if someone else takes them for you, as they can make sure that the tape is level and positioned in exactly the right place.

One of the best aspects of making your own garments is that, without too much effort, you can make them to measure. This doesn't just mean that they will fit your bust, waist, and hip measurements, which bought clothes should do, too. Off-the-rack sizes presume a perfect average body shape to which real people rarely conform. For example, some of us have a higher or lower waist, higher or lower bust, longer or shorter legs, or a bust of one dress size and hips of another.

On the back of every pattern envelope is a list of the standard body measurements for each size. Choose your basic size and then take your actual measurements as a comparison. The measurements illustrated opposite are the most important and your pattern will indicate where you can lengthen, shorten, or widen, as necessary, in order to accommodate your own dimensions.

Bear in mind that whatever foundation garments you are wearing at the time will affect the results of the measurements you are taking.

FULL BUST

Measure around the fullest part of your bust, making sure that the tape is level at the back.

BUST POINT

Measure from your shoulder to the point of your bust. Some people are built with a shorter upper rib cage and this can affect the position of darts.

BACK WAIST

Measure from the vertebra at the base of your neck to your natural waist. This will indicate whether the length of your torso and the position of your waist is standard, or a little higher or lower than the regular pattern.

WAIST

Pass the tape measure around the narrowest part of your waist.

HIPS

Choose the widest point to take this measurement.

BACK CROTCH

Sit up straight on a hard chair or stool and measure down your back from your natural waist to the seat. This is important when cutting pants, as if they don't fit properly into the crotch, they will either strain or sag.

SIDE LENGTH

Measure from your waist to the floor when you are standing. This is a useful measurement when making both pants and skirts.

SLEEVE LENGTH

Slightly bend your elbow and measure from your shoulder down the back of your arm to your wrist.

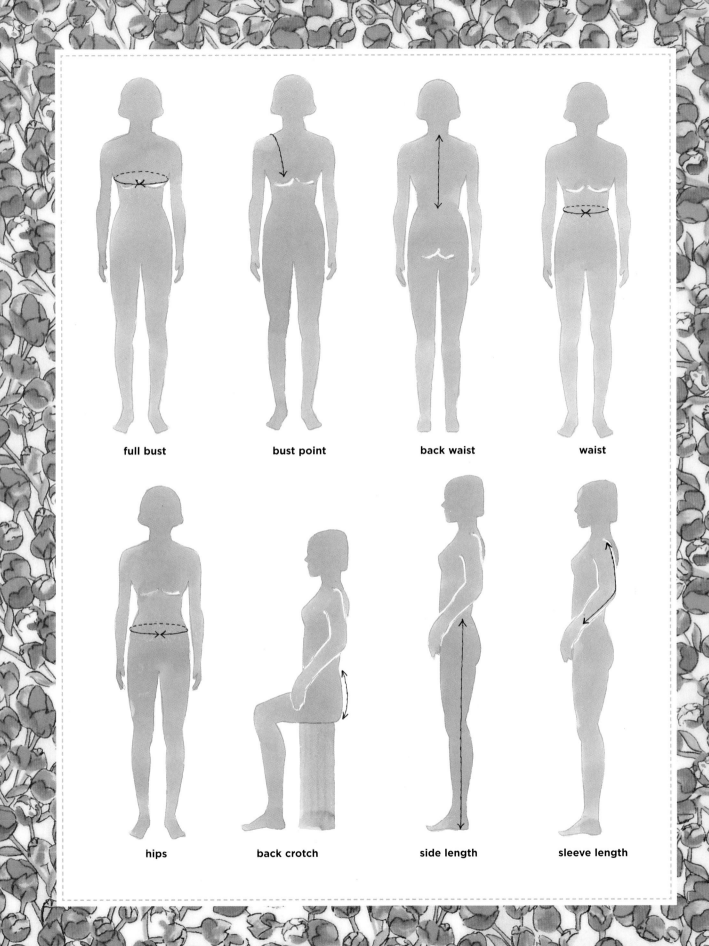

full bust

bust point

back waist

waist

hips

back crotch

side length

sleeve length

using the pattern

The accurate laying out of the pattern pieces and the cutting of the fabric are the foundation stones of sewing success. If the fabric is not folded accurately and the grain lines are not running straight along the grain, the finished garment will not hang well.

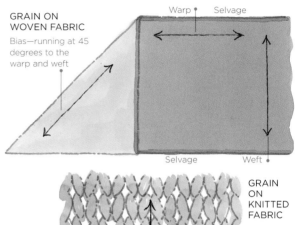

GRAIN ON WOVEN FABRIC

Bias—running at 45 degrees to the warp and weft

Warp   Selvage

Selvage   Weft

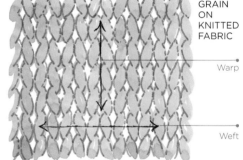

GRAIN ON KNITTED FABRIC

Warp

Weft

UNDERSTANDING FABRIC GRAIN

Woven fabrics are made up of warp yarns that run down their length with the weft yarns interlaced across them. The selvages are firm fray-free edges running along both sides of the fabric. The lengthwise grain is parallel with the selvages; the crosswise grain is at right angles to it. You will find the bias by turning down one corner so that the crosswise grain lies on the selvage.

The direction of the grain affects the look and comfort of the finished garment because the crosswise grain generally has more give than the lengthwise grain. For this reason, the fabric will drape better with the lengthwise grain running vertically down the garment. Sometimes, crosswise grain is used vertically for a special design effect, such as a border. When choosing striped fabrics, make sure that the grain is running the way you want the stripes to fall. For example, if you want to make a top with vertical stripes, make sure they run along the length of the grain. If they run crosswise, you would have to cut the garment across the grain to achieve vertical stripes, which would compromise the give, resulting in an unflattering fit.

Fabrics stretch most across the bias, and this can be used in the design. For example, a bias-cut skirt can be designed for a great fit without the need for darts. All bias-cut garments drape beautifully, but there is usually more fabric wastage than for garments cut on the straight grain.

PREPARING THE FABRIC

Before cutting, the fabric should be preshrunk, flat, and even. Start by making sure that the ends are straight along the cross grain. If the fabric is tightly woven, snip into one selvage, then tear along the cross grain. For a looser plain-weave fabric, pull out a cross thread to create a straight line for cutting. For jacquards, use a triangle or gridded ruler and tailor's chalk to draw a line along the raw edge at right angles to the selvage. If you don't have one of these, use a sheet of paper as a right-angle template.

If the fabric has not been preshrunk before you cut it, you may find that the garment no longer fits after you have laundered it. Check the care label when you buy the fabric. Dry-cleanable material should be stable; otherwise, wash the fabric as recommended. Press fabric well with a steam iron to eliminate even the smallest creases.

PREPARING THE PATTERN PIECES

The instruction sheet lists and numbers each pattern piece, shows each one in diagrammatic form, and indicates which are needed for each garment. The pattern pieces themselves usually come on large tissue sheets (although some are on sturdier paper). They are marked with numbers corresponding to the diagram and labeled as to what they are

(bodice front, skirt front, sleeve, for example). Cut out each pattern piece for your chosen garment using paper scissors (paper will blunt dressmaker's shears). If the pattern is multisized, cut along the cutting line for your size. Where there are notches, cut out around them. If you don't need to alter the pattern pieces (see page 58), you are ready to pin them onto the fabric.

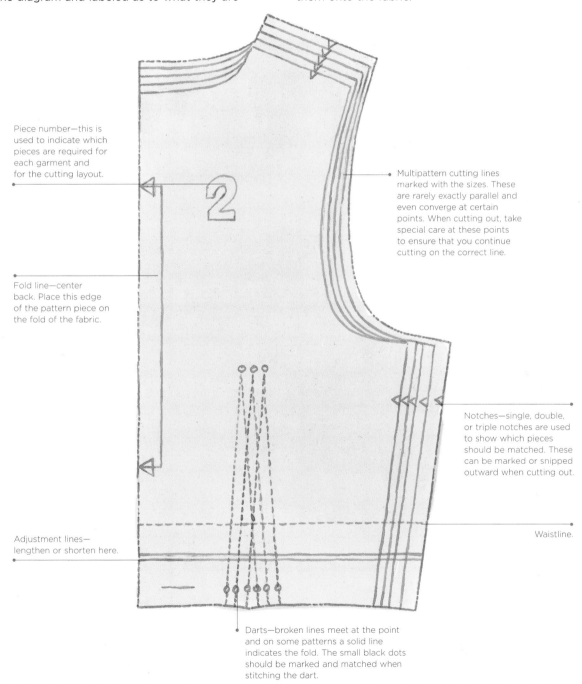

Piece number—this is used to indicate which pieces are required for each garment and for the cutting layout.

Fold line—center back. Place this edge of the pattern piece on the fold of the fabric.

Multipattern cutting lines marked with the sizes. These are rarely exactly parallel and even converge at certain points. When cutting out, take special care at these points to ensure that you continue cutting on the correct line.

Notches—single, double, or triple notches are used to show which pieces should be matched. These can be marked or snipped outward when cutting out.

Waistline.

Adjustment lines—lengthen or shorten here.

Darts—broken lines meet at the point and on some patterns a solid line indicates the fold. The small black dots should be marked and matched when stitching the dart.

ADAPTING THE PATTERN PIECES

One of the benefits of sewing your own garments is that you can adjust them to a perfect fit. Professional tailors and couturiers do this in two steps. First, they adjust the basic flat pattern to suit their client's measurements. Next, they make up a "toile," which is a muslin mock-up that can be fitted three-dimensionally on the body, adjusted, and then flattened out again so that the original pattern can be altered. Unless you are embarking on high-end tailoring, this should not be necessary because most commercial patterns are designed to help you with your own adjustments.

Whether you are lengthening, shortening, or altering the width of your garment, there are certain points on the pattern where this should be done, depending on where the darts or seam shaping is on the garment. These points are marked by lines on the pattern pieces. When you have adjusted a pattern piece, you may need to redraw the seam lines to smooth them out.

TO LENGTHEN

If you have a long torso, you may need to lengthen under the bust.

Lengthen sleeves at the upper arm and forearm.

To lower the skirt at the hipline, cut the pattern at this point and extend using a strip of tissue paper.

Add a strip of tissue to lengthen at the hemline.

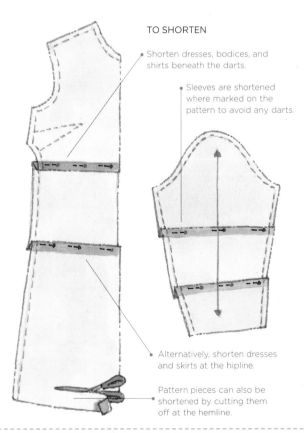

TO SHORTEN

Shorten dresses, bodices, and shirts beneath the darts.

Sleeves are shortened where marked on the pattern to avoid any darts.

Alternatively, shorten dresses and skirts at the hipline.

Pattern pieces can also be shortened by cutting them off at the hemline.

SHORTENING PATTERN PIECES

Commercial patterns have two shortening lines. Crease the pattern between these lines and make a fold half the amount needed to be shortened. Pin in position. Measure to check the length and readjust if necessary. Repeat the same fold with the back piece.

LENGTHENING PATTERN PIECES

To lengthen patterns, cut the relevant piece(s) between the shortening lines, then place a strip of tissue paper underneath the pattern. Adjust the distance between the two pieces to extend to the required length. Pin in position, check the length, and adjust if necessary. Repeat with the back pieces.

TO WIDEN

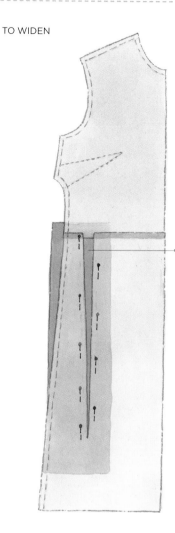

Cut pattern pieces for A-line dresses at the waistline before making a slash to widen from the hips down.

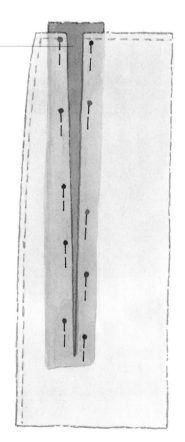

A fitted dress with a bodice will need enlarging in an inverted "V" from the dart to the waistline.

To widen a pattern for a fitted skirt at the waistline, slash down toward the hemline.

WIDENING PATTERN PIECES

When widening or taking in a pattern, remember that each major piece represents about a quarter of your body. If you are enlarging or reducing a measurement by less than 1 in/2.5 cm, do this by adjusting the seamline by a quarter of the overall adjustment. If you need to enlarge a piece by more than 1 in/2.5 cm, you will need to slash the pattern, place it over a piece of tissue, and spread it by a quarter of the enlargement. Pin, check the measurement, and adjust the position of the pins if necessary.

The quarter rule works for most patterns. If you are making a princess-line dress with more than four seams, divide the adjustment by the number of seams.

LAYING OUT THE PATTERN

First, you need to decide the best layout plan to suit both the garment you have chosen to make and the width of your fabric. You will find several cutting guides on the instruction sheet. There will be one for each garment and possibly one for each different fabric width. Each will show whether the fabric should be folded, and whether that should be a lengthwise or crosswise fold. To make sure you get it right, it will also show where the selvages should lie. The layout plan also shows the pieces marked with the relevant markings, such as grain direction and where they should be placed on the fold.

The layout plans included in patterns have been worked out so that the grain is running in the right direction, although you will need to take special care if the fabric you have chosen has a nap or large design.

SPECIAL LAYOUT: FABRIC WITH NAP

If the fabric you choose has a nap within the weave, such as velvet or velour, it will look different from different angles, so it is important to make sure that all the pieces lie in the same direction. This also applies if the fabric has a pattern with a strong direction, such as herringbone.

SPECIAL LAYOUT: LARGE OR STRONG DESIGNS

These need to be centered on the pattern pieces or matched to make the design work. Sometimes it is easiest to do this with single thicknesses of fabric, so you can hand-center each piece. If, however, you do need to fold the fabric for cutting, make sure you do this accurately so that the design repeat is aligned on both layers. Secure the fabric with pins at intervals to ensure that the design does not slip when pinning on the pattern pieces.

left Sketch diagrams are included on an instruction sheet in every pattern. There will be front and back diagrams for each design or variation shown on the pattern envelope. These diagrams are informative, showing the position of fastenings, darts, pleats, gathers, trimmings, and any other constructional details.

below A sample cutting layout for the dress, left, shows how to lay out all the pattern pieces required. Where relevant, several variations for each design may be shown for different fabric widths and nap.

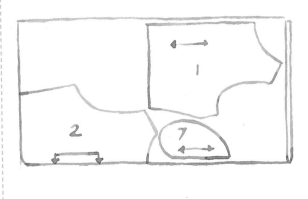

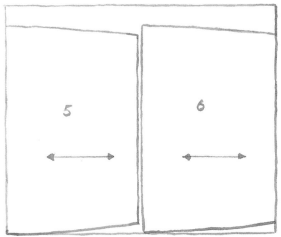

PINNING AND CUTTING OUT

Press the fabric well before you start. Work on the largest flat surface you have available and keep the fabric flat and smooth at all times.

1 Ensure the folds are accurate by correctly aligning the selvages.

2 Align the pattern pieces along the fold line where indicated and pin them in position.

3 For the other pieces, start by checking the straight grain by using a ruler to measure from the selvage to one end of the straight grain line. Repeat at the other end of the line. Pin along the grain line.

4 Smooth out the pattern using the flat of your hand, starting from the pinned straight grain and working outward. Pin in position. Pin diagonally at the corners.

5 If you are right-handed, keep the scissor blades to the right of the pattern piece. Rest the blades on the surface and make firm cuts the full length of the blades. Cut the notches outward from the edges of the pattern pieces as you reach them.

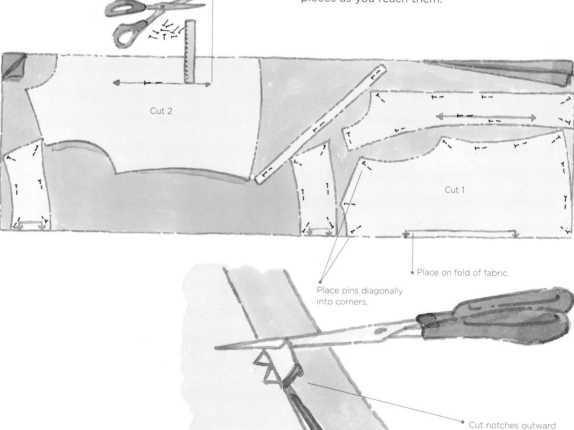

Straight of grain. Place on folded fabric away from the fold.

Cut 2

Cut 1

Place on fold of fabric.

Place pins diagonally into corners.

Cut notches outward from the edges of the pattern pieces as you reach them. This avoids the seam being weakened.

pattern marking

Once the pattern pieces are cut out, it is important that you mark them accurately to ensure that you stitch darts in the right place, position buttons and buttonholes perfectly, and match the right pieces to each other in the correct way that allows for any ease or fit. There are several ways of doing this.

ROTARY MARKER AND DRESSMAKER'S CARBON PAPER

This is a quick and easy way to transfer marks, particularly long lines. The rotary marker, or tracing wheel, is made up of spikes and, with dressmaker's carbon paper laid between the fabric and the pattern, when the wheel is run over the marks it leaves a line of tiny removable dots on the fabric. Dressmaker's carbon paper comes in several shades. Choose one that contrasts with the fabric—though not too strongly, as it may be difficult to remove.

1 Place a sheet of dressmaker's carbon paper with the wax side to the wrong side of each layer of fabric. You may have to remove some pins to slip it between the layers. Repin, then run the wheel along the marks on the paper pattern. Use a ruler for straight lines. The lines will transfer onto the fabric as a line of small dots. Where there are spot markings on the pattern, mark them as a small cross.

MARKER PENS AND PENCILS

These can only mark one layer of fabric at a time. It is best to make the marks on the wrong side of the fabric and don't iron the fabric before removing the marks, as the heat could set them.

1 Push the point of the fabric-marker pen or pencil through the mark on the pattern to mark the fabric below. Replace the pattern on the next layer of fabric and repeat.

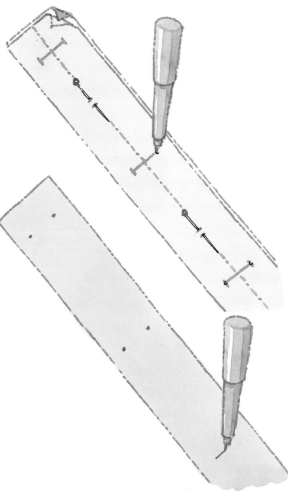

TAILOR'S TACKS

This is an easy, inexpensive, damage-free, and efficient way to identically mark all the layers of fabric. While other forms of marking can rub off, threads can be kept in position until you are ready to remove them. Use a color of thread that contrasts with the fabric so the marks are easy to see and easy to remove. If you are marking different kinds of symbols, you can differentiate between them using different colored threads.

These instructions show you how to mark single spot markings, such as the beginning and end of ease lines, or button and buttonhole positions. If you want to mark a line, then simply use the same principle along the length of the line, making long, loopy stitches (see page 113).

1 Using double thread with the end unknotted, make a stitch through the marking on the pattern piece and all the layers of fabric, leaving a tail of thread a couple of inches long. Make a second stitch over the first, inserting the needle where the tail of thread emerges. Instead of pulling the thread through, leave a loop on the surface. Snip off the thread, leaving another tail of thread. The more layers of fabric you want to mark, the longer the loop and tails need to be.

2 Cut through the loop and lift off the paper pattern.

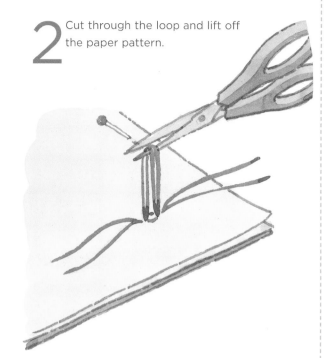

3 Carefully separate out the layers of fabric so that there is a length of thread between them, and cut the thread between each layer of fabric. You will be left with little whiskers of thread in exactly the same place on each layer of fabric.

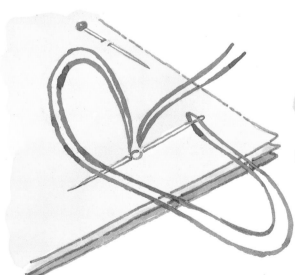

FABRIC CHOICES

Choosing fabric creatively is about much more than looking at the color and pattern. For a professional finish, you also need to consider the weight of the fabric and whether it is suitable for the particular garment or home furnishings that you are making. Look at how the fabric drapes and assess how it will gather or move. Lastly, check how hard wearing it is likely to be and how it needs to be laundered.

a buyer's guide

Fabric stores are a treasure-trove of design opportunity, and choosing all the materials and trimmings for any sewing project has to be one of the most satisfying and exciting moments. By the time you have made your choices and all the fabrics and trimmings are looking fabulous, folded up on the counter, you will have resolved the key design issues.

FABRIC OVERVIEW

Don't hurry the fabric-selection process. Take your time, visiting several stores, if you need to, and asking for swatches to take home so you can give the matter plenty of consideration. You may even want to take home several alternatives. One good reason to get swatches is because you may well need to buy the main fabrics and the trimmings in different places and it is good to give yourself time to consider them together.

There is no end to the variety of fabrics, but essentially, they fall into two main types: fashion and furnishing. There is no reason why these shouldn't be interchanged, depending on the situation, but you may find them in different stores or in different parts of a store.

FURNISHING FABRICS

These are usually heavier weight and wider than dress fabrics. They also fall into two further sub-types: upholstery, which is the most hard wearing, and drapery, which either has a special, less robust finish than upholstery fabric, or is lighter weight. Fabric sold specifically for lining drapes is mainly cotton sateen, which is usually slightly narrower than the main drape fabric. However, you can use any fabric for lining—from velvet to linen—or even self-line the drapes.

Most furnishing fabrics are at least 60 in/ 150 cm wide, although some come considerably wider. Since many furnishings, especially drapes, are made without a pattern, you need to work out how much fabric you will need yourself. Retail staff will always help you with this, and wider fabric will mean you need less drops for drapes. Take this into account when comparing the cost per yard for different fabrics.

FASHION FABRICS

These encompass fabrics suitable for all garments, ranging from delicate silks suitable for lingerie to heavyweight wool or cotton for outerwear. They are usually arranged in the store by fiber content. Printed dressmaking patterns list the types of fabrics suitable for the garment on the back of the envelope, but that still offers you plenty of scope. Most fashion fabrics come in widths of either 45 in/ 115 cm or 60 in/150 cm, although they can vary from this. The back of the pattern will tell you how much fabric to buy in each width.

THE SELECTION PROCESS

Whether you are buying furnishing or fashion fabrics, you will probably have a good idea of what you are looking for in terms of fiber, color, and pattern, but there are many other considerations.

Start with the pattern: unroll some of the fabric to check whether you like the color combination and to assess the pattern repeat. If it is a large repeat, make sure it is appropriate for your project: it may not be if the pattern pieces are small. However, you may decide to use a large repeat as part of the design. For instance, you may find a large animal motif, which could look fun "walking" all the way across a child's garment. Or there may be a dramatic flower motif that could be partly

cropped by a neckline. Large pattern repeats or directional designs (if there is a "top" and "bottom," for example) are likely to require more fabric. You will also need to buy longer quantities of fabrics that have a nap, such as velvet.

Next, assess the weight and drape. Is the fabric robust enough or delicate enough for its purpose? And how does it drape? To assess the drape, unroll a length of the fabric and gather it up in your hand. Does it have body and stiffness, or is it soft and flowing, and which is suitable for your project? A jacket, for example, will need plenty of structured body, while a camisole or evening dress may need to flow flatteringly over curves. For a gathered skirt or drape, gather up a section of fabric in your hand to see what bulk it makes and how it falls from the gathers.

Finally, check that the fabric-care requirements are appropriate for the use it will be put to. Clearly, most children's garments need to be robustly wash-and-wear; less clearly, if you are planning on making a dress, you may be rather less keen on that gorgeous fabric if it requires dry cleaning.

THE SUPPORTING ROLES

Once you have chosen the main fabric, you will need to choose those that take supporting roles: lining, interlining, and batting. These are the real unsung heroes lending body to garments and furnishings, helping them to hang appropriately, last longer, and provide warmth.

You can use purpose-made linings, such as the wide range of rainbow-colored acetates for garments and satin cottons for drapes. These are usually less expensive than the main fabric and are excellent at doing their job. However, for a more luxurious look, you can either self-line (using the main fabric as lining, too), or use an alternative contrasting main fabric.

Interlinings can provide extra body to both garments and drapes. They come in many weights and some are fusible using a hot iron. Nonfusible interlining needs to be basted into position to ensure that it doesn't move before being stitched. For very firm support, use buckram, which is an extremely stiff, loosely woven burlap used to make pelmets. Batting, which comes in different weights, is used for quilting or padding. Traditionally, it was made from cotton or wool, although nowadays, most people use the polyester version.

FABRIC CARE

Expect to find the same laundry information for fabric as you would find on any retailed garment. Laundry-care labels are not normally supplied with each sale, but there should be a label on the roll, along with the fiber content, price, and fabric width. Make a note of this, as following the manufacturer's care instructions will help to keep fabrics in good condition for as long as possible.

OPPOSITE 1. Buckram is a very stiff material used to make pelmets and wherever you need a similar strong shape. **2. Smart linings** lend a more expensive look to garments. If you need to keep an eye on costs, use a regular lining for most of the garment and add a special fabric where it will show, such as inside cuffs. **3. Interlinings** come in many different weights. Some, such as the folded one, can be as fine as lawn; others are as thick as card. **4. Polyester batting** for quilting is generally available in three weights: 2 oz/50 g, 4 oz/115 g, and 6 oz/170 g. **5. Fabric widths** affect the amount of fabric you need to buy. The pattern will state how many yards you need for each width. **6. Fabric drape** depends on the fiber content and the type and density of the weave. When you buy, handle the fabric to see how it will hang or gather to assess its suitability for your project.

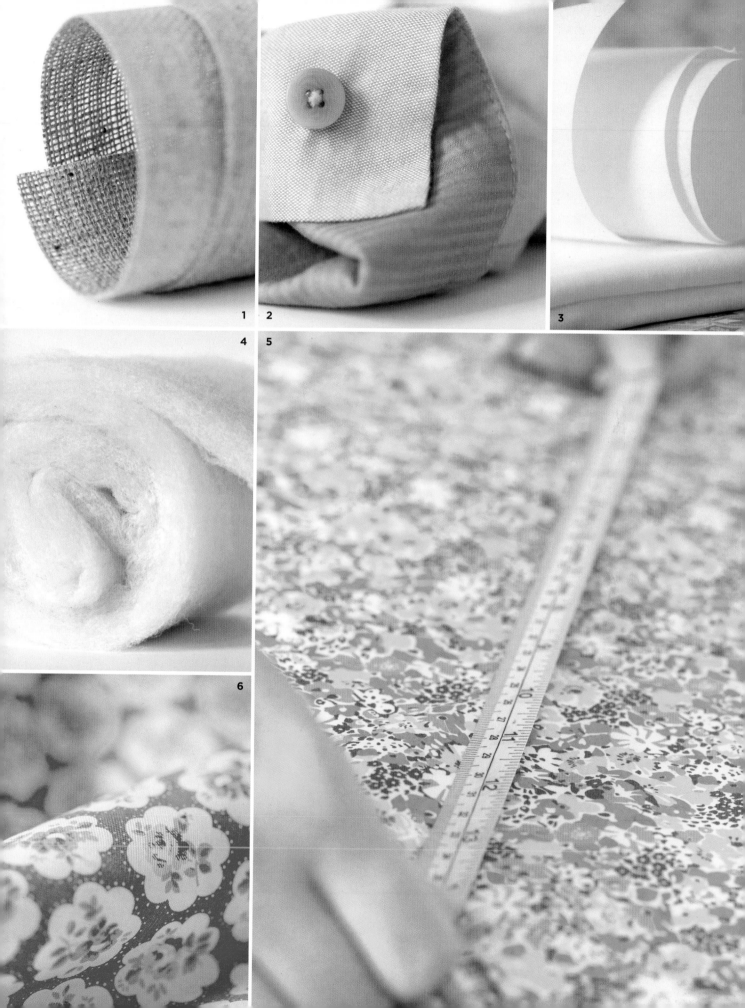

1

2

3

4

5

6

fabric weave

The weave of a fabric not only makes up its construction. It also affects the texture and drape, and can even influence its decorative pattern.

THE DIFFERENT FABRIC WEAVES

There are three basic weaves: plain, satin, and twill, all of which can be made up of any fiber: natural, synthetic, or a mixture. For special weaves, the yarns can be looped or twisted to create crepe and bouclé effects, or looped and cut to create a pile. Some more elaborate fabrics use a combination of two or more weaves or effects. However, the richest and most complicated designs, such as damasks and brocades, are created on jacquard looms, which can create intricate shapes in unlimited colors within the weave. Similar, but simpler, is the dobby loom, which uses the jacquard method to create designs that are typically small repeated motifs or stripes. To create the pattern, both looms carry threads along the back of the material, creating a dense fabric.

Knit (or jersey) is another form of fabric construction, popular for its naturally elastic quality, irrespective of the yarn used to create it. T-shirt material is an example of cotton knit.

Fabric can also be constructed by bonding. One of the best-known traditional examples of this is felt, which is made by matting the fibers using heat, moisture, friction, and pressure to produce a no-fray fabric. The introduction of synthetics has spawned many other nonwoven textiles, produced under intense heat and pressure.

PLAIN WEAVE

The basic weave is where crosswise yarns (weft) are woven under one/over one lengthwise yarns (warp), creating an even fabric. The quality and look of the fabric depends on how fine the threads are and how densely they are woven. The more threads used per inch, the finer and closer-weave the fabric. When two threads are woven under and two over, the result is a basketweave effect.

TWILL

Twill is woven over two vertical threads and under one. As this is offset with every successive horizontal thread, the finished fabric incorporates distinctive diagonal ribs. Denim, chino, drill, gabardine, plaid, ticking, and houndstooth are all examples. Twill is robust, drapes well, and recovers from creases more quickly than plain-weave fabrics. Herringbone is a twill variant with ribs running in two directions.

SATIN

Satin weave is created when the weft (horizontal) yarns are passed under several vertical yarns (warp) and then over just one. This creates a sheen on the right side of the fabric. The more warp threads showing on the right side, the greater the sheen. Usually created in silk or a silky thread, any fiber can be satin-woven.

SATEEN

This is a variation of satin, the difference being that more weft (horizontal threads) show on the surface, producing a softer sheen. This is often the weave of choice for fibers that are naturally shorter than silk, such as cotton.

WEFT KNIT

The basic knit construction is called weft knit, created using a single yarn in a similar way to hand-knitting. Manufactured weft knit is created in a circular fashion, creating a tube of fabric.

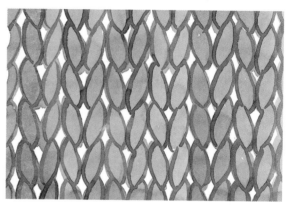

PILE WEAVE

This is any fabric where either the warp threads or the weft threads are woven as a loop to create a pile on the right side. Sometimes, the loop is cut to create a fabric such as velvet; sometimes it is not, to create cord.

WARP KNIT

Warp knit is created on a machine consisting of hundreds of needles, each of which takes a separate yarn that is "knitted up" vertically with a diagonal element. This creates a stable flat fabric.

patterned fabric

Patterned fabrics fall into two types: printed or woven. The production of both have become complex sciences, but here are the basics on a useful-to-know basis.

PRINTED DESIGNS

While technology has spawned many new ways to print pattern onto fabric, using chemicals, pressure, and heat, traditionally, there are three main methods: direct, resist, and discharge.

DIRECT PRINTING

This is where the dye is transferred directly onto the surface of the fabric, one color at a time using a screen, to build up the pattern. The three primaries (red, yellow, and blue) plus black are enough to produce richly colored designs. More expensive fabrics may use six or more color layers.

There are many other ways to transfer pattern onto fabric, using blocks, stencils, and engraved rollers, all of which usually produce simpler designs. More expensively, fabrics can be hand-painted.

RESIST PRINTING

In this method, part of the fabric is treated with a substance to stop the dye from penetrating in those places. Batik is an easily recognizable form of printing that uses wax as the resist, often built up in layers to produce elaborate colorful designs and distinctive veining where the dye has seeped between cracks in the wax.

DISCHARGE PRINTING

For discharge printing, the whole piece of fabric is dyed and then partly treated with a chemical or abrasion to remove some of the dye to create special effects or patterns. This method is used to create "distressed" fashion fabrics.

WOVEN PATTERN

While printing produces a surface design, woven patterns are integral to the very construction of the fabric, and generally look the same on the reverse. Plain weaves produce the simplest designs by using different colored threads along the weft and warp to create stripes and checks. However, more elaborate patterns can be created using the ikat method, which is characterized by its blurred-edged mirror-image designs. Traditional in Asia and South America, ikat designs are created by partly binding the yarns, treating them with wax, and dip-dyeing them before they are woven.

When the weave is more complicated, clever color choices can result in rich integral designs. Some of the best-known twill patterns, for example, are plaid and houndstooth check. Jacquard weaves, such as damasks, brocades, and dobbies, incorporate intricate patterns within the weave.

OPPOSITE **1. Ticking** is a densely-woven striped cotton twill. **2. Paisley** takes its name from the Scottish town that jacquard-wove the distinctive droplet motif into woolen shawls. This paisley is printed onto silk chiffon. **3. Printed patterns** can be reproduced on many fabrics; this colorful design has been printed on cotton. **4. Gingham** is a reversible, woven, checked cotton or cotton blend, featuring white and one other color. **5. Plaid** is a (usually) colorful wool cloth with a checkered design woven into the twill fabric. **6. Damask** comes in intricate designs woven into the fabric on a jacquard loom. **7. Dobbies** are typically simple repeated motifs woven into the fabric in a similar way to damasks but using a dobby loom. **8. Embroidered patterns** are created with surface decoration after the fabric has been woven. **9. Painted patterns** often have a watercolor effect, such as on this silk.

cotton

Cotton has the fresh appeal of a natural fiber that is relatively inexpensive. It takes dyes well and comes in a wide variety of weights, weaves, patterns, and colors. In manufacturing, it is resilient and, therefore, easy to treat with special finishes that improve both its looks and durability. It is easy to handle and makes up and presses well.

MATERIALS: **1. Cotton shirting:** A smooth, lightweight, closely woven cotton, with a high thread count, often incorporating a stripe. **2. Chambray:** A lightweight fabric with colored warp threads woven over white weft threads. The most common cotton chambray is in a denim blue. **3. Tana lawn:** A very fine closely woven cotton with a high thread count, capable of taking intricate printed designs. **4. Regency stripe:** Printed cotton incorporating a stripe. **5. Printed baby cord:** Fine corduroy, which has a ridged construction.

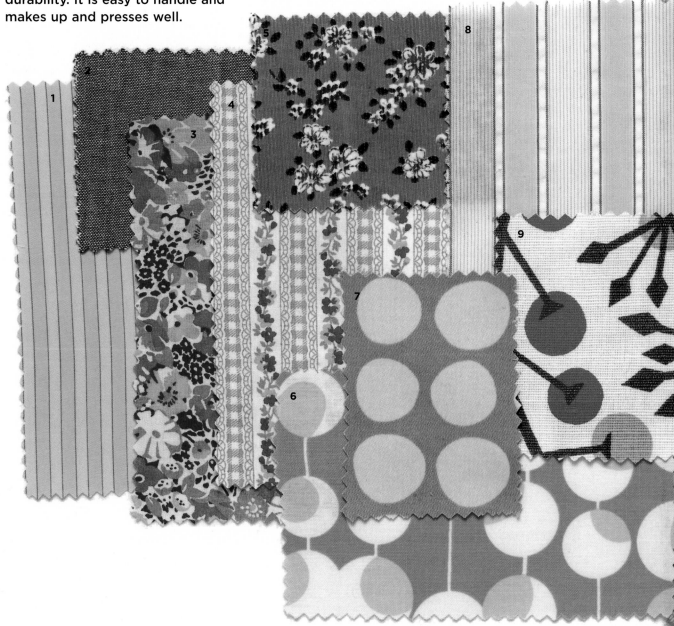

Usually plain, this baby cord has been printed with a pretty floral design. **6. Printed cotton:** Popular because the fiber takes colored dye well. This design has been printed on a plain-weave fabric. **7. Fine printed sateen cotton:** This is a firmer weave than the plain weave and has a slight sheen. **8. Seersucker:** A fine, light, often woven striped fabric that incorporates crinkles. These crinkles make the fabric very cool against the skin. **9. Printed cotton union:** A combination of cotton and linen that provides a firm, resilient fabric that is a popular upholstery choice. **10. Brushed cotton:** This brushed twill weave creates a fabric that is extremely soft to the touch. It is a perfect choice for babies' clothes and nightwear. **11. Gingham:** A popular yarn-dyed woven fabric, best known for its checks, which traditionally come in a variety of sizes. **12. Ticking:** This twill cotton, which is typically striped, is traditionally used for pillowcases and mattresses, as it is tightly woven to stop the feathers from escaping. This particular fabric is herringbone, a variation on twill. **13. Fine printed cotton:** This pattern, inspired by traditional East Indian designs, has a contemporary color combination of lime and emerald green. **14. Organdy:** An extremely sheer gauze with a very crisp finish that survives washing, created by treating it in acid. Best known in its white form; this one has woven colored stripes. **15. Cotton damask:** A patterned cotton that has been woven on a jacquard loom.

linen

Taken from the long, resilient fiber of the flax plant, linen has two to three times the strength of cotton and its wax content gives it a natural luster. Traditionally used for bedding and household "linens," it is also excellent for garments and home furnishings. It takes dye well and presses up beautifully, but it also creases badly.

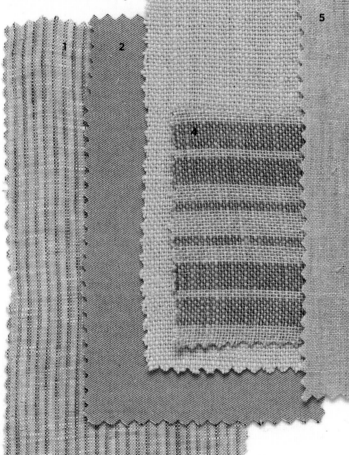

MATERIALS: 1. Fine stripes in different neutral colors work well in loosely woven linen. **2. Linen twill** creates a tightly woven cloth with a natural sheen for elegant garments. **3. Heavy-weave linen** makes an ideal furnishing fabric: in pastel shades, it lends a light, airy feel. **4. Linen voile** makes an elegant alternative to net curtains. This one has stripes incorporated into the weave. **5. Linen chambray,** like cotton chambray, is created using colored warp threads over white weft threads for a wonderful, subtle fabric. **6. Embroidered linen:** Monogrammed household linen is a centuries-old tradition. This outsized monogram-inspired embroidery makes a fabulous upholstery fabric. **7. Linen twill:** Two different thread tones and different twill gauges makes for a stunning striped fabric. **8. Linen shirting:** The woven stripe in bright colors of this fine-weave linen is inspired by cotton shirting, although the looser weave gives it a more relaxed feel. **9. Puppytooth linen:** The tiny version of houndstooth check, which is created using a twill weave. Normally associated with wool, in linen it makes up into elegant suitings. **10. Herringbone:** The textured quality to this weave is accentuated by the use of two different colored threads: pink and yellow. **11. Linen plaid:** The twill weave combined with a plaid design is more usually associated with a wool fabric. In linen, the fabric is finer with a clearer color range. **12. Heavyweight woven stripes** make a great contemporary upholstery fabric. **13. Heavyweight dyed linen** offers a wide range of colors that are excellent for upholstery and can be coordinated with stripes in a similar weight. **14 and 15. Dyed linen** is available in a wide range of colors, offering endless subtlety, as demonstrated by these two fine pink linens that would make up into exquisite dresses or blouses. **16. Natural linen voile** offers an elegant lustrous translucency—delightful for sheer curtains. **17. Printed linen:** As linen takes dye well, it can be printed with intricate designs.

silk

This fine natural fiber spun by silkworms has long been valued for the strong, smooth, shiny fabrics it can create. It has excellent insulating qualities, keeping you cool in summer and warm in winter. It dyes to rich colors and weaves into elaborate patterns.

is taken from cocoons in the wild that have been vacated by the silk moth. This Indian silk is generally heavier and slubbier than cultivated silk. **6. Tussah silk voile** with slubbed colored threads. This fabric has a stiff, organdy feel and would make exquisite sheer curtains or shades. **7. Painted silk:** The varying tones have a watercolor effect. **8 & 9. Silk velvet:** A fine pile fabric, shown here in green and gray. **10. Woven stripe Thai silk:** This densely woven design is sold in panels and used to make traditional

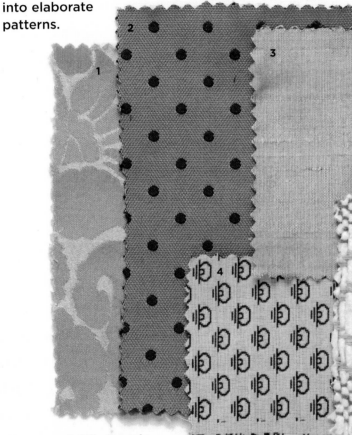

MATERIALS: 1. Silk damask: A richly patterned weave that originated in Damascus, along the ancient Silk Road from China. Nowadays, it is woven on a jacquard loom. **2. Silk dobby:** A jacquard woven on a simplified loom, the dobby. It is made up of a regular small motif to create typically spotted designs. **3. Silk satin:** A densely woven fabric that is matte on one side and very shiny on the other. **4. Silk jacquard:** A woven design created on a jacquard loom. This one incorporates sections of different patterns within the same fabric. **5. Tussah wild silk fancy weave:** Tussah

Thai formal suits. **11. Tussah herringbone weave:** Threads in two different colors have been used to weave this firm, textured fabric to highlight the herringbone weave. It would make up into an exquisite jacket. **12. Embroidered silk:** Woven silk has been surface embroidered with synthetic threads, beads, and sequins. **13. Woven stripes** can be created both by using different colored threads and different types of weave to create extra texture. **14. Printed silk** can be used to create rich, glowing designs. **15. Contemporary embroidered silks** can be created using threads plus pile for interest. **16. Silk chiffon** is fine and luxurious with a soft drape.

wool

This soft, warm animal fiber is generally made from sheep fleece, but high-quality wool fabrics can also be made from llama, goat, and rabbit fur. It dyes into soft tones and doesn't crease. There are two main types: woolens, which are usually bulkier fabrics used for outerwear and tweedy daywear; and finer, hard-wearing worsteds used for tailored clothing.

MATERIALS: 1. Plaid is a type of twill woven in a plaid design. **2. Herringbone:** This fine wool fabric has a slight sheen, is densely woven and crease-resistant; excellent for a fine suit. **3. Woolen fabrics** are woven with yarn that has been carded but not combed for a warm and comfortable suit. This green is a soft shade typical of dyed wool. **4. Jacquard woven:** This intricate geometric design in browns and greens has a charming contemporary feel. **5. Two-tone bouclé** makes a striking crease-free fabric with a soft, textured quality: perfect for a contemporary woman's suit. **6. Printed knit:** This fine jersey has natural stretch with the cross grain. Printing on jersey is unusual, but this one has a fine texture, so takes the dye well. **7. Textured knit** has an integral diamond pattern for extra texture and drape. **8. Plaids** come in many different color combinations. This one in black, gray, and damson makes an elegant alternative to the more usual reds and greens. **9. Fancy weaves** are easy to create using wool because of the natural crimp in the fiber. The seersucker texture of this fabric is accentuated using two different colors of yarn and by lengthening some warp threads and shortening others. **10. Wool satin** is an unusual dense fabric with a subtle sheen and wonderful drape. It would be excellent for elegant upholstery. **11. Wool damask** is a pretty woven design created on a jacquard loom. It is unusual in that silk and cotton are more usually made into damask weaves. **12. Wool twill** can be woven into glorious, subtly toned patterns. **13. Dramatic contemporary** twill can be achieved using bulky woolly fibers in contrasting colors.

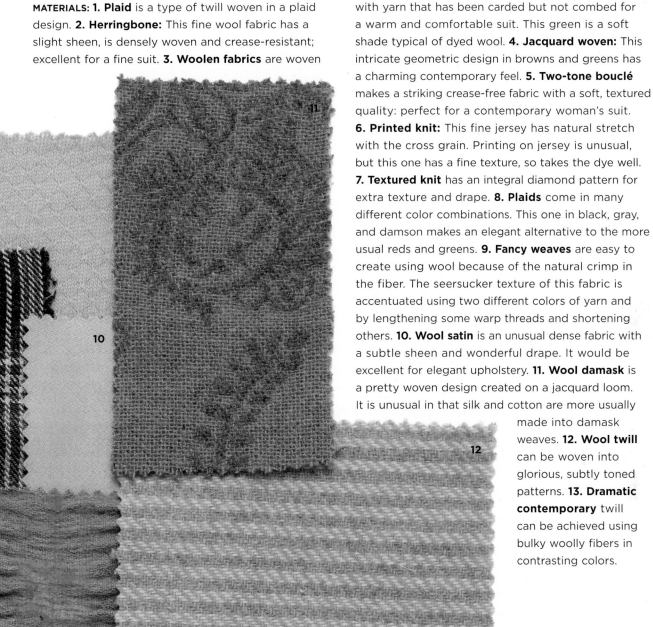

synthetic fibers and mixed-fiber fabrics

Nowadays, it is not so much natural fibers versus synthetic as the development of interesting mixes. Although synthetics are here to stay, most of us agree that natural fibers are more comfortable to use and wear, not least for their natural wicking qualities, which draw moisture away from the skin. But there are many reasons why manufacturers value particular properties of synthetics in combination with natural fibers to create a cloth of a particular durability, creasing (or, rather, noncreasing), and drape. It is also true that synthetics are mixed with natural fibers for economic reasons. Manufacturers also mix different natural fibers together to create special effects. All fabrics should be marked with the exact fiber content, expressed as percentages. Sometimes, it is only the decoration, such as embroidery, that is synthetic. All the exquisite fabrics opposite are made up of mixed fibers, both natural and synthetic.

Here, in simplified terms, is a rundown of the synthetic fibers you are most likely to come across, either in their pure form or as part of a mix.

ACETATE
This silky fabric, usually 100 percent acetate, comes in many hues and is sold for making dress linings. Colorfast and shrink-resistant, it should be warm-washed or dry-cleaned, as water weakens the fibers.

ACRYLIC
A wool-like fabric that is often mixed with natural wool because it keeps its shape, doesn't shrink as readily as the natural version, and has cost benefits. But it is not as warm as wool, and pills more easily.

POLYESTER
This cottonlike fiber is used in sheeting and clothing, both on its own and mixed with cotton (polycotton). It is easy to care for and crease-resistant.

RAYON
The original synthetic fiber, known as artificial silk, rayon comes in many forms, but viscose rayon is the most familiar today (see viscose, below).

SPANDEX
Also known as Elastane, or its trade name Lycra, this elastic fiber can stretch to 500 percent without breaking and can regularly stretch to 100 percent. Initially used in underwear, it is now associated with sportswear, but most retailers include it in their suitings to stop sagging knees and seats.

VISCOSE
This silky fiber is able to "breathe" like cotton and drapes well, so it is used in lightweight silky clothing. However, it wrinkles easily and is prone to shrinking unless it is carefully laundered or dry-cleaned.

OPPOSITE **1. Plaid in wool and linen** weaves into a finer fabric than the traditional pure wool version. **2. Wool and silk damask** makes a sophisticated crease-resistant drapery fabric. **3. Linen, viscose, cotton, and nylon**, jacquard-woven in blue and brown, makes a richly patterned upholstery fabric. **4. Cotton, silk, and linen**, woven into a coffee and cream damask, combine smart design with elegant drape. **5. Wool and mohair with a touch of nylon** team up in a loosely woven striped pattern for soft-to-the-touch curtaining. **6. Natural and synthetic fibers** can be mixed to create an appliqué effect. **7. Viscose and linen** combine in a dramatic green leafy design. **8. Cotton, linen, polyester, and viscose** herringbone weaves into a dense, hard-wearing fabric. **9. Linen and cotton**, plain-woven and honeycomb-embroidered, create a timeless design. **10. Wool and linen** can be dyed in subtle colors and twill-woven for a fresh plaid colorway.

fabric glossary

Acetate Often used as a lining, this silky synthetic is lightweight, available in a wide range of colors, and has excellent draping qualities.

Alpaca Fine, light fiber from South American llamalike animals. Difficult to dye, it is often used in its natural colors ranging from cream to brown and black, and mixed with wool for fine suitings.

Angora Long, silky rabbit hair, often mixed with wool.

Batik A method of printing rich designs using wax as a resist, traditional throughout Southeast Asia, India, and some African countries.

Batiste Traditionally, a fine, soft plain-weave linen used for lingerie, handkerchiefs, and household linen. Nowadays it is sometimes made from other fibers, such as cotton.

Bouclé A textured wool fabric made from a yarn incorporating loops and curls for a poodle effect.

Brocade Traditional to India and China, brocade is a richly woven and patterned fabric, often made with silk and gold fibers. Nowadays it is manufactured on a jacquard loom incorporating synthetic fibers.

Broderie anglaise Eyelet embroidery, usually on white cotton.

Buckram A very stiff plain-weave linen or cotton, often used for drape pelmets.

Cambric Fine, lightweight, densely woven, slightly glossy plain-weave fabric made from linen or cotton.

Canvas A firm, heavy, plain-weave cotton fabric used to make outdoor chairs, awnings, bags, and workwear.

Cashmere A fine, very warm, expensive wool fabric made from Kashmir goat hair, often blended with wool.

Cavalry twill A firm double-twill weave, originally used to make riding breeches.

Challis Traditionally a fine plain-weave wool, printed with a floral or paisley design against a dark background.

Chambray A plain weave where the weft (horizontal threads) are white and the warp (vertical threads) are dyed. Popularly made in blue cotton, it looks like a lightweight denim. Traditionally used for workerwear, hence the term "blue collar worker."

Chenille This is a soft (often wool) yarn that incorporates a pile, descriptively named after the French word for caterpillar. The yarn weaves up into a woolly velvetlike fabric that is also usually known as chenille.

Chiffon A very lightweight sheer with excellent draping qualities, traditionally made from silk.

Chintz A finely woven glazed cotton that is often printed with bright, traditional, often floral, designs. It is generally used for drapes and pillows, but is not suitable for upholstery, as the glaze could easily be worn off.

Corduroy A fabric woven with a weft pile that runs in vertical cords when cut. It is available in a variety of weights, including baby cord (fine) and elephant cord (heavy). It is usually plain, but baby cord can be printed.

Crepe Any woven or knitted fabric that has a crinkled surface created by twisting yarns, using irregularities in the weave or special heat and pressure treatments.

Crepe de chine A lightweight plain silk, where both weft and warp threads are highly twisted to give a muted sheen and soft drape. Nowadays, it is often made with polyester.

Damask Richly patterned, firm, reversible woven fabric, originally from Damascus, a trading post along the Silk Road from China. Traditionally handmade using silks, now it is woven on a jacquard loom in cottons and linens, as well as silk, and often incorporating synthetics.

Denim A strong cotton twill, originally used for workwear, as it is robust and resists soiling. Originally named serge de Nimes after the French town where it originated, it was soon shortened to denim.

Devoré This is a velvet pile fabric woven into a sheer base, where some parts of the pile have been chemically burned away to create a pattern.

Dimity A lightweight cotton with raised woven stripes or checks and sometimes with a small printed pattern.

Dobby Simple jacquard fabrics that are woven on dobby looms and are generally made up of repeated small woven designs or stripes. Dobby looms are faster, cheaper to operate, and more popular in the modern textile industry than the more complex jacquard looms.

Doupion Traditionally, a firm slubbed-silk fabric made from rough raw silk reeled from double cocoons, from which the name derives, and now often made from synthetic fibers.

Drill A cotton twill traditionally used in khaki army uniforms worn in the tropics. Still used for safari jackets, work clothing, and chinos.

Duck A heavy plain-weave cotton fabric.

Flannel Soft, closely woven cotton or woolen cloth, sometimes brushed.

Flannelette Plain-weave brushed cotton.

Gabardine Strong, heavyweight twill, often used for raincoats.

Georgette A lightweight plain-weave crepe fabric.

Gingham Cotton fabrics best known for their woven checked designs, although they can also be woven into stripes.

Grosgrain A strong ribbon made from strong cotton warp cords woven with silk or rayon to create distinctive ribbing. Grosgrain is available in a variety of widths and endless plain colors, as well as stripes.

Houndstooth check A distinctive checked pattern created by a special combination of contrast threads and twill weave. Available in smaller-sized checks, known as dogtooth check and puppytooth check.

Ikat Traditional in many countries in South America, Southeast Asia, India, and Japan, these distinctive designs, often with blurred edges, are created by part-dyeing bundles of threads before weaving.

Interlock A fine but firm cotton knit, traditionally used for underwear, but now used for outerwear.

Jacquard Nowadays, this term is used to describe any elaborately patterned woven fabrics, such as damasks, brocades, dobbies, even motif-woven ribbons or name tapes. Jacquards take their name from Joseph Marie Jacquard, who, in 1801, invented a loom with punched cards that were able to replicate intricate damasks from Damascus. The originals could only be woven with the help of small boys, who sat under the loom to raise and lower the warp threads as needed to create the designs. Jacquard's punched cards were a means by which hooks could be raised or lowered to create the designs: these have now been replaced by modern computers.

Jersey The general term for knitted fabrics in any fiber or fiber mix. T-shirt material is cotton jersey.

Lawn A fine plain-weave cotton, often printed.

Madras Lightweight plain-weave cotton from India with woven striped and checked designs.

Mohair A silky yarn or fabric made from the hair of the Angora goat.

Moire Silk taffeta with a watery effect. The synthetic version is often made of acetate.

Muslin Plain-weave cotton fabric, in a variety of weights, left unbleached. It is often used to make up toiles (prototype garments) and can also be used as interlining.

Nylon The trade name for polyamide, a silky synthetic fiber made popular in 1940, when it was first used to make women's stockings. Nowadays, it is often used mixed with other fibers.

Organdy A fine, sheer loose-weave cotton with a permanently crisp finish. Traditionally used to make little girls' dresses, but now more often used to make sheer curtains.

Organza A sheer, shiny, crisp silk organdy. Nowadays, it is more often made using synthetics, often with a metallic finish, and is available in a wide range of colors.

Oxford A cotton shirting fabric with a basket weave, often used for men's casual clothing.

Percale A fine, dense, firm, and smooth plain-weave fabric, mainly used for sheeting. The higher the thread count, the finer the sheeting. Percale typically has a thread count of 200 (measured per square inch of fabric), although highest-quality Egyptian cotton sheets can have a thread count of 800. Percale does not refer to the fiber, but it is usually made from cotton or a mix of polyester and cotton.

Pique A dobby-woven cotton fabric with a small raised geometric design within the weave: a popular choice for casual clothing.

Plush A thick, deep-pile fabric, similar to velvet, but made of wool or rayon, used mainly for upholstery.

Poplin Hard-wearing, tightly woven cotton fabric with a horizontal rib.

Polyester A versatile synthetic fiber that can be woven or knitted and is extensively combined with natural fibers such as cotton, or produced as microfibers for batting.

Raw silk Natural undyed silk reeled from the cocoons of cultivated silkworms before the protein sericin has been removed. The resulting fabric is usually slubbed.

Rayon Synthetic silk first produced in 1891. Viscose is a type of rayon that is often used, either on its own or mixed with other fibers, for fashion garments.

Sateen Sateen is similar to satin, except that more of the weft (horizontal threads) are seen on the right side of the fabric than warp (vertical threads), giving a softer sheen. Traditionally, long silk fibers were used to make satin and shorter cotton fibers to make sateen.

Satin This is a type of weave where more warp (vertical threads) are seen on the right side of the fabric for a lustrous shiny look, especially if it is woven from a shiny fiber, such as silk or, nowadays, synthetics.

Seersucker This all-cotton plain-weave fabric has a part-smooth, part-crinkled effect, and is very often striped or checked. The name comes from an anglicized Hindustani word meaning "milk and sugar," describing its texture. Cool and comfortable, it was a popular choice of fabric among the colonial British in India, because the crinkling held it away from the skin, allowing the air to circulate. In the USA, seersucker was worn by the poor until it was popularized by undergraduates in the 1920s.

Shantung A slightly rough silk or synthetic silk fabric created using slub yarn, mostly used to make formal eveningwear.

Slub yarn A yarn that is uneven along its length. This could be because of the natural properties of the fiber, or it could be the way in which it was spun. When woven, slub yarns create slubbed fabrics, which have an uneven knobbly effect.

Spandex A very stretchy synthetic fiber, often known as Elastane or its trade name Lycra. It can be used on its own for swimwear and sportswear, or mixed with other fibers to create fabrics that keep their shape.

Surah Silk twill often used for ties and quality headscarves, as it drapes better and resists soiling better than plain woven silk.

Taffeta A closely woven, smooth, crisp silk with a subtle rib and a distinctive rustle. Nowadays, sometimes made from synthetics.

Tartan A wool twill woven into plaid. The genuine tartan plaids belong to Scottish clans.

Thai silk Thai silk has a slightly knobbly texture often resulting in a slubbed fabric. It is often "shot" or two-tone, whereby the weft threads are one color and the warp threads are another, so the color looks slightly different, depending on which angle it is viewed from. Formal Thai clothes are made from elaborately woven panels.

Ticking A densely woven twill cotton that is very often striped, traditionally used to cover pillows and mattresses, as the fabric is strong enough to prevent feathers from working their way through.

Toile de Jouy A plain-weave cotton printed with a single-color design of Victorian pastoral scenes.

Tulle Fine netting, traditionally made of silk, but nowadays more often made of nylon. Used for bridal and dancewear.

Tussah Sometimes known as wild silk, this is made from the wild silkworms of India. It is thicker and slubbier than the silk from China's cultivated silk and is most often seen in its natural creamy colors.

Tweed Thick woolen fabric with characteristic slubs and flecks.

Twill This type of weave creates a distinctive diagonal ribbing within the fabric. Twill is robust and resistant to soiling.

Velour A knitted fabric with a thick, short, cut pile.

Velvet A luxurious cut-pile fabric, with the pile created by the warp (vertical) yarns. Traditionally made from silk, it can also be made from linen, mohair, wool, and cotton, although nowadays it is more likely to be made from synthetics.

Velveteen Similar to velvet, except the pile is created by the weft (horizontal) yarns.

Viscose A kind of rayon, one of the original silky synthetic fabrics.

Voile A plain-weave semisheer fabric traditionally made from cotton.

Woolen A fabric woven from soft wool yarn that has been carded but not combed, so it retains some of the shorter fibers.

Worsted Woolen yarn that has been carded and combed to remove the short fibers. Worsted fabrics are smoother and harder-wearing than woolens.

BASIC SEWING SKILLS

So, this is how you do it. Here are all the basic skills you will need to make almost anything you want. They are not academic: they are real, tried-and-tested, sometimes employ our favorite shortcuts, and they include 20 easy-to-follow projects. If you are a beginner, keep things simple to start off with: choose to make a project that involves only straight seams so you can develop your skills.

getting started

Working in the correct order not only makes the handling of your work easier, but it should also result in a better, more professional finish. Each project is different, so this list is meant as a guideline for general principles (such as aim to insert the zipper as soon as possible), rather than hard-and-fast rules. You will find all these steps in more detail in the relevant sections.

ORDER OF WORK

1. Prepare the fabric. Launder it, if necessary, press it thoroughly, and trim any ragged edges (see page 56).

2. Take measurements (see page 54).

3. Prepare the pattern. Cut out the relevant pieces, adjust them if necessary, and smooth them out (see pages 57–59).

4. Choose the most suitable cutting layout and temporarily place all of the pattern pieces in position to check that they fit on the fabric (see page 60).

5. Pin the pattern pieces in place on the fabric and cut them out (see page 61).

6. Transfer the pattern markings onto all the layers of fabric (see page 62).

7. Insert the zipper, if necessary, between the relevant pieces (see pages 129–33). Note: If a dress zipper runs through the bodice and the skirt, you will need to delay this step until those pieces have been joined together.

8. Sew any darts and pleats (see pages 113–15).

9. Stitch and finish the main seams (see pages 91–97).

10. For skirts and pants with elastic or drawstring waists, make the channel and thread the elastic or drawstring through it (see page 148).

11. Sew gathering stitches for gathered waists (see page 120–22).

12. Stitch waistbands to skirts and pants.

13. Stitch hooks to the waistbands of skirts or pants (see page 144).

14. For bodices, blouses, and jackets, insert sleeves if necessary (see page 122).

15. Join the facing pieces and then stitch the facings into position.

16. Join the bodice to the skirt. Insert the zipper if necessary.

17. Sew buttonholes and stitch on buttons, press studs, and hooks and eyes (see pages 137–39, 143, and 144).

18. Finish the hem (see pages 184–87).

seams

Seams are the basic building blocks of all sewing projects. Even if you are confident only about stitching a neat straight seam, the scope is endless: custom-made drapes, shades, tablecloths, napkins, and pillows are all well within your capability. Once you can master a straight seam, you will soon be able to add skills, such as curved seams and corners, which will have you transforming flat, two-dimensional lengths of fabric into unique three-dimensional pieces, such as garments, accessories, bags, stuffed toys, and more elaborate pillows and cushions.

Whatever you decide to make, the secret of success is to work methodically and as neatly as possible, aiming to make the item look as good on the inside as on the outside. That way, you can guarantee a more professional finish. The reason? Careful finishing and pressing-as-you-go means flatter seams at each stage that will fit together better at the next stage.

SEWING A PLAIN, STRAIGHT SEAM

Before you begin, check the length of the stitches and tension by stitching a short length across the bias on a small sample of two thicknesses of the fabric. Generally, you will need a longer stitch for thicker fabric and a shorter one for finer fabrics (see Tension, page 42). Make any necessary adjustments. The standard seam allowance is $5/8$ in/1.5 cm, which is etched on the throat plate of most sewing machines (see page 92). If it is not, measure the distance out from the needle and mark this point on the throat plate using a straight strip of low-tack tape.

1 Place the two pieces of fabric right sides together with the raw edges and any notches or markings matching. Pin them together, placing the pins at right angles to the seam.

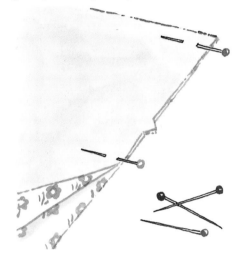

2 Position the fabric under the needle $1/2$ in/ 12 mm from the top edge, making sure the raw seam edges are aligned with the seam line etched on the throat plate.

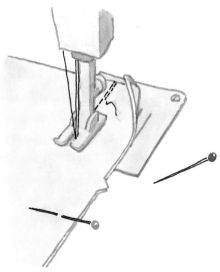

3 Backstitch to the top edge of the fabric and then stitch forward to the end of the seam, removing the pins just before they reach the presser foot. Backstitch ½ in/12 mm to finish. Trim off any spare threads at both ends of the seam.

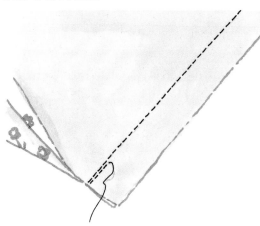

4 Using a steam iron, press the seam open on the wrong side of the work. Then turn the fabric over and press the right side flat.

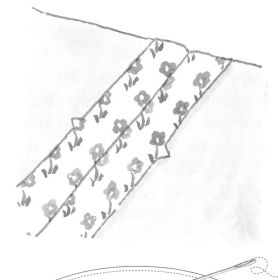

TIPS
STRAIGHT SEAMS
Before starting, check that both the bobbin thread and the top thread are pulled straight out behind the needle to ensure that they don't become ensnared in the seam.
• • •
Make sure that both pieces of fabric are absolutely flat.

MAINTAINING AN EVEN SEAM ALLOWANCE

Whether you are stitching a straight or curved seam, neat results can only be achieved if you keep the seam allowance even. The secret to success is to keep your eye off the needle and concentrate, instead, on lining up the raw edges of the fabric with a mark on the throat plate.

Most sewing machines have a throat plate that is etched with guidelines. The standard ⅝ in/ 1.5 cm seam allowance is marked on the throat plate by a long line, although there is also a choice of alternative seam allowances marked by shorter lines.

The throat plate is also usually marked with cross lines, which are there to help you stitch neat, accurate corners. If your machine's throat plate is not etched with seam allowances, you can measure them out and mark them yourself using low-tack tape. This is also a useful technique if you want to mark out a seam allowance that is different from any of the lines etched on the throat plate.

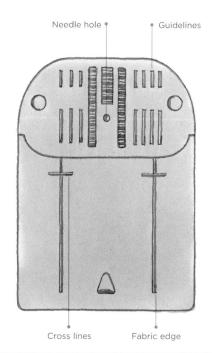

Needle hole • • Guidelines

Cross lines · · Fabric edge

SEWING A CURVED SEAM

Use the same basic technique as for a plain, straight seam, making sure that you keep the seam an even width from beginning to end. Once stitched, curved seams will need to be trimmed close to the stitching, then clipped or notched to reduce bulk and ensure that the seam lies flat.

Inward curves need to be clipped. Do this by using the points of sharp scissors to snip in toward the stitching, being careful not to cut into the stitches.

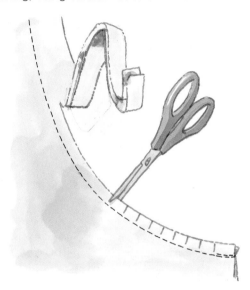

Outward curves should be notched, taking out small triangles of excess fabric. Do this in the same way as clipping, using the scissor points and making sure that you don't cut into any stitches.

TIP
CURVED SEAMS
Keep the seam line even by slowing down the machine speed as you stitch around the curve, carefully guiding the fabric so that the edges always align with the marking on the throat plate. It is even more important with a curved seam to keep your eye on the plate marking and not on the needle.

STITCHING AROUND A CORNER

1 Check that the throat plate has cornering cross lines. If it doesn't, measure out $5/8$ in/ 1.5 cm forward from the needle and use low-tack tape to mark a cross line. Stitch down one side in the same way as you would a straight seam, slowing down as you near the corner.

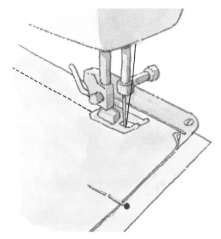

2 When the end of the fabric reaches the cross line, stop with the needle down through the fabric.

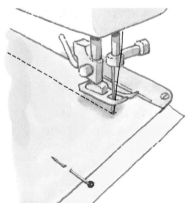

3 Raise the presser foot, swivel the fabric counterclockwise until the new edge aligns with the etched seam line on the throat plate. Lower the presser foot. Stitch down the new seam.

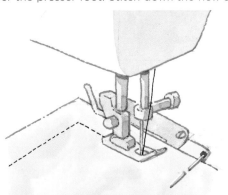

TIP
SEWING CORNERS
When sewing corners, reduce the stitch length a little for an inch or so on either side of the corners to provide reinforcement.

TRIMMING EXTERNAL CORNERS

The bulk of excess fabric at corners demands bold trimming to ensure a neat finish. On an external corner, before turning through, carefully cut the tip off, making sure that you don't cut into any stitches. Elongated points will also need the sides tapered to further reduce the bulk.

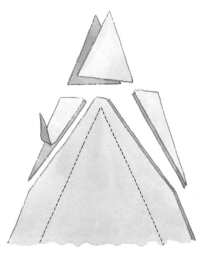

REDUCING BULK

While curved seams always need to be trimmed, there are also occasions when straight seams need to be trimmed to reduce bulk, depending on the position and shape of the seam. As a rule of thumb, this is usually where seams are enclosed within a facing, or where you are stitching an enclosed seam.

GRADING

Where there are several layers of fabric or the fabric is thick, cut the seam allowances to different widths so that the seam doesn't create too much bulk.

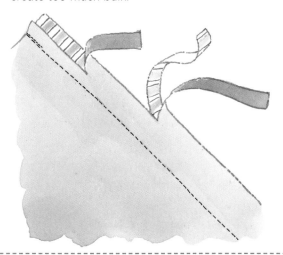

CLIPPING INTERNAL CORNERS

Clip into internal corners to create flexibility. It is important that you don't snip into the stitches, so start by putting a pin just inside the corner to protect the stitches. Make a straight snip into the point of the corner using the tip of the scissors.

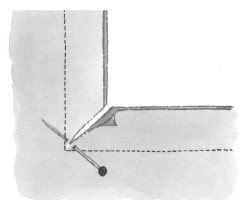

seam finishes

Generally, seams need to be finished, both to neaten them and to stop them from fraying, particularly if the fabric frays easily. However, those that won't be exposed to much wear and tear can be left without finishing. These are usually seams that are enclosed—inside a facing, for example, or if the garment is lined.

PINKING

This is the quickest and easiest way to finish seams, but it limits, rather than stops, the fraying, so it is best used on fabrics that don't fray too easily anyway. Use sharp pinking shears to trim off as little of the raw edge as possible. On finer fabrics, both layers of the edges of seams can be pinked together before being pressed open. For heavier fabrics, it is best to press the seams open first, then pink one side at a time.

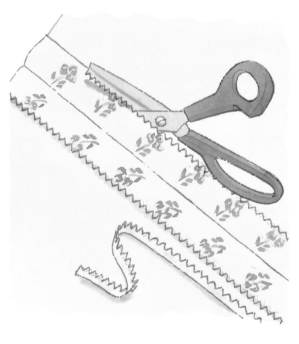

TURNING AND STITCHING

Use this neat and easy finish for lightweight fabrics. Turn under ⅛ in/3 mm of the raw edge of the seam and then stitch. It is best to finish the seams as you go, so that they lie flat when they are worked into the next stage of the garment.

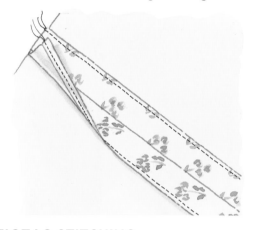

ZIGZAG STITCHING

Neat, quick, and effective, this is an excellent finish for any fabric, but in particular for bulky fabrics or those that easily fray. Set the machine to zigzag with a medium-width short stitch, then stitch down the seam allowance as close as you can to the raw edge. Then, if you wish, trim off any excess.

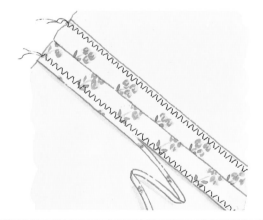

OVERLOCKING

Manufactured clothes often have seams finished by overlocking—and, indeed, sometimes the seam itself is stitched using an overlocker. This is a specialist machine that cuts the raw edge and stitches over it in one action. Few home-sewers own what is an expensive machine. Also, because it cuts the fabric as it sews, it needs an experienced hand, to ensure that it doesn't cut into the body of the garment. This can be overcome by overlocking the raw edges before stitching the seams.

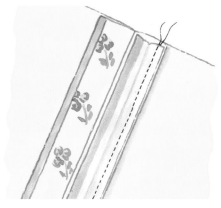

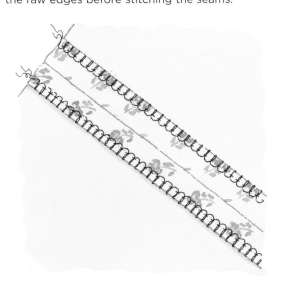

BIAS BINDING

This provides a strong, smart finish to seams. Ready-made bias binding has the raw edges pressed in and is pressed in half lengthwise so it has a central fold. It is available in several widths and colors. Bias binding has natural stretch, which means that it lies flat, even on curved seams. You can make bias binding from any lightweight fabric (see page 152). As well as the traditional application technique (below), there is a quick, one-step method (right); this requires a steady hand, as all the layers are machined at once, so some sections can slip out of alignment while stitching.

1 With right sides together, pin the raw edge of the bias binding to the raw edge of the seam allowance and stitch ¼ in/6 mm from the edge along the fold in the bias binding.

2 Fold the bias binding over to the wrong side of the seam allowance, with the raw edge of the bias binding turned in. Pin, and either topstitch on the wrong side close to the edge of the bias binding, or slipstitch by hand to finish.

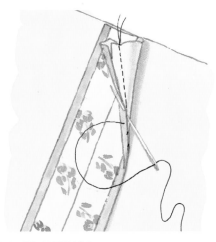

ONE-STEP METHOD

1 With the raw edges turned in, fold the bias in half lengthwise. Pin it over the raw edge and machine stitch through all the layers.

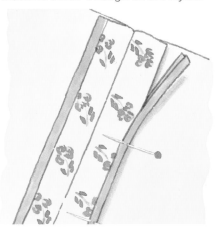

HONG KONG FINISH

This seam finish is similar to bias binding, but it is less fiddly, as there is one less fold in the fabric. For this reason, it is also a particularly effective technique for use on heavier fabrics.

1 With right sides together, pin the raw edge of the bias binding to the raw edge of the seam allowance and stitch ¼ in/6 mm from the edge.

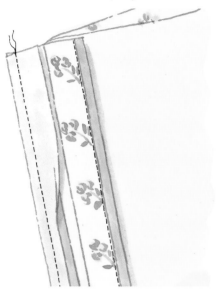

3 Working from the right side, stitch close to the seam. This is called "stitch in the ditch."

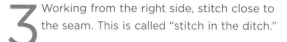

2 Turn the bias binding to the wrong side and, if you are using ready-made bias, unfold the pressed-in hem. Pin it in position.

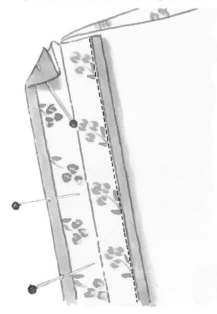

4 Turn to the wrong side again and trim off any excess bias binding.

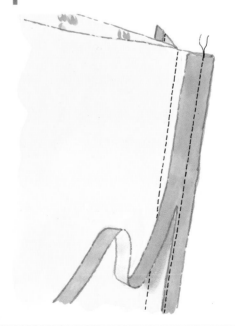

pressing

The importance of frequent and accurate pressing can't be overstated. There is nothing like a good shot of steam to transform an item at every stage from a somewhat shapeless piece of fabric into something altogether smarter and ready for the next step of construction.

Set up an iron and ironing board in your sewing room where it can't be knocked over, so there is always a hot shot of steam on hand. Press darts, seams, and facings at every stage, and then re-press the whole garment-in-progress before moving on to the next step.

PRESSING AIDS

Professional dressmakers and tailors use many different pressing aids. As a home-sewer, you only need the essential basics:

IRON

Steam irons are best, as they produce a continual stream of steam, softening creases and reducing the risk of scorching. As well as the classic steam irons, there is a new generation of steam irons that have a much larger reservoir of water that is pumped to the iron through a flexible cordlike pipe. The water is then converted to steam as it is released through holes in the sole plate of the iron. Extra shots of steam can also be pumped through the sole plate to the fabric when needed.

SOLE-PLATE CLEANER

It is essential to keep the sole plate of your iron clean, as surface dirt or dressing (any special coating or finish) from new fabrics can transfer as marks onto the pieces you are ironing. These can also restrict the gliding action of the sole plate.

TIP
PRESSING GATHERS
Never press across gathers, as this will flatten and crease them.

You can buy special wipes. Alternatively, look out for iron-cleaner sticks that are packaged in twist-up containers, much like a lipstick or glue stick. When the stick is run over the iron's warmed sole plate, it melts, both cleaning out any debris from within the iron and cleaning the surface.

Make sure that all the surfaces are thoroughly clean by pumping plenty of steam through the iron, then test it by pressing a spare piece of cloth.

IRONING BOARD

The largest you can find (and store) is the best choice. Make sure you replace its cover when necessary to provide a smooth, clean surface.

PRESSING CLOTH

Any clean, lint-free damp cloth will do, such as an old white or pale-colored tea towel. Don't use a new one, because it may still have dressing on it. Also, an old one will be well washed, so there will be no risk of color run.

PRESSING MAT FOR PILE FABRICS

Pile shouldn't be pressed flat, so instead, press it face down on another pile fabric, such as a piece of pale velvet or a towel.

PRESSING TECHNIQUES

Plain pressing is no mystery. The key is to be thorough and methodical, especially with larger pieces, to ensure that no areas are missed. However, different seams and areas of garments require different techniques.

PLAIN SEAMS

1 Start on the wrong side of the piece, pressing the seams open by working the point of the iron down the seam line. Once the seam is open, press along it firmly using the full sole plate and a shot of steam.

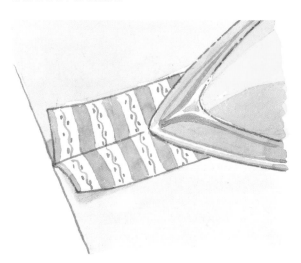

2 Turn the piece over to the right side and press firmly along the seam line using the full sole plate and a shot of steam. Then press the whole piece so that it lies perfectly flat.

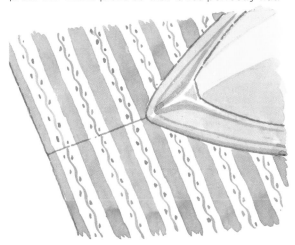

CURVED SEAMS

1 Clip or notch the seam allowance (see page 93) before pressing. In the same way as for plain seams (see left), press the seam open. However, depending on the curve of the seam, you may find that you have to lift one end, pressing from one edge toward the curve, and then turning the piece around and pressing from the other edge.

2 Press the inside using the whole sole plate, working from the outside edges toward the curve if necessary. Turn the piece over and press the right side in the same way.

GATHERS

1 Place the garment over the edge of the ironing board, then hold the gathered seam firmly, so that it is slightly raised up from the ironing board. Use the iron to press from the ungathered part of the fabric toward and into the gathers. Repeat along the length of the piece.

COLLARS AND CUFFS

1 Starting with the underside, press from the points toward the main part of the garment.

2 Now press from the outside edge of the collar toward the main part of the garment.

3 Repeat on the right side. This method prevents creases at the points.

SWEDISH SHADE

This delightful made-to-measure roll-up shade is easy to make, even if all you can do is sew in a straight line. Based on a classic centuries-old Swedish design—the original shades used a reefing system of pulleys and cords to roll them up—this variation uses ties in a coordinated fabric as an unfussy but pretty alternative.

MATERIALS

- Main fabric to the calculated length (see below)
- Lining fabric to the calculated length
- Lining fabric for the ties: four strips, each 3 in/8 cm wide and 6 in/15 cm longer than the shade. There may be enough spare width for these to be cut from the calculated length. If not, you will need to buy extra fabric length
- Dowel rod cut to 1 in/2.5 cm shorter than the calculated width
- Stick-and-sew Velcro to the calculated width
- Batten, 2 x 2 in/5 x 5 cm, to the calculated window width
- Thread
- Staple gun
- Wood screws

MEASURING

Shades lie within the profile section of the architrave, so measure from the flat part of the architrave on one side to the flat part on the other. Add 2 in/5 cm to the width. For the length, measure from the flat part of the architrave at the top of the window to the windowsill and add 6 in/15 cm for turnings.

1 Cut the main fabric and lining to the same size, as explained below left. Lay the main fabric wrong side down on a flat surface and place the lining right side down on top of it. Pin the sides and bottom together, placing the pins at right angles to the seam lines. Working with a seam allowance of 1 in/2.5 cm throughout, stitch along the bottom edge. Starting 1 in/2.5 cm above the bottom seam, stitch up one side. Stitch the full length of the other side, working from the bottom to the top. Trim off the corners, turn through, and press.

2 Place two tie pieces with right sides together and raw edges meeting. Pin and then stitch the long sides. Trim the seams and turn the tie through. Repeat to make up three more ties. Press.

3 Miter one end of each tie by folding and pressing the corner diagonally, and then cutting 3/8 in/1 cm below the fold. Turn in the raw edges and neatly slipstitch the end closed. Topstitch along the three seams on each tie.

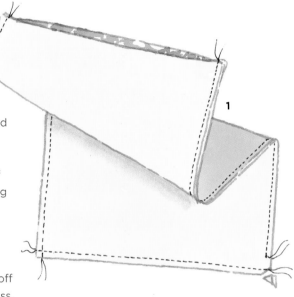

1

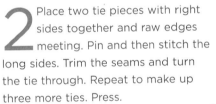

2

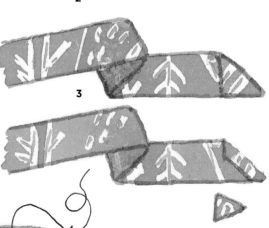

3

4 At the top of the shade, press a 1 in/ 2.5 cm hem to the wrong side. Using pins, mark one third in from each side. At the back, place the raw edge of two of the ties under the hem, centering them over the pin markers. Place the other two ties in the same position at the front of the shade, fold the raw edges over to the back, and pin. At the back, stitch the "sew" side of the Velcro to the top of the shade, covering the ends of the ties and the raw turned-in edge.

4

5

5 Topstitch along the fully-stitched side seam from bottom to top. Slip the dowel into the bottom edge of the shade through the opening at the bottom of the other side seam. Turn in the seam allowance and slipstitch the opening closed. Using a zipper foot, topstitch above the dowel along the bottom edge, sewing as close to the dowel as you can to keep it snugly in position. Topstitch the final side seam from bottom to top.

6 Cover the ends of the batten with the main fabric and secure it using a staple gun. Fix up the batten, screwing it to the flat part of the architrave at the top of the window. Peel the backing paper off the "stick" side of the Velcro and stick it to the front of the batten. Hang up the shade, joining the two parts of the Velcro to hold it in place. Roll up the shade to the desired position and use the ties to hold it in place.

6

above The main fabric and lining sewn edge-to-edge ensure the shade looks good from the inside and outside. Neat topstitching gives the edges a professional finish.

above right The ties have been made in the same fabric as the lining for a coordinated effect. They were cut wide for a bold look on large windows. For smaller windows, cut narrower ties. Simply roll up the shade to the desired height and tie the ties. When they are untied, the weight of the dowel will quickly unroll it.

right Firm fabrics, such as this cotton/linen blend, are ideal for large living-room windows. Pretty sheers with organza ribbon ties would create a completely different look.

TOTE BAG

Stitch up a fully lined shopper, adding a flirty pom-pom trim for fun. Clever fabric choice is the key to success. Here, the same striped fabric is used for the lining, the handles, and the top trim band, but given definition and interest by using the stripes vertically for the lining and horizontally for the band.

FINISHED SIZE

Height 14 in/35 cm, width at top 14½ in/ 37 cm, width at bottom 9 in/22.5 cm

MATERIALS

Quantities are for fabric 45 in/115 cm wide:
- ½ yd/50 cm main fabric
- 1 yd/1 m striped fabric
- 1 yd/1 m iron-on fusible interlining
- 1 yd/1 m pom-pom trim
- ⅓ yd/20 cm buckram
- Dot-and-cross paper or newspaper for the pattern
- Thread

CUTTING OUT

- Prepare the pattern templates on page 212 as indicated and cut them out in dot-and-cross paper or newspaper
- Cut two main bag pieces and one base piece in the main fabric
- Cut two top band pieces, two lining pieces, and one base piece in striped fabric
- Cut one slightly smaller base piece in buckram
- Cut two handle pieces, 20 x 3½ in/50 x 9 cm, in striped fabric

1 Iron fusible interlining onto the wrong side of all the striped lining pieces, and trim. Make up the lining. Place the front and back pieces with right sides together and raw edges aligned. Pin and stitch the side seams, leaving a 4¾ in/12 cm gap near the bottom of one side. Trim the seams and press them open. Match the side seams to find the quarter points and mark them on the front and back with pins. Fold the base lining in half both ways and mark the quarter points with pins. With right sides together and the pins matching, pin the base to the sides. Stitch and then trim the seam, clip the curves (see page 93), and press the seam open.

2 Make up the main bag as above. Measure down from the top edge and mark ⅝ in/1.5 cm. With the bag right side out, starting at one seam, turn in the end of the pom-pom trim and pin it along the marked line. When you get to the starting point, turn in the other end of the trim. Stitch in place using a zipper foot.

3 With right sides together, pin and stitch the side seams of the top band. Turn the band inside out and, with right sides together and raw edges matching, pin the shorter side of the band to the top of the bag, covering the stitching attaching the pom-pom trim. Stitch using the zipper foot.

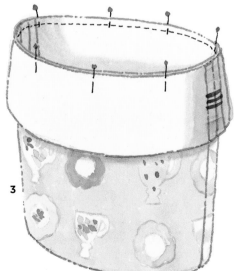

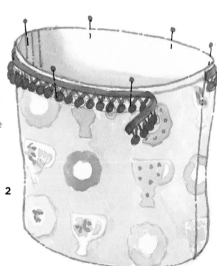

4 Fold each handle piece in half lengthwise and pin and stitch the long edge. Trim the seam and press it open. Turn the handles through by fixing a safety pin to one end and working it down through the handle. Press, then topstitch the handles down each long edge.

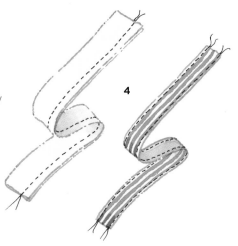

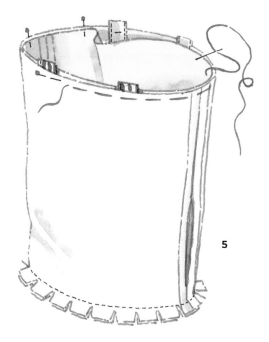

5 With the main bag right side out, measure 4 in/10 cm in from the side seams along the top edge of the bag on the front and back, and mark with pins. Pin the ends of the handles at these points, one on the front and one on the back of the bag, with raw edges together. Turn the lining inside out and place the main bag inside it, with the handles in between. Matching the side seams and raw edges, pin and then baste the top of the bag and lining together. Stitch, then trim the seam and turn the bag right side out by pulling the main bag through the gap in the lining and turning the lining right side out. Then tuck the lining into the bag.

6 Turn the whole bag inside out. Insert the buckram base through the gap in the lining and place it between the base of the bag and lining. Slipstitch the gap closed, then turn the bag right side out.

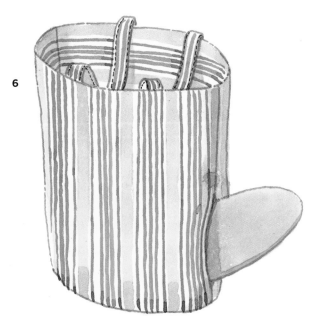

left Using fabrics of the same weight for both the lining and the outer bag adds strength and a quality feel to the finished piece. Once the main bag and lining are stitched together, it is turned to the right side through an opening in one side seam, then the lining is tucked back down into the outer.

enclosed seams

There are some occasions when you may need to use an enclosed seam. This is usually when you are using fine fabrics that might fray, especially where there will be close body contact (nightwear, for example), or, at the other end of the spectrum, when you are creating an item that needs to be particularly robust, such as heavy-duty workwear—traditional jeans are a good example.

FRENCH SEAMS

Seams in fine or sheer fabrics that easily fray, especially on garments that are in close contact with the body, such as lingerie, need to be enclosed. French seams are ideal, as they leave no raw edges. From the outside, they look like a plain seam; inside they are enclosed and look good enough to be on the outside.

1 With wrong sides together, pin the seams. Sheer fabrics are often slippery and trickier to handle than more robust fabrics, such as cotton. For this reason, you may like to hand-baste the seams before stitching them. Following the instructions for plain seams (see page 91), machine stitch ⅜ in/1 cm from the raw edge.

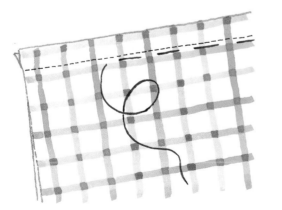

2 Trim the seam to ⅛ in/3 mm. Press the seam open, turn the piece over, and press the seam flat on the other side.

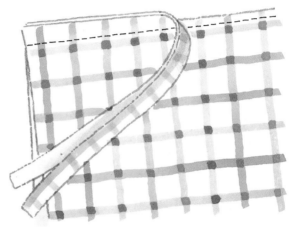

3 Repin the seam with right sides together, so that the original seam line runs along the top of the fold. Baste and then stitch as before, so that the seam encloses the raw edges.

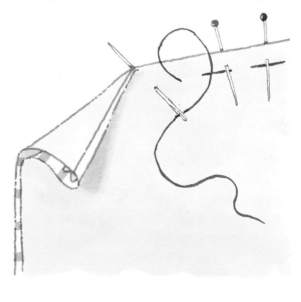

FLAT-FELL SEAMS

Robust, smart, and enclosed, flat-fell seams are typically used on workwear, reversible garments, and men's shirts. Topstitched on the outside, they can also be decorative (many jeans seams are worked in contrast thread), but only if the stitches are even and the stitching is meticulously straight. A felling foot, which folds the fabric under as it stitches, is available for some sewing machines.

1 With wrong sides together, using topstitch thread, sew a plain seam ⅝ in/1.5 cm from the raw edges.

2 Press the seam open and then toward the back of the garment. Trim the underneath layer to ⅛ in/3 mm.

3 Press in the raw edge of the untrimmed seam allowance by ⅛ in/3 mm, then fold and press this over the trimmed raw edge. Pin and then topstitch as close to the edge as possible.

SELF-BOUND SEAMS

Inside the garment, this looks a little like a French seam; on the outside, like a plain seam. It is more robust than an ordinary seam and is often used for children's clothes. It is especially useful where gathered fabric is stitched to a flat piece.

1 With right sides together, stitch a plain ⅝ in/ 1.5 cm seam and trim one side to ⅛ in/3 mm. If one side is gathered, then trim that side.

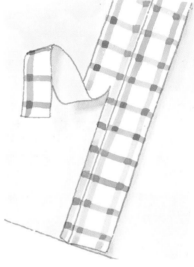

2 Press in the raw edge of the other side of the seam allowance by ⅛ in/3 mm, then fold it over again, enclosing the trimmed edge, and press. Pin or baste, then stitch the two parts of the seam allowance together, close to the stitch line.

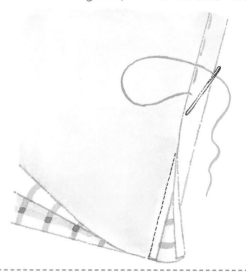

WELT SEAM

This looks similar to a flat-fell seam, except you can see only one instead of two lines of topstitching. It is robust, neat, and can be decorative, depending on whether or not you use a contrast thread. It is also less bulky than a flat-fell seam, making it an excellent choice for bulkier fabrics.

1 With right sides together, pin and stitch a plain seam ⅝ in/1.5 cm in from the raw edges.

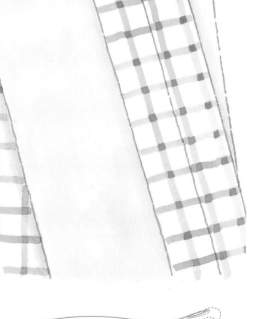

2 Press the seam open, then toward the front of the garment. Trim the under layer to ¼ in/6 mm.

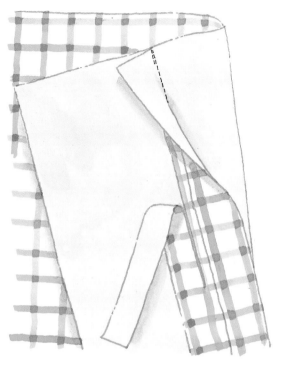

3 Turn the piece to the right side and then pin through all layers. Topstitch parallel to the seam line.

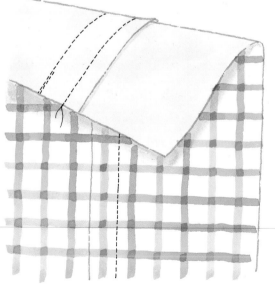

TIP
WELT SEAMS

Like flat-fell seams, the success of welt seams relies on even topstitching. One way of keeping it even is to align the outside edge of the presser foot with the original seam line. This will automatically give you an even line a presser-foot's width away from the first line of stitching.

PAJAMA PANTS

These simple drawstring pants, made in fine linen, have enclosed French seams to ensure they won't fray. Traditional Indian pajamas were generously cut with plenty of fabric gathered into a casing at the waistband. These are cut slimmer and are worn low on the hips for a smoother, updated look.

1

FIT

- To fit size small, hips 34 in/88 cm. For slightly larger sizes (up to hips 41 in/104 cm), measure the hips and divide by four. Add this to the long outside edge of the front and back pattern pieces. Extend the crotch line by the same amount and draw a smooth line from the point to about 2 in/ 5 cm down the leg

MATERIALS

- 2½ yd/2 m fabric 45 in/ 115 cm wide; or 1¾ yd/ 1.5 m fabric 60 in/ 150 cm wide
- 1¼ yd/1 m broad braid for waistband
- 2½ yd/2 m tape for tie
- Thread

CUTTING OUT

- Make up the pattern pieces on page 213 according to the instructions on page 212
- Cut two front leg pieces and two back leg pieces

1 With wrong sides together, pin one front leg piece to one back leg piece along the inner leg seams. Stitch. Repeat with the other leg. Trim the seams and press them open.

2 Turn both legs wrong side out and repin the seam with right sides together, to make French seams (see page 107).

3 With wrong sides together, pin the left and right legs together along the center seam, starting at the front waistline and finishing at the back waistline. Stitch, and trim the seam allowance. Turn the pants wrong side out and repin with right sides together as a French seam. Stitch.

3

4 In the same way, stitch the front of the pants to the back along the side seams, starting with the fabric wrong sides together and then sewing the seam again with right sides together. Hem the bottom edges of the legs (see pages 184–87).

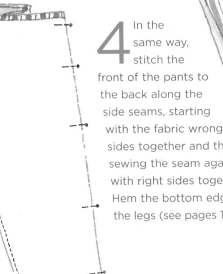

4

5 At the top edge, fold and press a ½ in/12 mm hem to the right side. To make a channel for the pajama tape, cut a piece of the main fabric, 1¼ in/3 cm wide to the measurement of the top of the pants. Turn in one end by ⅝ in/1.5 cm. Starting 1¼ in/ 3 cm in from the center seam, pin this strip around the waistline, about 1¼ in/3 cm from the top of the pants. Turn in the other end by ⅝ in/1.5 cm so that you finish 1¼ in/3 cm from the center seam. Stitch in place along the top and bottom edges. Fix a safety pin to one end of the pajama tape and thread it through the channel. Tie a knot at each end.

5

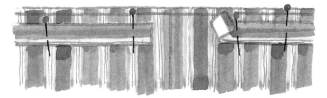

6 To stitch the wide braid over the top of this channel, first turn in ⅜ in/1 cm at one end of the wide braid and align it with the center seam. Pin the braid in position around the top of the pants, covering the turned-in hem. When you reach the center seam again, trim the braid, allowing ⅜ in/ 1 cm to turn under at the end. Stitch the braid in place along the top and bottom edges.

6

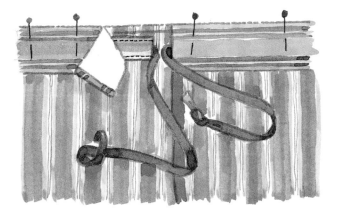

above top The naturally frayed raw edge makes a pretty hemline that doesn't need stitching. Not all fabrics have this detailing, so you may prefer to hem the pajama bottoms.

above middle French seams look as good on the inside as they do on the outside. They give a strong fray-free finish and are often used on fine fabrics and lingerie for this reason.

left The wide webbing makes a striking detail, but would have provided too wide a channel for the tie, so a narrower channel was stitched onto the waistline before the decorative braid was applied.

shaping and contouring: darts

Transforming two-dimensional pieces into a three-dimensional garment traditionally relies on shaping in the form of darts and curved seams. These allow fullness at the bust and hips with cinching at the waist.

TAILOR'S TACKS

Traditional tailor's tacks transfer pattern markings to two (or more) layers of fabric. Also called thread markings, they should be made with thread that contrasts with the fabric. Thread the needle with a long length of double thread. Do not knot the ends. The dart will be marked on the paper pattern by lines, with one dot at the point and more dots at intervals along the lines. Mark each of these dots with thread once the pattern has been cut out and while it is still pinned onto the fabric.

1 Start with one of the dots at the open end of the dart. Take a small stitch through all layers of fabric, putting the needle in at the top of the dot and out the opposite side, leaving a long tail of double thread. Leaving a long, loose loop, stitch across the next dot in the same way.

2 Repeat to the point of the dart, and in the same way, work your way up the other side, taking a stitch at each dot. Then cut through the center of each loop.

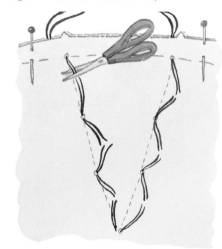

3 Unpin the pattern and carefully lift it off, leaving the tailor's tacks in position. Now separate the layers of fabric so that there are equal lengths of threads on each one. Snip the threads in the center between the layers of fabric.

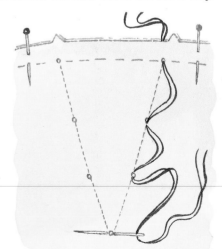

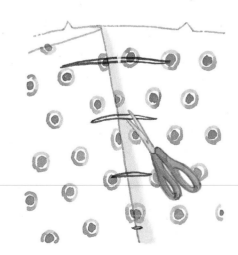

SINGLE-POINTED DARTS

These are the basic darts. The aim is to stitch them accurately along the marked line, finishing with a sharp point.

1 Mark the darts as described on page 113. With right sides together, match the dots on either side of the darts to fold the dart from the point to the widest part at the raw edges. Pin in place and then hand-baste along the stitch line.

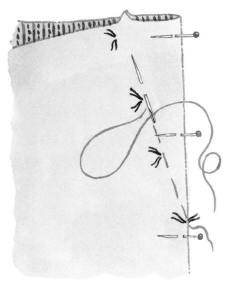

3 At the point end, tie the two tails of thread together in a double knot to secure. Repeat at the top end of the dart.

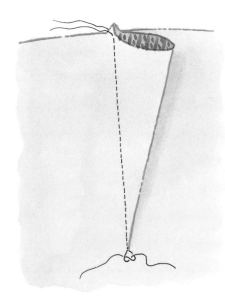

4 Firmly press the folded dart, taking care not to press beyond the point. Do this by opening out the fabric and placing it right side down on the ironing board. Press the dart to one side so that the top raw edges align. You will be able to see by the cut of the pattern which side matches best.

2 Remove the tailor's tacks and pins. Leaving long tails of thread, stitch from the raw edges to the point. Remove the basting.

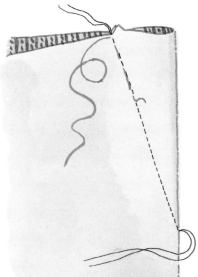

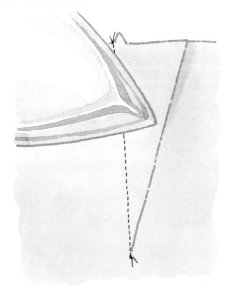

CONTOUR DARTS

These are sometimes called double-pointed darts because they are used to nip in fabric, for example, at the waistline, tapering to a point at each end to follow the contours of the body.

TIP
DARTS
For perfect sharp darts, work along the stitch line to the fold, then make an extra couple of stitches along the fold.

1 Use tailor's tacks to transfer the dart markings (see page 113). With right sides together, fold the dart along the center line, matching the thread markers. First pin the center part, double checking that the thread marks match, then work out toward one point, matching and pinning. In the same way, pin toward the other point.

3 Stitch just outside the line of basting from the widest point in the center toward the point at one end. Break off the threads, leaving long tails for finishing. In the same way, stitch toward the point at the other end of the dart. Finish by tying the two thread tails at each point of the dart into a knot.

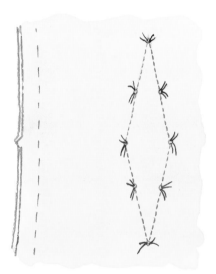

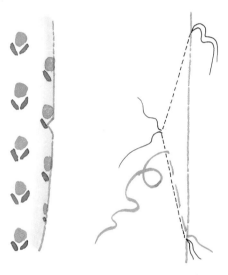

2 Hand-baste the dart just inside the thread-marked stitch lines. Remove the pins and thread markings.

4 Place a pin just inside the stitch line at the widest central point of the dart. Use the point of the scissors to cut into the fabric, straight toward the pin.

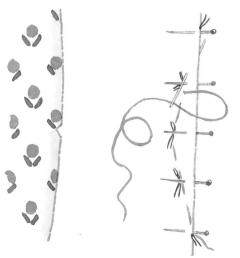

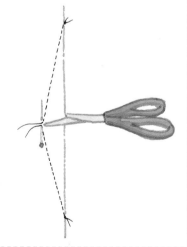

CAMISOLE

Pintucks are not difficult, but making sure they are centered and working out the extra fabric you need to allow for them can be tricky. Solution: stitch the pintucks before cutting out the front. This lined silk camisole is bias-cut to flow flatteringly over the contours. Depending on the fabric you choose, the camisole doesn't have to be lined.

FIT

- To fit size small, bust 34 in/86 cm. For other sizes, adjust the pattern by enlarging or taking in down the center front and center back. To do this, divide the difference between 34 in/86 cm and your bust measurement by four. Fold the pattern pieces in half lengthwise and increase or decrease the pattern at both the center front and the center back fold by this amount

MATERIALS

- 2½ yd/2 m fine silk 45 in/115 cm wide
- Thread

CUTTING OUT

- Make up the pattern pieces on page 214 according to the instructions
- Cut one main back piece and one each of the front and back lining pieces (which are slightly shorter)
- Cut two shoulder straps, 17 x 1½ in/ 43 x 4 cm

1 The pintucks need to be worked before you cut out the top-layer front piece. So pin the pattern piece on the bias on the remaining fabric and cut a generous square around it, making sure that there is a minimum of 4 in/10 cm of fabric on either side of the pattern piece.

2 Fold and press the fabric in half lengthwise. Using tailor's chalk and a ruler, draw a line 14½ in/37 cm down this fold. This is the position of the central pintuck. Draw the rest of the pintucks in decreasing lengths of 13¾ in/ 35 cm, 10¾ in/27 cm, 8¾ in/ 22 cm, 18 cm (7in), and 6 in/ 15 cm on either side, spacing them ½ in/12 mm apart.

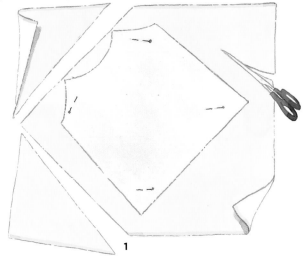

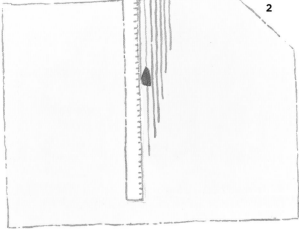

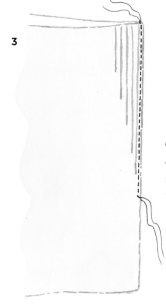

3 Starting with the central pintuck, fold the fabric along the marked line and place a pin at the end position of the pintuck. Stitch as close as you can to the fold and leave long threads at the end. Refold the fabric at the position of the second pintuck and repeat the process. Stitch all the pintucks in the same way. Thread each of the threads at the bottom of the pintucks onto a needle and pass them through to the back of the fabric. Tie each pair of threads together securely and then trim the ends.

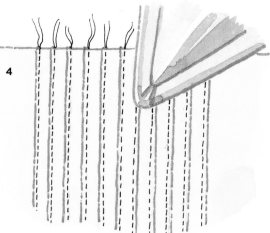

4 Press the finished pintucks so that those on the left of the central pintuck are pressed to the left and those on the right are pressed to the right.

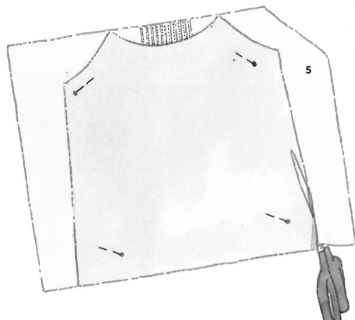

5 Now lay the pattern piece onto the pintucked fabric, aligning the center front of the pattern with the central pintuck. Cut out the front of the camisole.

Pintucks add tailored texture to a garment and the graduated lengths of these make an elegant detail.

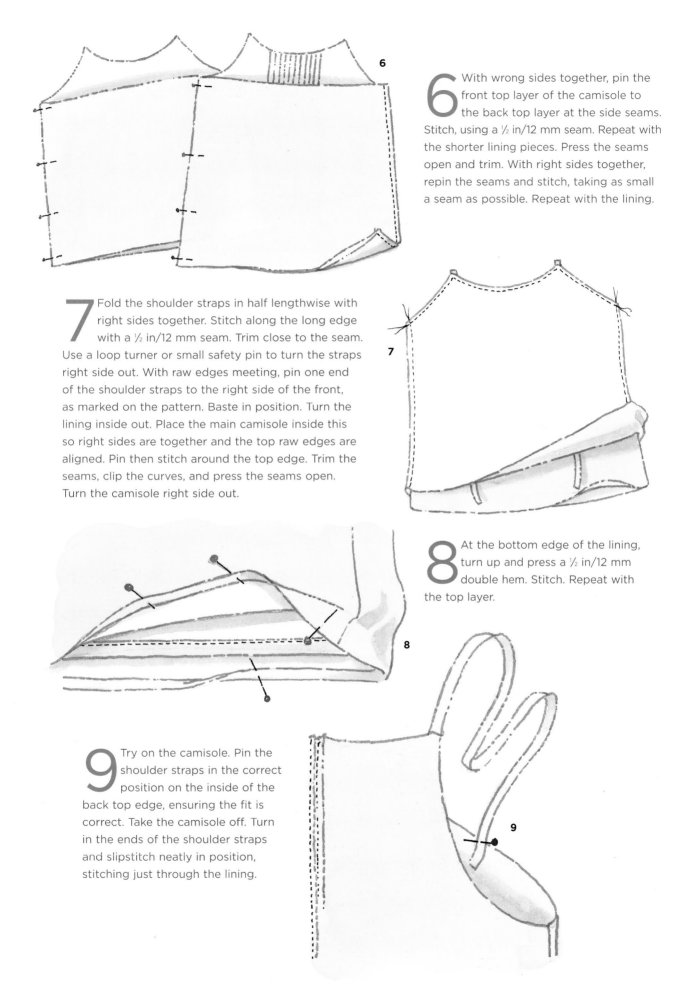

6 With wrong sides together, pin the front top layer of the camisole to the back top layer at the side seams. Stitch, using a ½ in/12 mm seam. Repeat with the shorter lining pieces. Press the seams open and trim. With right sides together, repin the seams and stitch, taking as small a seam as possible. Repeat with the lining.

7 Fold the shoulder straps in half lengthwise with right sides together. Stitch along the long edge with a ½ in/12 mm seam. Trim close to the seam. Use a loop turner or small safety pin to turn the straps right side out. With raw edges meeting, pin one end of the shoulder straps to the right side of the front, as marked on the pattern. Baste in position. Turn the lining inside out. Place the main camisole inside this so right sides are together and the top raw edges are aligned. Pin then stitch around the top edge. Trim the seams, clip the curves, and press the seams open. Turn the camisole right side out.

8 At the bottom edge of the lining, turn up and press a ½ in/12 mm double hem. Stitch. Repeat with the top layer.

9 Try on the camisole. Pin the shoulder straps in the correct position on the inside of the back top edge, ensuring the fit is correct. Take the camisole off. Turn in the ends of the shoulder straps and slipstitch neatly in position, stitching just through the lining.

gathering and easing

Gathering is one of the easiest, most forgiving sewing techniques with satisfyingly professional-looking first-time results. Once you have mastered the technique, you will be able to gather drapes for fullness, quickly run up dart-free gathered skirts, and make endless ruffles. The same basic principle is also used for more advanced sewing techniques, such as "easing," which uses a subtle form of gathering to coax gentle three-dimensional curves from flat fabric to fit, for example, over and around a shoulder as a set-in sleeve.

HAND GATHERING

Many people choose to gather by hand rather than machine, because it is quick and easy to do; the double threads are stronger than general machine thread, making them robust and easy to pull up.

1 Traditionally, gathering is worked by hand. Thread a needle with double thread, tie a knot in the end, and make a line of running stitches just inside the seam line along the edge to be gathered.

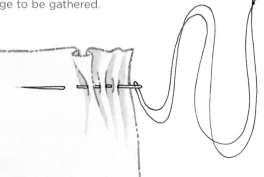

2 When you get to the end, pull up the threads until the gathered edge fits the straight edge it is to be sewn to.

MACHINE GATHERING

For speed, you can use the sewing machine to stitch your gathering threads, although you need to spend time adjusting and checking the tension before working on the project piece. This is especially useful where you have long lengths to gather.

1 Loosen the upper thread so that the bobbin threads pull through more easily. Do this by adjusting the tension dial to between 6 and 9.

2 Adjust the stitch length to between 6 and 12 stitches per inch/2–4 mm—the shorter setting for lightweight fabric and the longer setting for more heavyweight materials.

3 Check the tension on a test piece of fabric and experiment with pulling up the gathers.

GATHERING INTO A WAISTBAND OR BODICE

1 Stitch the garment seams. Next, use pins to mark the quarters on the garment. First, mark the two side seams with pins, then fold the garment, bringing the pins together, and mark the position of the folds in the fabric with two more pins. One of these positions may well be the back seam or opening. Run the gathering threads along the appropriate edge. You may do this as one long piece of doubled thread, or, if the length to be gathered is very long, you may decide to break the threads off at the quarters and wind them around a pin to anchor them. This not only protects against the threads breaking as you gather them, but it is also a manageable way to keep the gathers even along the length of the fabric.

2 Mark the quarters on the waistband or bodice. The overlap for fastening will be marked on the pattern. Place a pin in this position. Now fold the band so that the seam allowance at the end meets the pin. Insert another pin here. Place another pin at the fold. Refold the band so the end pins match and add another pin at each of the two new folds.

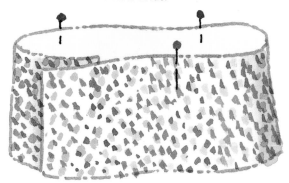

3 Turn the skirt inside out. With raw edges meeting and right sides together, pin the gathered edge of the skirt to the straight edge of the waistband or bodice, matching the openings and the quarter pins. Pull up the gathering threads until the skirt fabric matches the straight edge and secure by winding the ends of the threads around one of the pins.

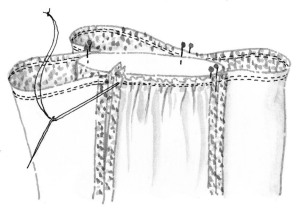

> **TIP**
> ### SEWING A GATHERED EDGE
> When machine stitching the gathered edge to the waistband or bodice, place the piece under the needle with the gathered side uppermost. If you place the gathered edge downward, the gathers will become trapped in the teeth of the feed dogs.

4 Add more pins between the quarter pins to hold the two edges together, then hand-baste and remove the pins.

5 With the gathered side up, stitch along the seam line. Remove the basting and gathering threads. Trim the seam.

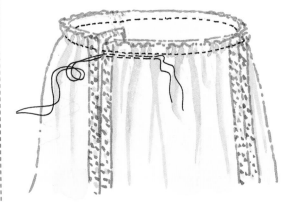

6 Press, working the tip of the iron vertically into the gathers so that you don't flatten them (see page 99).

EASING

Following the same principles as gathering, easing is used where one piece of fabric is to be attached to another slightly larger piece, to give as flat a finish as possible, such as hemming a flared skirt. Easing can also lend a three-dimensional effect to part of a garment, for example, where a set-in sleeve needs to curve around the shoulder. Sometimes, only part of a piece needs to be eased, and this will be marked at each end on the pattern as a small circle. Easing can be done by hand or on the machine.

1 Mark the start and end position of the required ease with tailor's tacks (see page 63). Choose a long stitch length, then work two parallel lines of stitching just inside the seam allowance.

2 Turn the garment inside out. With right sides together and matching the easing positions, pin the sleeve into the armhole. Pull up the gathering threads so that the larger piece perfectly matches the smaller piece. Anchor the threads by taking two small stitches on top of each other. Baste into position.

3 Remove the pins and stitch just outside the baste lines. Remove the basting.

SWEETEST SUNDRESS

Gathering a skirt into a waistband or bodice is a basic technique that is easy to do, yet, depending on your choice of fabric and trimming, can look like a million dollars. The contrasting cotton prints, together with the bias hem and bodice trimming, lend a professional look to this simple dress. Make it in heavier fabric for the winter and she can wear it as a pinafore over a fine sweater.

FIT

- To fit age 4, chest 23 in/ 58 cm. For other sizes, divide the difference between the child's chest measurement and 23 in/ 58 cm by four. Add this figure to the center front and center back pattern pieces

MATERIALS

Quantities are for fabric 45 in/115 cm wide:

- 1 yd/1 m printed cotton for the skirt
- ¼ yd/20 cm coordinating cotton for the bodice
- 4¼ yd/4 m folded bias binding 1 in/2.5 cm wide or ½ yd/50 cm plain fabric to make your own
- 5 shell buttons, (¾ in/ 2 cm diameter
- Thread
- Dot-and-cross paper

CUTTING OUT

- Cut one front skirt piece 31 x 16 in/78 x 40 cm
- Cut two back skirt pieces 15½ x 16 in/39 x 40 cm
- Cut one skirt placket 8 x 2 in/20 x 5 cm
- Trace the bodice pieces on page 215 onto the dot-and-cross paper and then cut two front pieces and four back pieces
- Cut four ties 1½ x 15 in/ 3 x 38 cm
- Cut 4¼ yd/4 m bias strips 2½ in/6 cm wide (see page 152)

1 For the ties, cut four strips of contrasting bias to the same length as the ties. Fold both long edges of the ties into the center so they meet, with wrong sides together, and press. Repeat with the bias. Then, with wrong sides together, center the tie on top of the bias, and pin. Topstitch along both edges of the printed fabric. Turn in and slipstitch one end of each tie to neaten. Next, make the rouleau loops by cutting a length of bias 12 in/30 cm long. With right sides together, fold it in half lengthwise and stitch a narrow seam. Use a safety pin at one end to turn it right side out. Cut it into five equal lengths.

2 With right sides together, pin and stitch two back bodice pieces to a front bodice piece along the side seams. Repeat with the other bodice pieces to make up the lining. Trim the seams and press them open.

right Button and rouleau loop fastenings look enchanting and are less fussy than classic buttonholes or zippers.

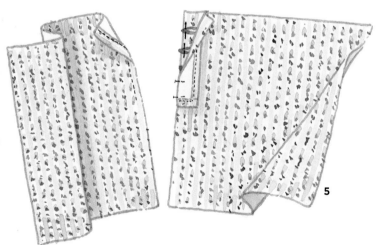

3 Lay one bodice right side up on a flat surface. With raw edges meeting, pin one rouleau loop onto the center back seam allowance of the right back bodice, ¾ in/2 cm from the top. Pin another ¾ in/2 cm from the bottom. Pin one tie at the top edge of each back bodice, just inside the armhole seam allowance. Pin the last two ties just inside the armhole seam allowance on both sides of the front bodice. Lay the bodice lining right side down on top of the main bodice. Pin together, then stitch up one center back seam, across the top back, around the armhole, across the front neckline, around the other armhole, and down the other center back seam. Turn through and press.

4 Cut a piece of bias 27 in/68 cm long and, with wrong sides together, fold it in half lengthwise and press. Overlap the edge of the back bodice with one end of the bias by ⅜ in/1 cm, then pin the bias to the bottom edge of the bodice with raw edges meeting. Overlap the other end of the bias over the other side of the back bodice. Stitch in place.

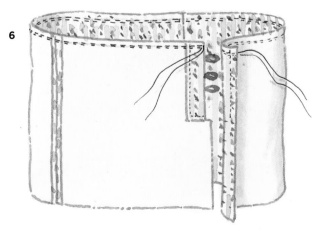

5 Lay the right back piece of the skirt right side up. With raw edges meeting, pin one rouleau loop to the center seam allowance 1½ in/4 cm from the top edge; pin two more at 1½-in/4-cm intervals. On the placket piece, press in and stitch a ½-in/12-mm hem along one long side and one short side. Place the placket right side down over the rouleau loops, aligning the raw edges with the top and center seam allowances of the skirt. Pin and stitch. Turn the placket to the wrong side of the skirt. On the left back skirt edge, turn in a double ⅝-in/1.5-cm hem and stitch down 8 in/20 cm from the top edge.

6 With wrong sides together, pin and stitch the side seams of the skirt. Run gathering stitches along the top edge of the skirt. Match the side seams of the skirt with the side seams of the bodice and pin in place. Pull up the gathering threads and secure. Pin, baste, and stitch the waist seam (see page 121). Stitch the remainder of the center back seam. To finish, apply bias to the hem (see page 187). Sew buttons onto the back left bodice and skirt, to align with the rouleau loops.

CLASSIC DRAPES

Drapes are surprisingly easy to make, especially if you use ready-made heading tape, which comes with the gathering cords already threaded through and is available in several different styles. For long drapes like these, use a deep heading tape, such as goblet, and cut the drapes slightly long for a luxurious look. Cotton-linen blend, such as shown, is a good fabric choice for full-length drapes, as it falls into beautiful folds.

MATERIALS

- Main fabric calculated, as right, to fit the window
- Lining fabric calculated, as right, to fit the window
- Heading tape the width of the window plus 2 in/5 cm for turnings
- Thread
- Curtain hooks and/or rings—allow one for every 6 in/15 cm of rod or rail

CALCULATIONS

There is a particular order for calculating the materials needed.

1. Measure the width of the window across the architrave and add 6 in/15 cm on either side. This will be the length of the rail or rod and it is the required width for the drape. Measure the length of the drapes from the rail or rod to the floor or windowsill, depending on your requirements. Add 6 in/15 cm to the length for turnings.

2. Choose the heading tape. Each style of tape requires a different amount of fabric width to create the correct fullness of gathers. This is called the fullness ratio and will inform the width of drape you need to make up. Measure the rail or rod and multiply it by the fullness ratio. Now divide this by your fabric width and round up to the next full number. This is the number of drops you will need. If you are making two drapes for the window, you may need to cut one drop in half, so, for example, you have two drapes, each one-and-a-half fabric widths.

3. Multiply the number of drops by the length, including turnings. This is the length of fabric you need to buy.

1 Cut both the main fabric and the lining to size. If the window width requires it, seam the drops together, ensuring half widths are positioned at the outside edges. Cut the lining 4 in/10 cm narrower and 4 in/10 cm shorter than the main fabric. At the lower edge of the lining, turn up a single 2-in/5-cm hem to the wrong side and stitch. At the lower edge of the main fabric, turn up and press 2 in/5 cm to the wrong side. Use pins to mark the center width points at the top and bottom of both the main fabric and the lining.

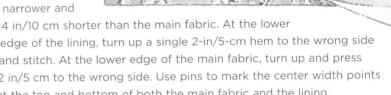

2 With the main fabric and lining right sides together and the top raw edges meeting, pin the side seams together, working from the top downward. Stitch the side seams, working from the top downward on both sides. Press the seams open.

3 With the drape still inside out, lay it lining side up on a flat surface. Match the central marking pins to center the lining on the main fabric. Baste the top edges together and then stitch. Trim the seams and clip the corners.

above A goblet heading, with large gathers alternating with clean, flat intervals, makes an elegant choice for very long drapes. The modern twist on classic toile de Jouy is a witty fabric choice.

4 Turn the drape right side out. Lay the drape lining side up on a flat surface. Ensuring the hook pockets are facing you, free the gathering cords on the heading tape that will be on the outside edge of the drape. Knot the ends, then trim the tape to within 1 in/2.5 cm of the knots. Measure out the heading tape along the top of the drape, free the cords at the other end, and trim the tape to within 1 in/2.5 cm. Starting with the knotted end, and double checking the pockets are facing you, turn in 1 in/2.5 cm at the cut end and pin the gathering tape ⅛ in/3 mm below the top of the drape. When you get to the other end of the tape, turn in 1 in/2.5 cm. Following the stitching lines near the top and bottom edges of the heading tape, stitch the tape to the top of the drape. Stitch down the sides, being careful not to catch the freed cords.

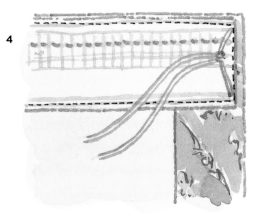

5 Thoroughly press the drape, then lay it right side down on a flat surface to finish the hem. You will have already pressed up a single 2 in/ 5 cm hem (see step 1). Now fold up and press a 3-in/7.5-cm hem to cover the lower edge of the lining. Pin in position, then either slipstitch or machine stitch the hem to finish. Neatly slipstitch the sides where the hem is folded up. At the top of the drape, pull up the gathering cords and make a half-bow at the end to secure. (This will be easier than a knot to undo when you want to take down and flatten out the drapes for cleaning in the future.) Insert curtain hooks and hang the drape.

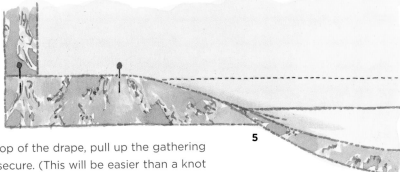

fastenings

Fastenings can be discreetly utilitarian, such as zippers, hooks, or press studs hidden within a seam or placket, or they can be flamboyantly part of the design, such as extrovert buttons on a double-breasted jacket. Some let us in and out of our garments; others, such as cardigan and jacket fastenings, are designed to be used only some of the time. Stitched with care and used with flair, they speak volumes about the finish and detailing.

ZIPPERS

From lightweight and concealed to chunky and open-ended, zippers come in many sizes and types. They make an efficient form of fastening for both garments and home furnishings. Depending on the zipper and how it is inserted, it can be neatly concealed within a seam, revealed as a design detail, or hidden behind laps. Inserting a zipper is a fussy job that repays dividends if you are methodical and take your time.

TIPS
INSERTING ZIPPERS
Hand-basting a zipper is time well invested, as it gives you greater control over the exact positioning of all the parts.

• • •

To get past the zipper tab, stitch down part of the zipper. Leave the needle in the fabric, raise the foot, then move the tab to the stitched section. Lower the foot and stitch the rest of the tape.

CENTERED ZIPPER

Best for beginners, this is the easiest technique for inserting a zipper. It works well in many situations, both for garments and soft furnishings.

1 Use the zipper to measure the opening. Do this by aligning the raw ends of the top of the tape with the raw edges at the top of the opening. Use a pin to mark the position of the end stop. With right sides together and raw edges matching, pin the seam downward from the pin to the bottom edge. Stitch. Remove the pins and use them to pin the seam from the top of the stitching to the top edge of the garment. Using contrast thread, baste the seam from the stitching to the top edge.

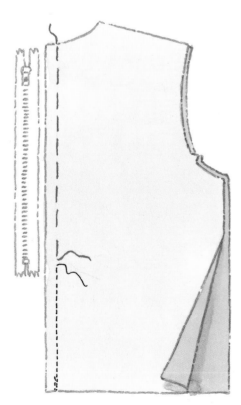

2 Press the seam open. With the garment right side down, lay the zipper right side down with the teeth centered on the seam line. Ensure that the top ends of the zipper match the top raw edges of the seam. Pin through one thickness of fabric (the seam allowance) with the pins parallel with the length of the zipper. Working from the bottom, hand-baste one side of the zipper to the seam allowance. Repeat on the other side.

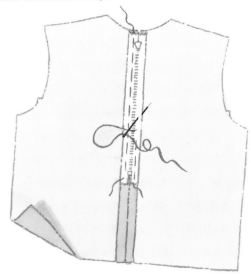

3 Turn the garment to the right side and, starting at the bottom end and working through all thicknesses, hand-baste one side of the zipper in position. Repeat on the other side, working from the bottom up. Turn the garment to the wrong side to check that the basting is stitched through both tapes along their full length.

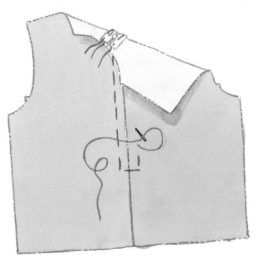

4 Attach a zipper foot so that the needle is nearest to the seam line. Start by stitching across the bottom end of one tape. When you get to the baste line running up the length of the zipper, leave the needle down, lift the foot, reposition the fabric, lower the foot and stitch to the top of the zipper, just inside the line of basting. Reattach the foot so that the needle is nearest the other side of the seam line and repeat on the other side. Remove all the basting and press lightly.

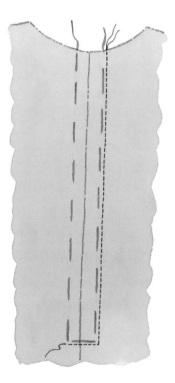

TIP
SEWING ZIPPERS
It is much easier to handle the machining of a zipper if you are working with flat fabric. So, for best results, insert it as soon as you can in the order of work: certainly before the final seam is sewn.

LAPPED ZIPPER

Sometimes, it is neater to have a single flap covering the zipper, especially if it is positioned in the side of a garment, such as a skirt.

1 With right sides together and raw edges matching, pin the seam. Use the zipper to measure the opening by aligning the raw ends of the tape with the raw edges at the top of the opening. Use a pin to mark the position of the end stop. Stitch a ¾ in/2 cm seam from this point down to the bottom of the garment. Press the seam open and extend this to the top of the garment. This should be ¾ in/2 cm all the way up.

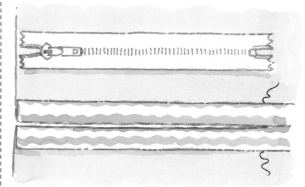

2 On the left-hand side, fold the seam in a further ¼ in/6 mm, making the seam on that side ½ in/12 mm. Close the zipper and slip it under this fold. Pin and hand-baste into position. Stitch from top to bottom. When you get near to the slider, leave the needle down, slide the slider out of the way of the needle. Stitch that section, then, leaving the needle down, pull the slider up again and past the needle. Finish stitching that side of the zipper.

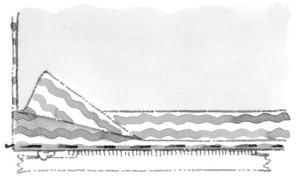

3 With the zipper closed, lay the fabric flat, right side up, on your work surface. Fold the lap over the line of stitches you have just made and pin it in position. Hand-baste the fabric to the other side of the zipper tape.

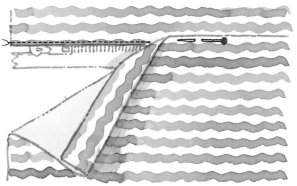

4 Place sticky tape on the right side of the fabric along the stitch line and along the bottom of the zipper, just beneath the end stop, to guide you. Stitch from top to bottom. When you get to the end, leave the needle in, turn the fabric and stitch the end of the zipper. Finally, thread the loose end of the thread on the right side of the fabric onto a needle and pass it through to the wrong side. Knot it together with the loose end of the bobbin thread to finish and remove all of the basting and the tape.

INVISIBLE ZIPPER

Invisible zippers are designed to sit behind the seam so that once they are closed, all you see is the pull. Instead of teeth, they have coils that connect behind the tapes. They need to be stitched in very close to the coil, and to do this you will need an invisible-zipper foot, which has two grooves to accommodate the two parts of the zipper coil. While regular zippers are stitched in from the bottom upward, invisible zippers need to be stitched from top to bottom; otherwise you will be left with a bubble of fabric at the end. For the same reason, the rest of the seam is stitched after the zipper has been inserted.

1 Open the zipper and, using a very cool iron, press it flat so that the ridge of the coil is on the front side of the tapes. Mark the seam allowance on both sides of the enclosure using tailor's chalk or basting. Close the zipper. With right sides together and the top raw edges of the tape aligned with the top raw edge of the garment, place the zipper face down with the coil over the basting. Pin and baste into position.

TIP
INVISIBLE ZIPPERS
Invisible zippers are much easier to insert if you first press the coils so that they lie next to, rather than behind, the tapes. However, the coils are made of nylon, so do this using the coolest iron possible.

2 Open the zipper, then, starting from the top of the tape, lower the invisible-zipper foot, so that the coil is under the right groove, and stitch down the zipper until you reach the pull.

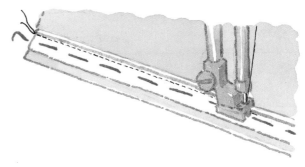

3 Close the zipper. Position it face down over the baste line on the other piece of fabric, aligning the top raw edges. Pin it into position and baste.

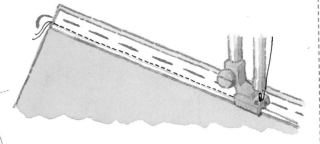

4 Open the zipper and stitch from top to bottom with the coil under the left groove.

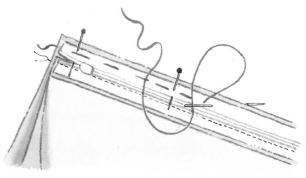

5 Pin the seam from the bottom of the zipper to the hem. Using a regular presser foot, machine stitch in place.

SEPARATING ZIPPER

Open-ended separating zippers are generally designed for outer garments, such as cardigans and jackets that can be worn open or closed and can also be slipped off easily. Finer versions are also available, which can be used for corsetry in place of traditional lacing. At the other end of the scale, heavy-duty separating zippers are used for tents and camping gear. Because they can be opened at the end and extend along the complete length of the seam, separating zippers are the easiest to stitch into place, as there is no fussy conjunction where the zipper meets the rest of the seam.

1 The edges need to be finished before inserting an open-ended zipper. The way you do this depends on the design of the garment, but it is likely to be a case of turning them in by at least half the width of the zipper plus ³⁄₈ in/1 cm. On some designs, the hem is finished before the edges; on others, it is finished afterward. At this stage, the neck edge will be unfinished. Baste the two edges together and press the seam open. Pin the zipper into position face down on the inside of the garment with the teeth centered on the seam. The raw edges of the zipper tape should meet the raw edges of the neckline. Baste through all layers.

TIP
STITCHING SEPARATING ZIPPERS
Topstitching will be much easier if you open the zipper—then you have only one half of the front to handle.

2 Remove the seam basting and open the zipper. Check that the basting holding the zipper in position has caught through all layers down the full length of the tape.

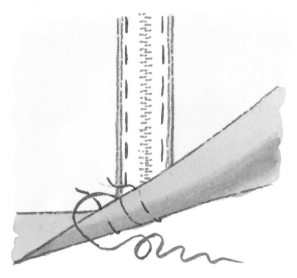

3 Turn to the right side and topstitch just inside the basting line—about ³⁄₈ in/1 cm from the teeth. Remove the basting and press.

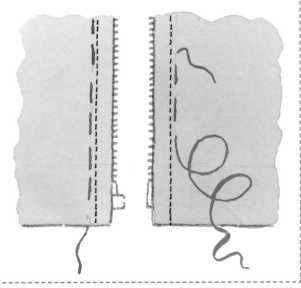

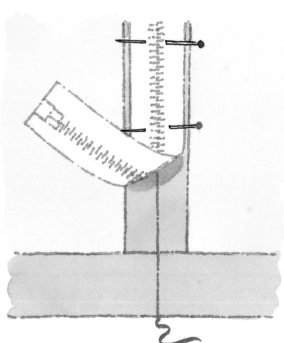

TRAVEL KIT

The exposed white zipper on this travel kit is an integral part of its design. The three-dimensional quality of the bag itself makes it one of the more tricky projects and not the best choice for a beginner, as sewing round the corners does require a little skill. Make the lining first as practice before you tackle the outer.

FINISHED SIZE

Height 7 in/18 cm, width 11¼ in/28.5 cm, depth 5½ in/14 cm

MATERIALS

Quantities are for fabric 45 in/115 cm wide:

- 1¼ yd/1 m firm cotton fabric
- ⅔ yd/60 cm iron-on interlining
- 16 in/40 cm robust nylon zipper
- Thread
- Dot-and-cross paper or newspaper for the pattern

CUTTING OUT

- Trace the template on page 215 onto dot-and-cross paper and cut out four side pieces
- Cut two pieces 6¾ x 25⅝ in/17 x 55 cm for the main gusset
- Cut four pieces 4 x 17¼ in/10 x 44 cm for the top gusset
- Cut two pieces 2¾ x 4 in/7 x 10 cm for the pulls

1 Start by making the bag lining. Fold one main gusset piece in half, end to end, and mark the center point with a pin at each side. Fold the two side pieces in half, end to end, and mark the center point at the top and bottom edges with a pin. With right sides together, match one of the gusset center pins with the center pin on the bottom edge of one of the bag side pieces. Starting at this point, pin and then baste the gusset along the bottom edge and up one end. Return to the center point and baste in the same way to the other end. Repeat with the other side piece. Stitch, easing the gusset fabric carefully at the corners. Start and stop stitching ⅝ in/ 1.5 cm before the ends. Clip the corners, trim the seams, and press them open.

2 Press in ⅝ in/1.5 cm along one long edge of two of the top gusset pieces. In the same way as you attached the main gusset, center, baste, and stitch the raw edge of one top gusset piece to the top edge of each side piece. Baste and then stitch the ends of the top gussets to the ends of the main gusset. Trim the seams and press them open.

3 For the outer shell, lay all the remaining pieces except the pulls wrong side down on the interlining. Iron to fuse. Trim around the pieces. Re-press with the interlining uppermost.

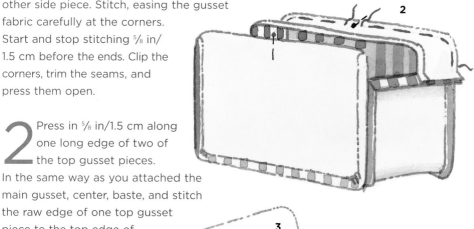

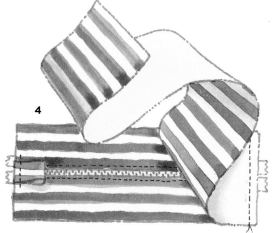

4 Now insert the zipper into the top gusset pieces (see page 129). Press in ⅝ in/1.5 cm along one long edge of the gusset pieces. With the zipper and gusset pieces right side up, place one folded edge close to the teeth on one side so that it projects past the zipper teeth by ¾ in/2 cm at each end. Baste into position. Repeat with the other side. Using the zipper foot, stitch the zipper in place. Make up each pull by folding both long sides in to the center and then folding it in half end to end, so the raw edges are enclosed. Lay the zipper gusset wrong side down. With raw edges meeting, pin and baste one pull to each end, centering it over the zipper teeth. Use a zipper foot to stitch it in position. Then, with raw edges meeting, pin one end of the main gusset piece right side down over one end of the zipper gusset, and stitch.

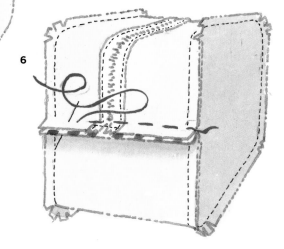

5 Using pins, mark the center points on each long edge of the zipper gusset and on the top and bottom of the outer-shell side pieces. With right sides together, match the zipper-gusset pins to the pins on the top edge of each side piece. With the zipper part open, baste the zipper gusset into position, starting at the center point of one side and basting to the pull, and then returning to the center and basting to the other pull. Repeat with the other side.

6 Starting at the end that is stitched to the top gusset, baste the main gusset to one side piece, with right sides together, stopping ¾ in/2 cm from the end. Repeat with the other side. Make sure the main gusset fits without any creases and, if necessary, trim the end. Pin and baste the end of the main gusset to the end of the zipper gusset, then stitch in place.

7 Turn the bag right side out and turn the lining inside out. Place the lining inside the bag, aligning the seams. Pin and baste the turned-in edge of the lining's top gusset close to the underside of the zipper teeth. Slipstitch along both sides to finish.

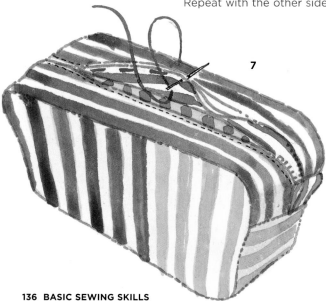

BUTTONS AND BUTTONHOLES

To stitch on a button securely, use a doubled thread—preferably extra-strong button thread—and attach it through a double thickness of fabric. This is not usually a problem, since the edge of the garment often has a facing. If you do need to add extra strength, you can sew a piece of nonfraying fabric or a small button to the underside.

SEWING ON BUTTONS WITH HOLES

Buttons with holes are the basic sew-through type, and need a thread shank to allow space for the fabric that will be buttoned onto it. This should be equal to the thickness of the fabric plus ⅛ in/3 mm. Use the same method to sew on both two- and four-hole sew-through buttons.

1 Start by threading a needle with double thread and knot the ends together. Using a marking pen or a pin, mark the position of the button on the garment. Pass the needle from under the fabric to the right side and through one of the holes. Place a toothpick or matchstick over the top of the button and stitch over this into the other hole and down through the fabric. Repeat twice or three times to make a firm fixing.

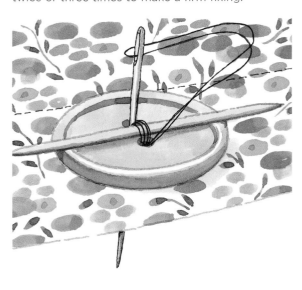

2 Remove the toothpick and push the button up to the top of the stitches. Pass the needle down through the hole to the underside of the button and wind the thread tightly around the threads under the button to form the shank. Pass the needle down through to the underside of the garment and finish with two small stitches on top of each other.

SEWING ON A BUTTON WITH A SHANK

Some buttons have an integral shank, so they simply need to be sewn directly onto the fabric, as above, but with no slackness. Finish on the underside of the garment with two small stitches on top of each other.

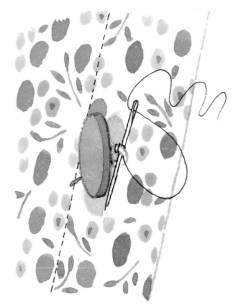

BUTTONHOLES

Badly executed buttonholes can ruin a garment, so aim to do the neatest job possible. Nowadays, we are so used to the neat finish of machined buttonholes that the hand-stitched versions scream homemade garment and only work well on more bohemian styles. If you want a smart finish, you will need to machine-stitch your buttonholes.

Some computerized sewing machines have the capability to stitch buttonholes that automatically fit your chosen buttons. Simply put a button into the buttonhole foot and the buttonhole will be programed into the machine's memory and can be stitched in one step. Less sophisticated machines have four-step buttonholes, which entail setting the stitch dial to the four different stitch components of the buttonhole as you need them. These usually consist of a close stitch used to zigzag along one side (known as satin stitch), followed by a bar tack at one end, close zigzags, or satin stitch, along the other side, and a bar tack at the other end.

Whatever the system, it is a good idea to practice the buttonhole on a spare piece of fabric, so that you can check both the tension and the fit of the button. You will need to assemble all the relevant layers—facings, interlining, and top fabric—to make it an accurate test of tension.

1 Mark the position of the buttonholes. These will be marked on commercial patterns, so transfer the positions using tailor's chalk, a temporary fabric-marker pen, or tailor's tacks. Calculate the length of the buttonhole. This should be the diameter of the button plus its depth.

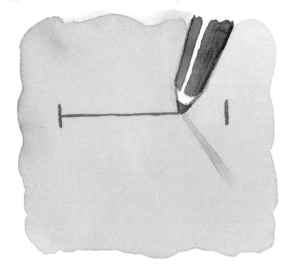

2 Set the machine at the first buttonhole position to stitch along one side.

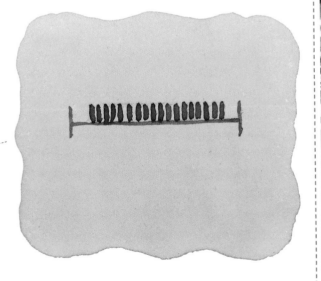

TIP
CHEAT'S BUTTONS
Always test buttonholes on a spare piece of fabric until you are absolutely sure that the tension is correct and you are confident of a neat finish. If you are not, don't risk spoiling the project. Stitch the buttons into position and use press studs behind them for the actual fastening.

3 Adjust the dial to stitch the end bar.

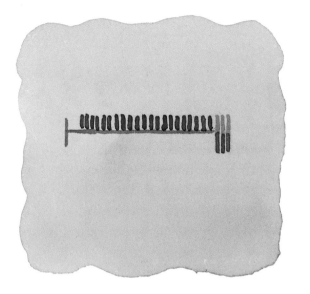

5 Finally, stitch the other end bar.

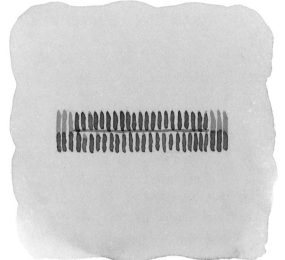

4 Adjust the dial again to stitch along the other side.

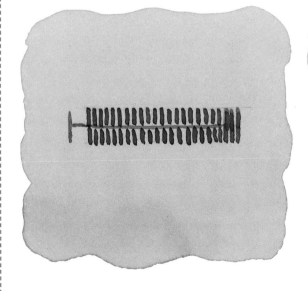

6 Once the buttonhole is stitched, place a pin at both ends of the buttonhole, just inside the side bars. Using a sharp pair of scissors and starting in the middle of the buttonhole, snip between the rows of satin stitch.

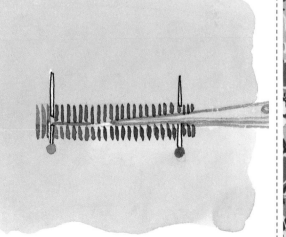

TAILORED PILLOW

Heavy linen in three tonal hues make up into the most elegant of pillows. The cover is put together like a large pillowcase and trimmed with five shimmering shell buttons fastened into machined buttonholes. Try out a buttonhole on a sample piece of fabric. If you are not confident that you can get them tailor-neat, stitch the buttons to the top flap and fasten the pillow cover using snaps underneath.

FINISHED SIZE
18 x 18 in/45 x 45 cm

MATERIALS
- 18-in-/45-cm-square pillow form
- ½ yd/50 cm each of three different colors (sky, heather, and slate) of upholstery-weight linen
- 5 shell buttons, ¾ in/ 2 cm diameter
- Thread

CUTTING OUT
Cut the linen as follows:
- Sky: 19 x 15½ in/ 48 x 39 cm
- Heather: 19 x 28½ in/ 48 x 72 cm
- Slate: 19 x 20 in/ 48 x 50 cm

1 To keep the edge from fraying, stitch one 19-in/ 48-cm side of the piece of sky linen using zigzag stitch. With right sides together, pin the other end of the sky linen to one matching end of the heather linen. Pin the other end of the heather linen to the matching end of the slate linen. Stitch the two seams. Clip the corners diagonally and press the seams open. Stitch along the other edge of the slate linen with zigzag stitch.

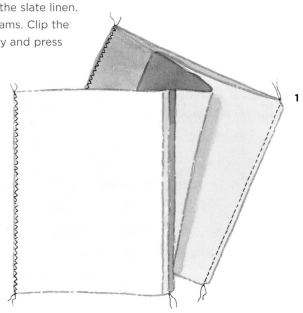

1

2 Turn in and press a 2-in/5-cm hem on the zigzagged edge of the slate piece and stitch. Fold the slate piece over the heather. Pin and stitch the side seams.

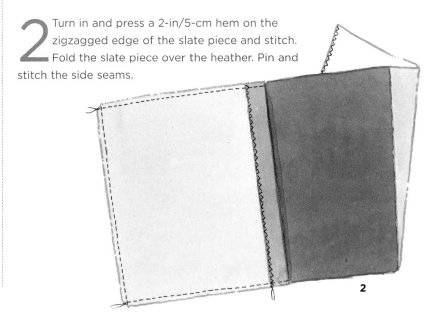

2

3 For the sky trim at the bottom edge of the front flap, measure 1 in/2.5 cm away from the seam joining the sky and heather pieces, and fold and press the sky piece at this point. Fold the rest of the sky piece back over the heather, overlapping the hemmed edge of the slate piece. Stitch along both sides. Clip the corners and clip into the seams at the point where all three fabrics meet. Press all the seams open and turn the pillow cover through. Make sure that the front corners are properly turned through and sharp, then press the whole cover using a good shot of steam.

4 Mark the buttonhole positions on the front flap so that they just encroach on the sky trim. The first one should be 3 in/7.5 cm in from the side and the rest should be spaced at 3-in/7.5-cm intervals. Mark the positions with pins and double check that they are equally spaced. Using tailor's chalk, mark the buttonhole lengths, which should be 1¼ in/3 cm. Stitch the buttonholes through both thicknesses.

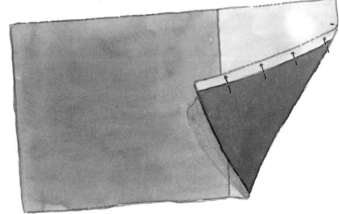

4

5

3

5 Re-press the pillow cover and lay it on a flat surface. Fold the flap over the main part of the cover and, using tailor's chalk or a marking pencil, mark the positions of the buttons through the buttonholes. Use a measuring tape to check that they are even and straight before stitching the buttons in position using double thread (see page 137).

left As well as being practical, pretty buttons make a textural, and sometimes colorful, decorative feature on furnishings and clothing.

PRESS STUDS (SNAPS)

Easy to snap together and pull apart, press studs are surprisingly strong; unless they have become very worn, they hold fast until they are prised open. Also known as snap fasteners or snaps, press studs can be used to secure just the top part of an opening, or they can be spaced apart to close the whole opening in a similar way to buttons. They come in two parts: the ball and the socket. Both parts have a hole in the center, which can be used for alignment, plus four holes around the perimeter for sewing them into position. They come in a range of sizes, from the smallest nickel for securing delicate lingerie, to robust plastics for outdoor wear, luggage, and camping gear, designed to withstand the stresses of wind and weather.

1 Start by sewing the ball part to the underside of the overflap. Mark the position of the press stud using tailor's chalk. Thread the needle with double thread and knot the ends together. Take a small stitch through the facing section only, so that the knot does not show on the front of the garment. Position the press stud over the knot, then stitch four stitches through each hole into the facing to secure the press stud without the stitches showing on the front of the garment.

2 To mark the position of the socket part, either rub tailor's chalk on the ball and use that to make an imprint on the underlap, or push your needle through the hole in the middle of the ball and use that to align with the hole in the socket part. Now stitch the socket part to the underlap. As the back of this will be against the skin, you can stitch through all layers. Finish with two or more tiny stitches on the underside.

TIP
MULTIPLE PRESS STUDS
When stitching on more than one press stud, take care to mark their positions accurately before sewing them in place, because even slight misalignment makes for an untidy row. Do this using a ruler and tailor's chalk or a marker pen.

HOOKS AND EYES

Even tiny hooks and eyes can take strain where necessary, such as at the top end of dress zippers to stop them from opening. Hooks for skirts and pants are generally heavier duty to cope with the extra strain around the waist. Whatever their size, hooks are stitched into position using the same method. The hook section should be stitched onto the top flap and the bar onto the underlap.

1 Position the bar directly above the teeth of the zipper. Using double thread knotted at the end, pass the needle through all the layers from the underside and make at least four stitches through the hole at one end of the bar. Repeat with the other hole. Finish with at least two small stitches on top of each other on the underside of the fabric.

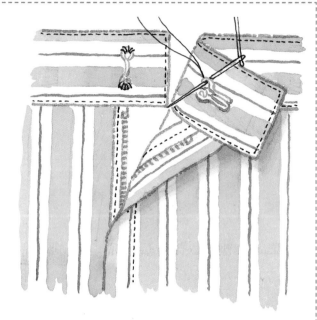

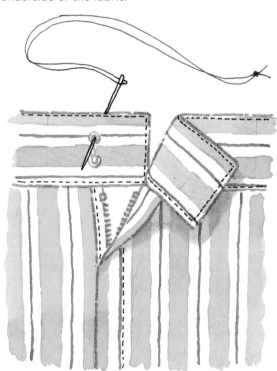

2 In the same way, position the hook above the zipper teeth on the corresponding side of the opening. Stitch it in position using the same method as for the bar, but only stitch through the under layer of fabric so that the stitches do not show on the outside of the garment.

TAPE FASTENERS

Snaps, and hooks and eyes are also available evenly spaced on tape, which can be bought by the yard. Most patterns allow for turnings where there are to be closures. If not, allow double the seam allowance and fold back one half before applying the tape.

HOOK-AND-EYE TAPE

This is primarily used for garments where you need edge-to-edge fastening. Traditionally, hook-and eye tape was used for undergarments, although now it is also often used for fitted outerwear. If you want to reveal the hooks, you can fold the tapes in half lengthwise before stitching them into position.

1 To ensure that the hooks and eyes will align exactly once stitched in place, hook the tapes together, then cut them exactly under one hook-and-eye pair. Use the tape to measure the length of the opening, then cut it as near to the top end of the next hook-and-eye pair as possible. This will also provide a seam allowance for the next stage.

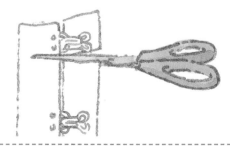

2 Fold back the required turning on the garment, ensuring that it is wider than the hook tape. Then, with the tape hooked together, pin the hook tape right side up on the edge of one side of the garment. Repeat to pin the eye side of the tape onto the other side of the garment. Baste, then remove the pins and unhook the hooks and eyes. Using a zipper foot, first stitch down the straight edge and across the bottom, then around the hooks, making sure you lower the needle into the fabric and lift the foot before turning, then lower the foot before stitching in the new direction. Repeat with the eye section.

1 Cut the tape to the length of the opening. Pin the hook side to the upper side of the underlap and the loop side to the underside of the overlap. Machine stitch both pieces of tape in position around all four sides.

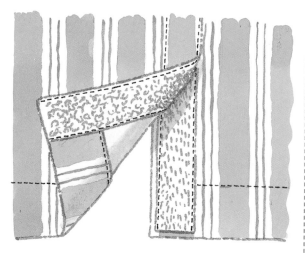

2 For the dots, position the hook side on the underlap and pin it in position. Pin the loop side to the underside of the overlap. Check the positioning by fastening it to the hook side. Baste in position with one large stitch. Remove the pins. Stitch around the perimeter of the dots.

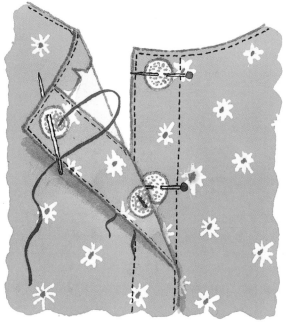

HOOK AND LOOP

Commonly known as Velcro, hook-and-loop fasteners are more commonly used for home furnishings than garments, although they can be useful for children's clothes or outerwear. They come in several widths in the tape form, or as dots. Tape should be used where the closure is lapped.

SNAP TAPE

Useful for home furnishings, such as pillow and duvet covers, these work in the same way as single snaps and are designed for use where one side of the item overlaps the other to create the closure.

1 To ensure that the snaps will align correctly when stitched in place, cut the tape exactly under one snap. Use the tape to measure along the opening, then cut the tape to length as near to the next snap as possible. This will also provide a seam allowance.

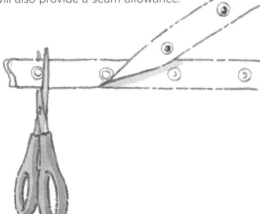

2 Place the socket tape wrong side down close to the edge of the right side of the underlap. Ensure that the cut edge matches the raw top edge of the underlap. Pin it into position.

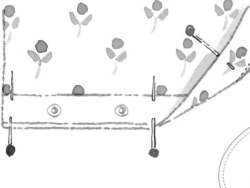

3 Starting about 1 in/2.5 cm from the top edge, stitch down the length of one side. When you get to the corner, lower the needle through all layers, lift the presser foot, swivel the fabric, lower the foot again, and stitch along the bottom edge. Continue in the same way around all the corners and continue by a few stitches once you get to the starting point.

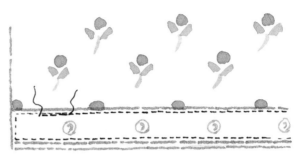

4 Place the ball tape wrong side down on the underside of the overlap and stitch it in the same way as the socket tape.

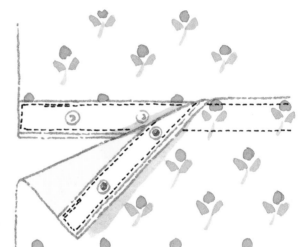

TIP
STITCHING TAPE FASTENERS

For extra control, you might find it easier to stitch on tape fasteners using a zipper foot on the sewing machine, so that you can stitch close to the edge of the tape while keeping clear of the fasteners.

NO-SEW FASTENERS

There are many robust workwear fasteners, such as jeans buttons; heavy-duty snaps for bags, outdoor equipment, and clothing; and eyelets of all sizes available from notions stores. These are riveted, rather than sewn, into position, using special pliers or tools. The tools are sometimes supplied as part of a kit with the fasteners; other times they are sold separately.

Whether you are attaching jeans buttons or eyelets, the process of riveting is basically the same: the aim is to pass one side of the fastener through the fabric and flatten it by gently tapping it with a hammer to fix it into another piece of metal on the other side of the fabric. Some jeans buttons are fixed using a metal tack that is supplied in the kit. Each kit is a little different but is supplied with full instructions. Here are some examples.

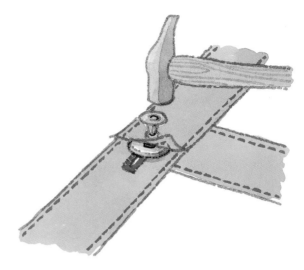

JEANS BUTTONS

Jeans were the original American workwear pants that moved into the fashion arena in the 1950s and are now a staple in everyone's closet. Designers and mass-market retailers alike adapt the basic cut to meet current fashion trends, extending the style to jackets, skirts, and dungarees.

If you want to make your own jeans garments, to retain integrity, they need to incorporate the hallmark riveted stud-buttons. Thankfully, notions stores can facilitate this by supplying a variety of easy-to-no-sew kits.

1 Push the tack that makes up the back of the button through the fabric from the underside. Place the button upside down on a flat surface, then put the fabric right side down on top of it, so that the point of the tack locates into the hole in the stem of the button. Gently hammer the tack into position.

HEAVY-DUTY SNAPS

Generally used for bags and outdoor clothing and equipment, heavy-duty snaps are available in a range of styles and are supplied with a simple punching tool so that you can rivet them into position yourself.

You need to rivet each part separately. To ensure that the ball part and the socket part align properly on the garment, start by marking the positions of both parts of the snaps. These will be marked (probably by circles) on the paper pattern. Transfer the marks using your preferred method (see page 62).

Each kit comes with slightly different tools and instructions on how to fix the snaps. Essentially, the method involves making a hole in the fabric, pushing a shank through this from the underside, and fixing the top part by using a spreading tool and a light tap with the hammer to flatten a metal flange and secure it in position. Fix the ball to the underlap and the socket to the overlap.

EYELETS

Eyelets come in a huge range of sizes—from the tiny, designed to provide holes for laces, to those that are a couple of inches or so in diameter, designed to accommodate curtain poles. Small eyelets can be fixed using special pliers. Larger ones come supplied with their own tools that are designed to pierce the fabric and rivet the eyelet into position on the other side of the fabric.

DRAWSTRING AND CASING

In garments, drawstrings are usually used to gather in the fabric around the waist or hips, dispensing with shaping, such as darts, and other more complicated fastenings, such as zippers or buttons. Drawstrings can also be used to fasten simple bags. They are kept in place by casings, which, at their simplest, are a deep hem. You can see three variations on the basic casing on the pajama pants (page 110), bias-cut skirt (page 188) and drawstring bag (opposite). Casings can also be used to contain elastic.

CASING FOR AN ELASTICATED WAIST

1 Stitch the main seams of the garment or bag. Then, at the top edge, turn in and press a ¼ in/6 mm hem to the wrong side. Measure the width of your elastic and add ½ in/12 mm to this measurement. Turn the edge down by this measurement, creating a double hem, and press.

2 Undo the stitching on one seam on the inside of the folded-over hem, up to the top fold. Pin the hem and stitch. Cut the elastic to length, allowing for a 1 in/2.5 cm overlap. Attach a large safety pin to one end of the elastic and push this into the casing through the opening in the seam. Use the safety pin to feed the elastic through the casing until you get back to the other side of the open seam. Pin the 1 in/2.5 cm overlap at the other end of the elastic in place at the opening so that it doesn't get pulled into the casing.

3 Overlap the elastic ends by 1 in/2.5 cm. Fold in the ends, if necessary, and slipstitch into position. Oversew the sides where they overlap. Slipstitch the open seam to close.

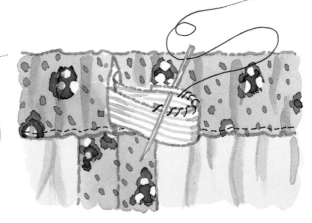

TIP
THE DRAWSTRING
Insert a drawstring in the same way as described for elastic. You can use a length of ribbon, braid, or tape, or make your own drawstring. To do this, fold both long edges of a strip of fabric to the wrong side, then fold the strip in half lengthwise with wrong sides together. Turn in the ends and press, then topstitch all around.

DRAWSTRING BAG

Keep the kids organized by making drawstring bags for their various school kits, such as gym, ballet, and soccer. Make up a simple appliqué to put on the front to make sure they grab the right one in the morning rush. Use a firm fabric, such as gabardine, used here, denim, or cotton duck, and then trim it, if you wish, with a fresh and pretty fabric like this tiny blue gingham check, which is also used in the appliqué.

FINISHED SIZE

Height 19 in/48 cm, width 12 in/30 cm

MATERIALS

- ½ yd/50 cm white cotton gabardine
- 8 in/20 cm smallest check blue gingham
- Scrap of denim 4 x 8 in/10 x 20 cm
- Double-sided fabric bond (Bondaweb) at least 8 x 8 in/ 20 x 20 cm
- One white shoe lace
- 2½ yd/2 m of ribbon or braid
- Red thread
- White thread
- Safety pin or loop turner

CUTTING OUT

- Cut two pieces of white cotton gabardine, each 14 x 16½ in/36 x 42 cm
- Cut four pieces of blue gingham, each 14 x 5¼ in/36 x 13 cm
- Following the instructions for appliqué on page 177, fuse fabric bond onto the back of the denim and a piece of blue gingham the same size. Using the templates on page 216, cut one complete shoe shape in denim and cut one of both shoe details in blue gingham

1 Start by making up the sports-shoe appliqué (referring to page 177). Peel the fabric-bond backing paper off the gingham shapes and pin or baste them in position right side up on the denim shoe shape. Iron the gingham shapes to fuse them to the denim. Use close zigzag stitch and red thread to stitch the gingham onto the denim, following the outline but avoiding the outside edges of the shoe shape. Pin the white shoelace into a lace configuration on the shoe, then stitch in place using straight stitch and white thread. Trim to length and tie a knot at each end.

2 Peel the fabric-bond backing paper off the denim and position the shoe shape centrally on the right side of one piece of gabardine, 3¾ in/9.5 cm from the bottom edge. Baste in place, then iron to fuse it to the front of the bag. Use close zigzag stitch and red thread to stitch around the outline of the shoe.

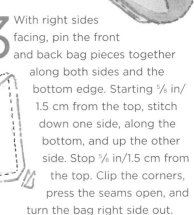

3 With right sides facing, pin the front and back bag pieces together along both sides and the bottom edge. Starting ⅝ in/ 1.5 cm from the top, stitch down one side, along the bottom, and up the other side. Stop ⅝ in/1.5 cm from the top. Clip the corners, press the seams open, and turn the bag right side out.

4 To prepare the gingham top, fold one long edge of each of the four pieces ¼ in/6 mm to the wrong side, and press. Place two pieces with right sides together and pin along the three raw edges. Starting 1 in/2.5 cm from the pressed-in edge, stitch down one side, along the top edge, and down the other side, finishing 1 in/2.5 cm from the pressed-in edge. Clip the corners and turn right side out. Turn in and press the remaining 1 in/2.5 cm of the side seams to align with the seam allowances. Repeat with the other two pieces.

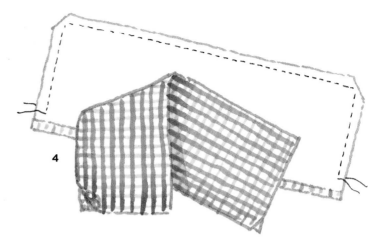

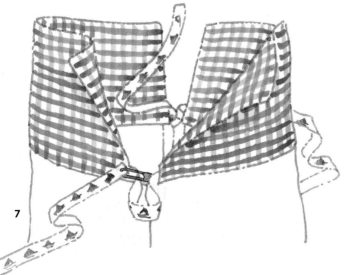

5 Place one gingham section over the top edge of the front of the bag, making sure the raw edge of the bag lines up with the end of the stitching on the side seams of the gingham section. Baste through all three layers to hold it in position. Stitch along the folded edge of the gingham. Attach the other gingham section to the top edge of the back of the bag in the same way.

6 Sew another line of stitching 1 in/2.5 cm above the first line on the front and back. This should align with the bottom of the gingham side seams, making a channel through which you will be able to thread the ribbon or braid.

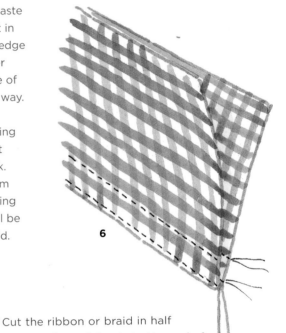

7 Cut the ribbon or braid in half and attach a safety pin to the end of one length. Thread one piece of ribbon in through one end of the front channel to the other end, then into the back channel and out at the other end. Take the next piece of ribbon and thread it in the other direction, starting where you finished at the back channel and threading it back through to where you started. Knot the ends of each pair of ribbons together and pull both loops at once to close the bag.

trimmings

Design flair lies in the detail. The trimmings you choose can completely change the personality of the project. Small and neat, bias binding, piping, and cording will smarten it up. Add a frill, ribbon, or braid, and it will immediately become prettier. Short frills and pleats generally look more elegant than larger, blousier frills, while pom-poms and fringes add a flirty feel. You can use trimmings to add accent color—the smaller the trimming, the louder you can afford to go with the color.

BIAS BINDING

Learn to make bias binding and you will open the door to a whole array of useful dressmaking skills. Made from strips of fabric cut on the diagonal and joined together end to end, bias binding has a natural stretch that neatly contains raw edges and lies flat around curves. It can be used to finish seams and hems, and it can be used as a trimming—either matching the garment, or contrasting with it as a neat design detail. Better still, once you have mastered making bias binding, you will be able to adapt the technique to make piping and cording.

TIP
CUTTING BIAS STRIPS
An easy way to ensure that you cut bias strips of equal widths is to use the full width of your ruler each time, or cut a strip of firm card to the desired width and use that as a straight edge to draw the lines using tailor's chalk.

MAKING BIAS BINDING

1 Bias binding is cut at 45 degrees to the fabric grain. The easiest way to work this out accurately is to first pull out a thread running between the selvages at one side of the fabric to establish the true straight line of the grain. Then, using sharp scissors, cut along the thread position. Fold this straight trimmed edge diagonally to one of the selvages and press the fold with your hand to make a crease.

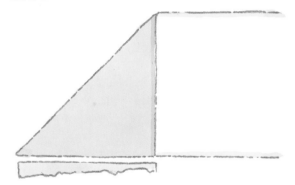

2 Use a ruler and tailor's chalk to mark the line of the crease. Draw another line parallel to the first, the desired width of the bias—2½ in/6 cm is a standard width. Continue drawing parallel lines of the same width across the width of the fabric. Cut along the lines using scissors or a rotary cutter on a cutting mat.

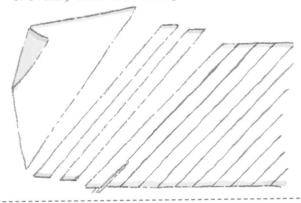

3 If you have cut the strips using this method, the ends of the bias strips will be on the selvage, which is the straight grain. Any ends that don't have a selvage should be trimmed on the straight grain. Then, with right sides together, align these edges, so that the strips form a V shape. Pin and then machine stitch them together.

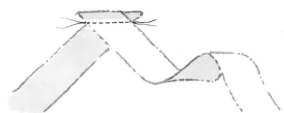

4 Repeat with all the strips until you have made up the desired length of bias binding to trim all the raw edges that are to be bound. Press the seams open and trim off the excess corners. Press a hem of ¼ in/6 mm along both long edges.

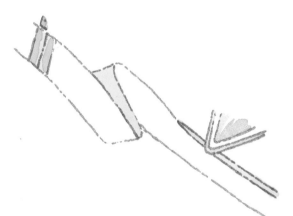

APPLYING BIAS BINDING

1 Unfold one edge and, with right sides together and raw edges meeting, pin it to the main piece, putting the pins in at right angles to the long edge. Stitch along the bias fold, which will help you both to keep the stitches perfectly straight and make it easier to neatly turn the bias to the wrong side of the main piece.

2 Turn the bias binding to the wrong side of the main piece. With the folded edge turned under, pin it into position, then either hand-stitch it into place using uneven slipstitch (see page 48) or machine stitch just outside the original line of stitches. If you are hand-stitching, place the pins parallel with the stitches, unpinning each section before you come to it. If you are machine stitching, place the pins at right angles to the line of stitching so the machine can run over them.

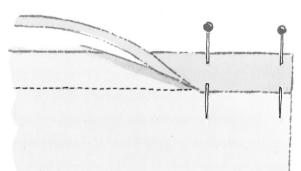

TIP

MACHINE STITCHING BIAS BINDING

Achieve a neatly machined finish by spending time on accurately and neatly pinning the bias to the wrong side. If the folded edge of the tape closely follows the first line of stitching, when you stitch the final line, it will appear neatly on the front just below the bias tape.

PIPING AND CORDING

Both piping and cording might provide small detailing, but the addition of either will have a huge effect on the finished design. Use it in the same fabric as the main fabric to neaten seams elegantly, or make it in strong accent shades to spice up the color scheme.

Piping is made up of lengths of bias-cut fabric, but instead of being used to encase an edge, it is folded in half lengthwise and inserted between two pieces to form a trim. Piping can be flat or it can be wrapped around piping cord to make a rounded trim known as cording.

MAKING PIPING

1 Make up bias strips, as described on page 152, to a width that is twice the width that you want the exposed piping to be plus 1¼ in/3 cm for turnings. Do not press in the hem edges. With wrong sides facing, fold the strips in half lengthwise and stitch ½ in/12 mm in from the raw edges.

MAKING CORDING

As well as your chosen piping fabric, you will need to buy lengths of piping cord. This comes in a range of widths. Use it small and neat for a sophisticated finish, or go larger for a bold look.

1 To work out the correct width to cut the bias strips so that the fabric encloses the cord and provides a seam allowance, fold a corner of the fabric over the cord and allow an additional seam allowance of ⅝ in/1.5 cm. Place a pin through both thicknesses of fabric so that the cord is encased snugly. Check the seam allowance and cut along this line.

TIP
PIPING VERSUS CORDING
Unsure whether you want piping or cording? Cording gives a neat finish and is generally more used than piping—so much so that, confusingly, it is now usually known as piping. True piping—without the cord—is rather less formal, but can be used to provide accents of color.

2 Unpin the fabric and use it as a template to mark out the width of the bias strips with a ruler and marking pencil or tailor's chalk. Cut the strips and join them end to end (see page 153).

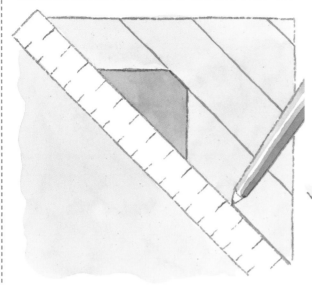

3 With wrong sides together, fold the bias strip in half lengthwise, snugly enclosing the length of piping cord within the center fold, and pin in position. Use the zipper foot to machine stitch close to the cord to encase it.

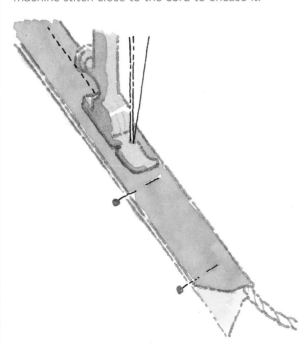

APPLYING PIPING AND CORDING

Piping and cording is encased into the seam between two pieces of fabric to provide a neat trim from the right side. The same method is used to encase trims such as fringing and pom-poms.

1 Trim the seam allowance to ⅝ in/1.5 cm. Align the raw edges of the piping with the raw edge of one piece of main fabric; pin, then baste it in position. Using a zipper foot set to the right of the needle, stitch just inside the piping stitches. If you need to stitch around a corner, notch the seam allowance in the piping at the corner to provide ease.

2 With right sides together, pin the main seam, sandwiching the trimming in between. Stitch. Trim the seam, grading it to reduce bulk (see page 94). Clip or notch the seam if necessary. Press the seam open.

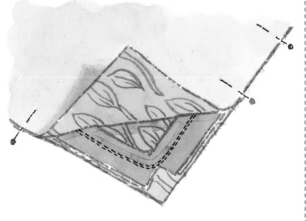

BOLSTER

Make up a pair of bolster pillows in elegant aqua damask trimmed with gold braid and piping for an opulent Regency look. The braid was mounted onto some of the piping fabric, both for coordination and to create a wider-looking braid.

FINISHED SIZE
Length 18 in/45 cm, diameter 8½ in/22 cm

MATERIALS
For each bolster:
- Bolster pillow form, 8½ in/22 cm diameter x 18 in/45 cm long
- Invisible zipper, 14 in/ 36 cm long
- ¾ yd/50 cm silk damask
- ¾ yd/50 cm shot silk for the piping and trims
- 1½ yd/1.5 m fine piping cord
- 1½ yd/1.5 m gold braid
- Thread
- Paper for the pattern

CUTTING OUT
- Cut one piece of damask 28¾ x 19¼ in/ 73 x 48 cm
- Cut a paper circle with a 9¾-in/25-cm diameter and use this as a pattern to cut out two circles of damask for the ends
- Cut two strips of shot silk, 29 x 3 in/74 x 7 cm for the trims

1 On the two cut strips of silk, fold both long edges into the center on the wrong side and press. Cut the braid in half and pin one piece onto the right side of each strip of folded silk, positioning it centrally along the length. Hand-stitch it in place along both edges of the braid, taking tiny stitches on the right side and long stitches on the reverse.

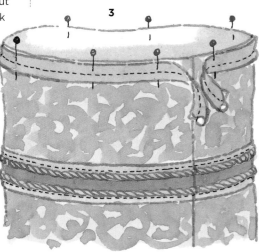

2 Pin and baste one silk-and-braid strip 2½ in/6 cm in from one long edge of the damask. Repeat with the other strip along the other long side. Using a zipper foot, stitch close to the braid along both sides of the trim. Now insert the zipper, which is positioned centrally in the single seam. Do this following the instructions for invisible zippers on page 132. Stitch the section of seam remaining at each end of the zipper.

3 Make up the cording in shot silk, following the instructions on page 154, and cut the length in half. With the raw edges of the cording meeting the raw edge of the right side of the bolster cover, pin the cording around one edge; leave 1½ in/4 cm of excess cording at the ends and start and stop pinning 1 in/2.5 cm away from the seam line. Baste the cording in place and then, using a zipper foot, stitch close to the cording.

4 Now join the ends of the cording together. First, snip open about 1 in/2.5 cm of the silk seam on both ends to reveal the piping cord. Pin one side of the seam allowance to the damask. Then, allowing a joining seam allowance, trim the silk along the straight grain. Stitch the seam to join the two pieces of silk. Cut the piping cords to length and hand-stitch the ends together. Wrap the silk back around the cord and, using the zipper foot, finish off stitching the cording to the damask. In the same way, apply cording to the other end of the bolster cover.

4

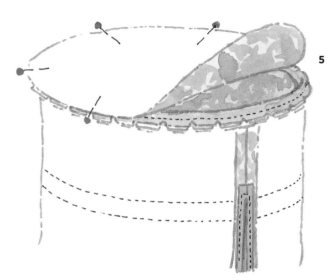

5

5 Unzip the zipper and turn the bolster cover wrong side out. With right sides together, pin one circular piece of damask to one end of the bolster. Use the zipper foot to stitch it in place, following the stitch line securing the cording. Repeat for the other end. Cut notches into the curved seam, then turn the cover through to the right side and insert the bolster pillow form.

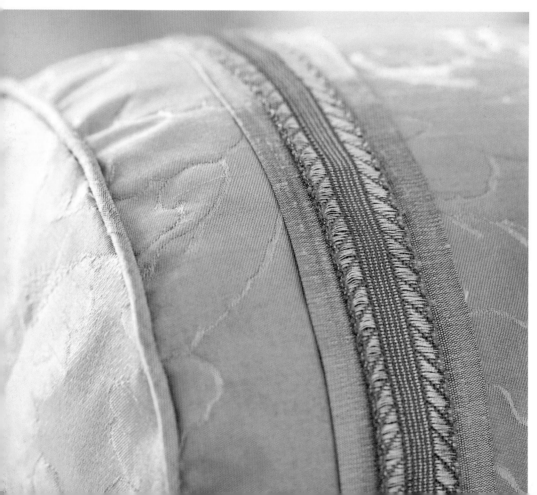

left The cording has been made from Thai shot silk in gold woven with purple, resulting in a luxurious look that isn't too gaudy.

STRAIGHT FRILL

Use frills, or ruffles, to introduce a soft touch to any garment, pillow, or drape. They don't always have to be huge feminine flouncy ones: depending on their size and how they are cut, ruffles can offer quite different design elements. Use them small and crisp as an elegant edging; make them double for extra flounce; cut them straight for a classic frill, or make them circular (see overleaf) for a waterfall effect. Straight frills, in particular, are wonderfully quick and easy to make, yet they can transform any design.

MAKING A STRAIGHT FRILL

Use this for:
• Garment edges with facings
• Edges of lined drapes
• Sides of pillows, pillowcases, and duvet covers.

1 Cut a piece of fabric that is double the length of the edge to be trimmed and double the width of the frill. Make a small double hem at both ends. With wrong sides together, fold the fabric in half lengthwise. Run a line of gathering stitches through the two thicknesses of fabric, ³⁄₈ in/1 cm from the raw edges.

2 Fold the fabric in half widthwise and mark the center point of the top edge with a pin, then fold it in half again and mark the two quarter points with pins. Pull up the gathering threads until the gathered edge fits the edge of the garment or item that is to be trimmed. Wind the spare gathering thread around a pin to hold the gathers in place.

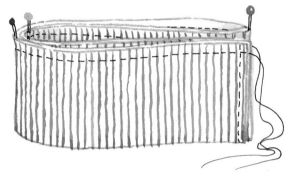

3 To insert the frill into a single seam, lay one piece of fabric that is to be trimmed wrong side down on a flat surface. Place pin markers at the half and quarter points along the edge of the fabric. With raw edges meeting, lay the gathered edge of the frill on top of the fabric. Pin the two pieces together at the half and quarter points and adjust the gathers. With the wrong side up and raw edges meeting, lay the other piece of fabric on top of the frill, matching the half and quarter points as before. Pin all the layers together and stitch. Turn the main fabric pieces right side out and the frill will hang from the bottom seam.

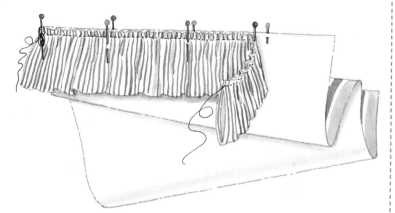

RUFFLE STYLE

Romantic ruffles soften a basic shirt such as this one. They can simply run down both sides of a blouse or cardigan, or around the neck, too. While, nowadays, we associate ruffles with womenswear, there is also a great tradition for them in menswear, dating back to the eighteenth-century dandies and highwaymen, which had an influence on some men's fashion in the 1960s and the 1980s.

Ruffles don't have to go all the way around a pillow. A smarter solution is to add them to just two sides. Stitched into the ends of a long pillow, straight frills are an elegant way to add softness.

A frill or ruffle around the hem of a dress adds gorgeous girly flounces. Use a single ruffle, as here, or add them in layers. A ruffle is also a great way to update a garment or add extra length to the hemline.

CIRCULAR RUFFLES

If you cut a circular piece of fabric to make a ruffle, the fullness comes from how the fabric falls, rather than from the gathers as it does on a straight frill. The end result is more elegant than frilly and looks good both when stitched to curved edges, such as necklines, and when stitched to straight edges, such as hemlines.

1 Before you start, you will need to make a pattern. Measure the length along which you want to stitch the ruffle and add 1¼ in/ 3 cm for seam allowances. On a large piece of paper (dot-and-cross paper is best, if you can get hold of it; newspaper will do), draw a circle with a circumference of the measured length. Now draw a line straight out from the edge of the circle (with your ruler aligned on the center point) to equal the width you would like to make the ruffle. Next, draw another circle outside the first, with a diameter from the center of the original circle to the end of the "width" line. Cut out the pattern and pin it to the fabric with the "width line" along the straight grain.

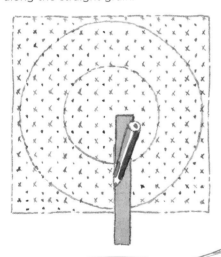

TIP
CIRCULAR RUFFLES
If you prefer a faced ruffle, make up two matching lengths. Then, with right sides together, stitch the outer edges together, trim the seam, press it open, and then turn the ruffle right side out and press again.

2 Cut around the outer circle first, then straight up the line along the straight of the grain. Finally, cut around the inner circle line. Stitch a line of straight stitch ⅝ in/ 1.5 cm inside the inner circle—this is known as staystitching and will prevent the curved fabric from distorting, then clip notches at regular intervals around the inner edge.

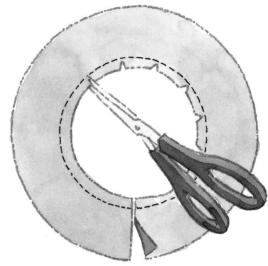

3 When you open out the circle, the fabric will naturally fall in soft ruffles. For long lengths, cut out and prepare several circles, the inner circumferences of which add up to the desired length, remembering to add seam allowances. Stitch the straight edges together, then press the seams open. Hem the ends and bottom edge of the ruffle with a double-folded hem (see page 184). With right sides together, pin the staystitched edge of the ruffle to the edge of the piece that is to be trimmed. Stitch it in place, finish the seam, and press it open.

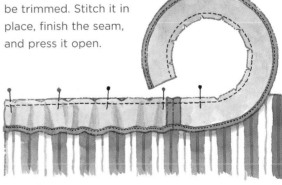

CUSTOMIZED T-SHIRT

If you don't want to stitch from scratch, customize what you already have. Here, a basic and inexpensive T-shirt has been given a frill hem to make a quick and easy fashion garment. Use white T-shirt fabric for the frills and stitch them onto a white T-shirt, so that you can then dye the finished piece any color you like.

MATERIALS
- Loose white cotton T-shirt
- 1½ yd/1.5 m white cotton jersey 55 in/140 cm wide or 2½ yd/2m white cotton jersey 45 in/114 cm wide
- White thread
- Gray fabric dye
- Dressmaker's dot-and-cross paper

CUTTING OUT
- Using the master frill template on page 217, trace and cut out three patterns for the small, medium, and large frills
- Fold the fabric to fit the widest frill. Pin the pattern piece in place, aligning the straight edge with the fold, and cut out. Measure the circumference of the T-shirt hem. Stretch out the frill and measure the top edge. Add 1½ in/4 cm for seam allowances. If the length of the frill is shorter than the hem of the T-shirt, you will need to cut more frill (see page 161). Adding an extra 1½ in/4 cm for seam allowances, measure the additional length needed around the inner edge of the frill, and cut this extra section in fabric
- Refold the fabric to fit the medium frill and cut it to the same length
- Repeat to cut out the smallest frill

1 If you had to lengthen the frills to fit the bottom edge of the T-shirt, stitch those seams together first to make three frills the correct length. Work zigzag stitch along the bottom edge of all of the frills. Layer the frills, with the widest at the bottom and the narrowest on top. Align the top edges and pin, then stitch all three layers together with zigzag stitch. Place a pin ¾ in/2 cm in from each end on the top edge. Fold the frill in half widthwise, matching the pins, and mark the halfway point with a pin. Fold the frill in half again and mark the quarter points with pins.

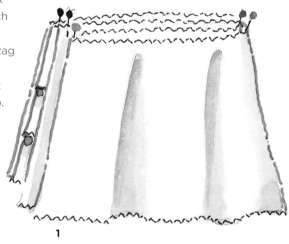

1

2

2 Decide where on the T-shirt you would like to position the frills. This may be the bottom edge or it may be a little higher up. Measure up from the bottom edge and mark this position at several points around the T-shirt using tailor's chalk or a fabric-marker pen. Fold the T-shirt so that the side seams meet and mark the center front and back with pins. Matching the pins, pin the frill onto the T-shirt at the center back, side seams, and center front. Starting at the center back, stitch the frill into position using zigzag stitch. With right sides together, stitch the ends of each of the frills together and trim the seams. Following the manufacturer's instructions, dye the T-shirt.

TIP
DYEING KNOWHOW
If you plan to dye the finished garment, ensure the fabric is at least 95 percent cotton, as home dyes don't take on synthetics. Using polyester thread will result in a contrast detail.

VINTAGE APRON

Pretty gingham and rickrack trims set against illustrations of Paris scenes are the perfect combination for a 1950s-style apron. Aprons were typically the first garment our mothers and grandmothers made at school, as girls could practice their gathering and trimming skills without the challenge of complicated darts and fastenings.

FIT
Fits sizes small to large

MATERIALS
- 1 yd/1 m patterned cotton fabric 45 in/ 115 cm wide
- 1 yd/1 m smallest check pink gingham
- 3¼ yd/3 m turquoise rickrack
- White thread
- Turquoise thread
- Paper for the pattern

CUTTING OUT
- From the patterned fabric: cut one skirt, 31 x 18 in/78 x 46 cm
- Draw a paper pattern for the bib: first draw a rectangle, 12 x 12 in/ 30 x 30 cm, then measure 1 in/2.5 cm in from the top corners. Draw a line from each of these points to the corresponding bottom corner. Cut out the paper shape and use it to cut two bib pieces
- From the gingham: using the top of the pattern piece, cut a top bib band 3 in/8 cm deep
- Cut two waistbands, 2½ x 22 in/6 x 56 cm
- Cut four waist ties, 2½ x 32 in/6 x 82 cm
- Cut one bottom frill, 2½ x 57 in/6 x 144 cm
- Cut four neck ties, 2 x 22 in/5 x 56 cm

1 With right sides together, fold the frill in half lengthwise. Pin and then stitch the short seams. Clip the corners and trim the seams. Turn the frill right side out and press.

2 Using double thread, run gathering stitches along the top edge (see pages 120 and 159). Fold the frill in half widthwise and mark the center point with a pin. Fold in half again and mark the quarter points.

3 On each side of the skirt piece, fold in a double hem, press, and then stitch (see page 184). Fold the skirt in half lengthwise and mark the center point on the bottom edge with a pin. Fold it in half again and mark the quarter points. With right sides together, pin the frill to the bottom edge of the skirt at the marked quarter points. Pull up the gathers to fit. Baste the gathered edge to the skirt. Stitch in place using a 1 in/2.5 cm seam allowance.

4 Make a self-bound seam (see page 108). First, trim the gathered edge to neaten the seam. Then turn in the raw edge of the skirt seam allowance by ¼ in/6 mm. Fold the turned-in edge over the raw edge of the frill and stitch in place.

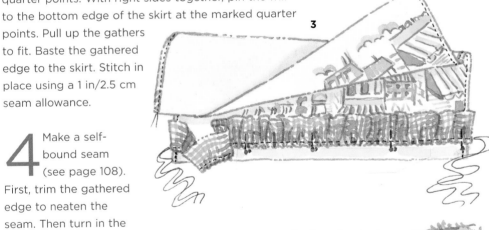

5 Sew a line of gathering stitches along the top edge of the skirt. Mark the halfway position with a pin. Use pins to mark 2½ in/6.5 cm in from each end of both waistband pieces. Place these pins together to mark the halfway positions. Lay the waistband lining piece wrong side down on a flat surface. Lay the skirt piece wrong side down on top of it, matching the raw edges and halfway marker pins. Pin the outside edges of the skirt to the waistband lining at the pin markers. Pull up the gathers until the skirt fits the waistband, then wind the threads around the pins to secure. Now place the front waistband piece on top of the pile, right side down, and pin it at the halfway and edge points. Baste all the layers together. Stitch, and then trim the seam allowance.

5

6 Make up the neck ties by placing two pieces with right sides together and stitching along the two long sides. Trim the seams and press them open. Turn through to the right side using a safety pin or loop turner, and press. Repeat with the other two pieces to make the second neck tie. Turn in and press one end of each tie. Topstitch around all three sides, leaving one end of each tie open.

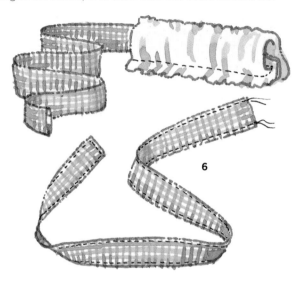

6

7 Press the bottom edge of the gingham bib trim ¼ in/6 mm to the wrong side and stitch. Place the trim wrong side down on the right side of the front bib, aligning the raw edges, and pin. Stitch the top edge and sides. Clip the corners.

7

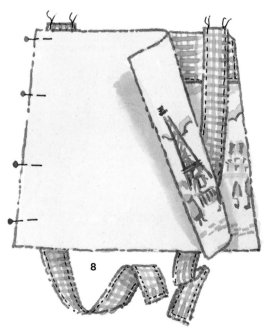

8

8 Lay the trimmed bib piece wrong side down on a flat surface. Place one neck tie on either side of the top edge, in line with the seam allowance and with the raw ends of the ties meeting the top edge of the bib. Now lay the bib lining right side down on top. Pin and stitch through all layers, up one side, along the top edge and down the other side, taking care not to catch the length of the neck ties in the stitching. Clip the corners, trim the seams, and press them open. Turn through to the right side and press.

9 Mark the halfway point of the lower edge of the bib with a pin. With right sides together and raw edges meeting, pin the front of the bib to the front waistband, matching the halfway pins. Stitch in place, then press the seam open. Turn in the raw edge of the waistband lining by ½ in/12 mm and press. Fold the waistband lining up into position, making sure it matches the front waistband. Fold in and press the seam allowance on the unstitched parts of the waistbands. Pin in position.

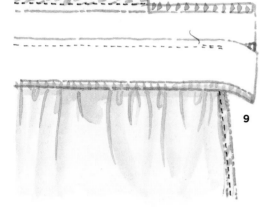

The seam joining the contrast frill to the bottom edge of the skirt has been self-bound, meaning that the raw gathered edges have been covered by the main fabric for a strong, neat, fray-free finish.

10 Now attach the waist ties. With right sides together, pin one waist-tie piece to each end of the front waistband and one to each end of the waistband lining. Stitch, then trim the seams and press them open. Turn in the seam allowances all around, and press. Pin the front and back of both waist ties together. Topstitch along the end and length of one tie, across the waistband, along the length of the other tie and end, and then all the way along the other edge of the ties and the waistband.

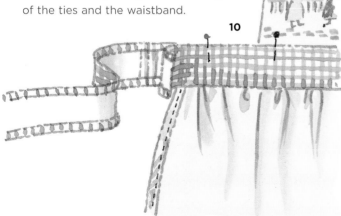

11 Pin rickrack along the top and bottom edge of the gingham bib trim, around the waistband, and along the bottom edge of the skirt. Turn in the ends neatly and stitch in place with matching thread.

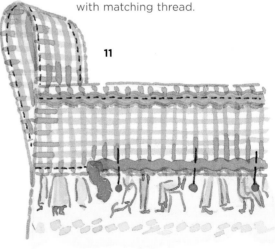

APPLYING BRAID OR RIBBON

Braid and ribbon can be used to provide surface embellishment both for garments and home furnishings. Apply it as early on in the project as you can, while the piece is still flat, as you will find it easier to keep the trimming straight. This is not always appropriate, however: for example, it is better for braid on a skirt to run over the finished seam, rather than be sewn into the seam, which it would be if you applied the braid as a first step.

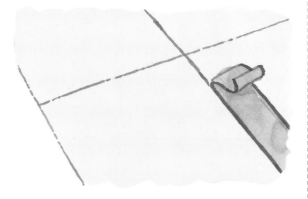

1 Decide where on the item you would like the braid to be: 4 in/10 cm up from the hem, for example. Measure up this amount at regular intervals along the edge and mark with tailor's chalk or a fabric-marker pen. Allowing an extra 1 in/2.5 cm for turnings and/or overlaps, cut the braid or ribbon to the required length.

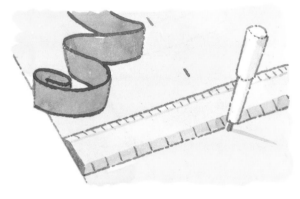

2 Using a ruler and the chalk or marker, join up the marks to draw a guideline. Turn in the raw end of the ribbon or braid and butt it up to a seam line on the item (or overlap the end with a raw edge if the item is unstitched at this stage), then align the bottom edge of the trimming along the guideline. If you think that you may not be able to completely remove the guideline, position the ribbon or braid just over the marked line.

3 Pin the trimming in position, placing the pins at right angles to the ribbon or braid. Turn in the other end when you reach the starting point and pin it in place.

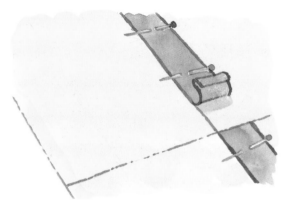

4 Use a zipper foot to stitch as close to one edge as you can. Go back to the beginning and reposition the zipper foot so you can stitch the other edge in the same way. Always stitch both sides in the same direction to avoid crinkling.

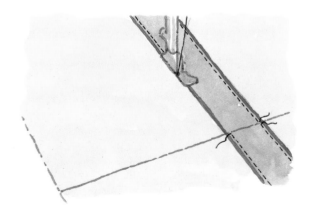

PRETTY PILLOW

Clever use of trimmings can turn plain into pretty. Here, the combination of cream pom-poms set against charcoal grosgrain ribbon and short silk frills transform a simple pillow into something special. The key is to keep the frills neat and restrict them to the short sides of an oblong pillow.

FINISHED SIZE
12 x 20 in/30 x 50 cm

MATERIALS
• Pillow form, 12 x 20 in/ 30 x 50 cm
• 1/2 yd/50 cm printed cotton
• 1/3 yd/20 cm striped silk
• 3/4 yd/60 cm grosgrain ribbon at least 1 1/4 in/ 3 cm wide
• 3/4 yd/60 cm pom-pom braid
• 12 in/30 cm zipper
• Thread

CUTTING OUT
• Cut one pillow front piece in printed cotton, 13 x 19 1/2 in/33 x 49 cm, and two pillow back pieces, each 7 1/2 x 19 1/2 in/ 18.5 x 49 cm
• Cut two pieces of striped silk, each 4 x 24 in/10 x 60 cm for the frills

1 Press in a 5/8 in/2 cm seam allowance along one long edge of each of the two pillow back pieces. Following the instructions on page 131, insert a lapped zipper and sew up the seams at both ends.

2 Prepare the frills (see page 159). With right sides together, fold one strip of striped silk in half lengthwise, and pin and stitch the short ends. Repeat with the other strip. Clip the corners, trim the seams, turn right sides out, and press. Run gathering stitches along the raw edges. Pull the threads and gather up the material until each frill measures 11 1/2 in/29 cm.

3 With right sides together and raw edges matching, pin and then baste one frill onto each end of the back zippered pillow piece. The frill should lie just outside the seam allowance.

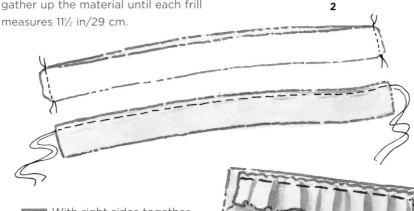

4 Cut the ribbon and braid in half. Place one length of ribbon on top of each of the frills. Turn in the ends and pin. Stitch in place along the outer edge, close to the raw edge of the pillow cover. Turn in the ends of the pom-pom braid and pin it on top of the grosgrain ribbon. Baste, then use the zipper foot to stitch it in place.

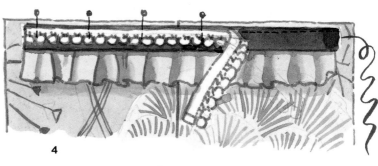

5 Open the zipper and place the trimmed pillow back right side up on a flat surface. Place the pillow front piece right side down on top of it. Pin and baste along all four edges. Stitch the trimmed ends together using the zipper foot.

6 Change to the general foot and stitch the long seams, making sure you don't catch the frill and trimmings. Trim the seams and corners. Turn the cover right side out through the zipper opening and insert the pillow form.

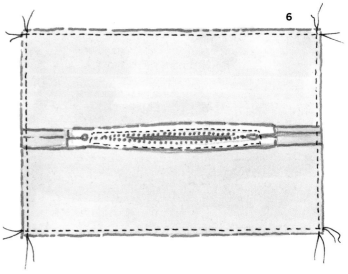

left Pillow covers do not require huge quantities of fabric so you can afford to splurge on special materials and trimmings to make them gorgeous. Aim to make the covers a little on the tight side for plump, sumptuous pillows.

embellishments

Beads, sequins, and pretty buttons make excellent surface decoration. Tiny rocailles (seed beads) and bugles can be used to create endless elaborate designs. Sequins can be sewn on singly, or you can buy them already sewn together in lengths, for stitching on as a trimming. Buttons, big and small, can also be sewn on in rows or patterns as embellishment.

SEWING ON BEADS

1 Thread a beading needle with double thread and knot the ends together. Pass the needle from the underside of the fabric to the top side and thread on a bead. Slide the bead to the bottom of the thread.

2 Pass the needle from the right side of the fabric to the wrong side, as close to where it came up as possible, so the threads pass over the side of the bead and hold it securely in place. Then pass the needle up to the right side of the fabric, wherever you would like to position the next bead. When you have used up most of the thread, pass the needle to the wrong side of the fabric and take several small stitches on top of each other to secure, preferably in a place that will not show on the front.

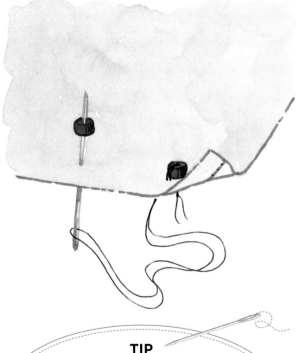

TIP
SEWING ON BEADS
Double threads can easily knot, so make sure that both threads are completely pulled through and are of even lengths before taking the next stitch. When moving on to the next bead, leave enough slack in the thread at the back of the work to ensure that the fabric lies flat.

SEWING ON SEQUINS

Single sequins are sewn on in the same way as beads. Use a silk thread that matches the sequin. Here's how to sew on sequin strings.

1 Using tailor's chalk or a marker pen, mark where you would like the sequins to go. You could apply them in a straight line or in a curved design. If you are applying them straight, along a hemline, for instance, measure up from the hemline in several places and mark this position. Using a ruler and tailor's chalk or marker pen, join up the marks, then pin the sequins along this guideline, placing the pins at right angles to the sequin string.

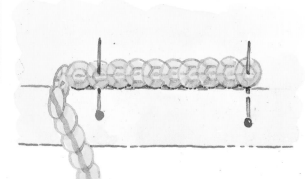

2 Use a zipper foot to stitch the sequin string in position. Choose a straight stitch set to the longest stitch length—if possible, the length of the sequin. Stitch through the center of the sequins, sewing in the direction of the sequins.

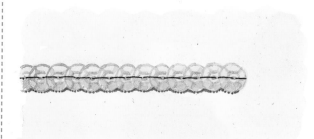

SEWING ON DECORATIVE BUTTONS

1 Either mark where you would like the buttons using tailor's chalk or a marker pen, or position them as you go. Thread a needle with double thread and knot the ends together. Position the first button and pass the needle from the wrong side through the fabric and the first hole in the button.

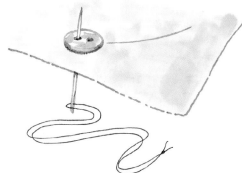

2 Pass the needle back down through the second hole and up again through the fabric and the first hole. Repeat three times. Pass the needle to the back.

3 Position the next button and bring the needle up through the first hole of the next button. Repeat the process with all the buttons. Finish by passing the needle to the wrong side of the fabric and taking several small stitches on top of each other in a concealed place.

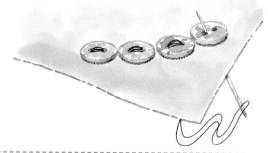

EVENING PURSE

This pretty little evening purse, made from coffee-colored Thai silk and lined with floral printed cotton lawn, has been embellished on each side with a simple spiral of shell buttons, sewn on with contrast thread for added interest. The silk has been interlined to give it strength to support the buttons.

FINISHED SIZE
Height at center front 5 in/14 cm, width 8 in/ 21.5 cm, depth 1½ in/4 cm

MATERIALS
- ½ yd/50 cm silk
- ½ yd/50 cm printed cotton lawn
- 12 in/30 cm iron-on interfacing (sewable)
- 92 off-white round shell buttons, ¾ in/ 2 cm diameter
- 1 skein mulberry-colored stranded embroidery thread (floss)
- Thread to match the silk
- Paper for the pattern

CUTTING OUT
- Using the templates on page 218, cut two bag pieces in silk and two in cotton lawn
- Cut one gusset piece in silk and one in cotton lawn
- Cut one shoulder strap in silk and one in cotton lawn to the desired length, 2½ in/ 6 cm wide

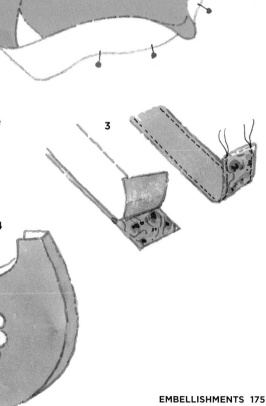

1 Lay the silk front and back bag pieces and gusset piece wrong sides down on the iron-on interfacing. Following the manufacturer's instructions, iron to fuse the fabrics together. Cut out the shapes.

2 With right sides together, pin the outer edge of one silk bag piece to the silk gusset piece, and stitch. Pin and stitch the other silk bag piece to the other side of the gusset. Trim the seams, clip the curves and press the seams open. Make up the cotton lawn lining in the same way.

3 Make up the shoulder strap. With right sides together, pin the silk strip to the cotton lawn strip and stitch them together along both long edges. Trim the seams and press them open. Turn the strap through to the right side using a safety pin or loop turner. Topstitch along both long sides.

4 Starting in the center of one side and using embroidery thread (floss), stitch half of the buttons in a spiral pattern onto the front of the bag and the other half onto the back.

5 Turn the lining inside out. With cotton lawn meeting cotton lawn, pin one end of the shoulder strap centrally to the top edge of one side of the gusset, with raw edges aligning. Making sure the strap isn't twisted, pin the other end to the other gusset. Put the silk outer bag into the lining, so right sides are together and the shoulder strap is between the two layers. Pin the lining and outer bag together around the top edge. Stitch in place, leaving a 4-in/10-cm gap in the center of one side to turn the bag right side out.

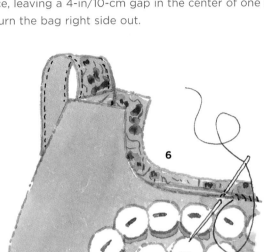

6 Trim the seams and turn the bag right side out through the gap in the seam. Tuck the lining inside the bag. Turn in the seam allowance and slipstitch the gap closed (see page 48).

below The deep pink of the roses on the printed Liberty Tana Lawn lining is echoed in the embroidery thread used for stitching on the buttons. As the thread makes a fine line on the buttons, you can use a darker shade than expected. This mulberry-colored thread matches the very darkest part of the roses.

appliqué

This is a decorative technique whereby you use fabric shapes to embellish your work. This can be done by hand or machine, using plain or patterned fabric to make up your own motifs, or cutting motifs from one fabric and applying them onto another. Appliqué has been made much easier with the introduction of iron-on fabric-bond web. This is applied to the back of the appliqué fabric using a hot iron before the motif is cut out. The backing paper is peeled off and the motif is fused in position using a hot iron before the outline is stitched.

MACHINE APPLIQUÉ

1 Place the wrong side of your appliqué fabric to the sticky side of the fabric-bond web and, following the manufacturer's instructions, iron to fuse them together.

2 Draw or trace a template of your chosen design onto a piece of paper and cut it out. Place the paper template right side down on the paper side of the fabric bond— this is particularly important if the motif is not symmetrical. Draw around the motif and neatly cut out the shape.

3 Peel off the backing paper. Place the fabric motif right side up on the main fabric. Use a hot iron to bond it into position. If your appliqué fabric is silk or wool or has a nap, lay a cotton cloth over it before you apply the hot iron to prevent it from becoming shiny.

4 Set the sewing machine to a close zigzag and stitch around the outline of the motif to secure.

BRODERIE PERSE

This is the correct name for appliqué where a printed motif that is part of the design of one fabric has been cut out and used as appliqué on another fabric. The cute owl on the pocket of the child's craft apron (page 181) is an example of this.

1 Cut a rough square around the motif you wish to use. Place it wrong side down on the nonpaper side of the fabric bond and iron to fuse.

2 Carefully cut out the motif and peel off the backing paper.

3 Position the motif on the main fabric and pin or tack it in place. Use a hot iron to fuse the fabrics together, as before.

4 Set the sewing machine to a close zigzag and stitch around the outline of the motif to secure.

HAND APPLIQUÉ

The principle is the same as for machine appliqué, but instead of zigzag stitching around the edges of the motif, you can hand-stitch it in position using slipstitch, tiny running stitches, or blanket stitches (see pages 47–48). If you use a fray-free fabric, such as felt, for your appliqué motif, you don't need to turn in the raw edges before stitching.

1 Draw or trace the motif onto a piece of paper, to make a template. Place the paper template on the fabric and draw around the shape using a fabric-marker pen or pencil. Cut out the fabric motif, adding a ¼ in/6 mm seam allowance.

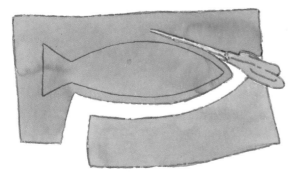

2 Clip or notch the seam allowance to accommodate any curves in the shape.

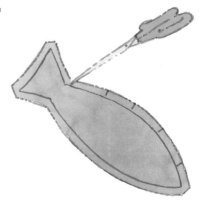

3 Pin the motif into position on the main fabric and then baste it in place, sewing ½ in/12 mm in from the edge.

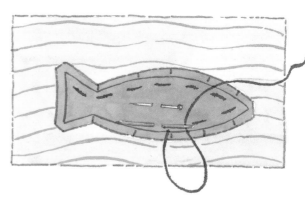

4 Neatly slipstitch the motif into position, turning in the seam allowance as you go.

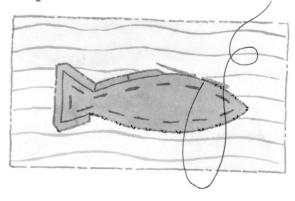

CHILD'S CRAFT APRON

The enchanting owl appliqué on the pocket of this craft apron will guarantee that any child will want to put it on before engaging in messy play. By cutting an animal motif from another fabric, you can easily create a professional finish. Raglan sleeves are the easiest to sew, as they don't rely on any easing or fitting.

FIT
Loose fit for ages 3 to 6. Finished garment size: chest 32 in/80 cm; sleeve length from neckline 16 in/40 cm; length 18 in/ 46 cm. Adjust the width, sleeve length, and length along the adjustment lines

MATERIALS
• 1 yd/1 m main fabric
• 1 yd/1 m contrast fabric
• Animal character cut from another fabric
• Fusible interfacing, 12 x 8 in/30 x 20 cm
• Double-sided fabric bond (Bondaweb) to fit the animal character
• Matching thread for the garment
• Contrast thread for the appliqué

CUTTING OUT
• Using the templates on pages 220–221, cut one apron front, two apron backs, and two apron sleeves from the main fabric
• Cut one pocket from contrast fabric, 12 x 8 in/30 x 20 cm
• Cut 6 yd/5.5 m of bias strips, 2 in/5 cm wide, from contrast fabric (see page 152)
• Cut out one animal motif from other fabric to fit the pocket

1 Place the front and back apron pieces with right sides together. Pin and then stitch the side seams and press them open.

2 With right sides together, pin the raglan sleeves into the armholes, ensuring that you match the front of each sleeve to the front of the apron and the backs of the sleeves to the back of the apron. Stitch, and press the seams open.

3 With right sides together, pin the seam along the top of each sleeve. Stitch, and press the seams open.

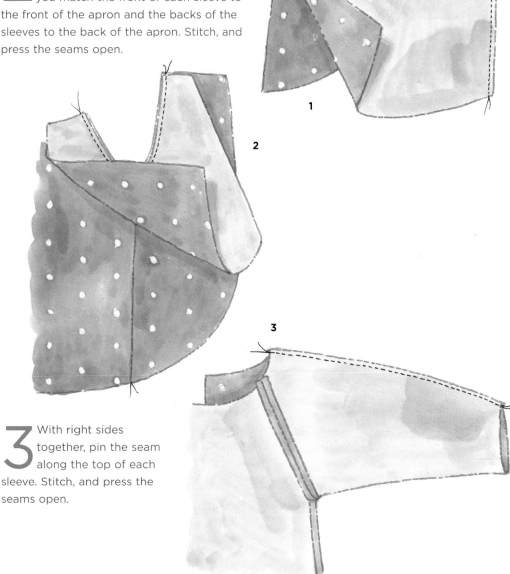

4 Referring to the instructions on page 153, apply the bias binding to the raw edges of the craft apron. Starting at the top of one side of the back opening and allowing an extra ³⁄₈ in/1 cm to turn in the end, with right sides together, pin bias binding down one side of the back, around the bottom, and up the other side of the back opening. Cut the bias binding at the neckline, allowing an extra ³⁄₈ in/1 cm to turn in the end. Fold the bias binding over to the right side of the craft apron and stitch along the folded edge. In the same way, apply bias binding to the cuffs.

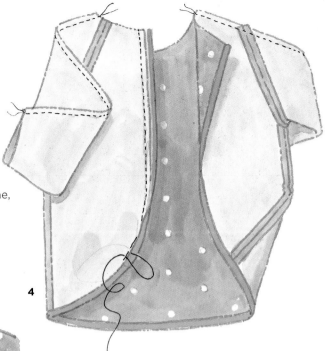

4

5

5 Fold in and press ³⁄₈ in/1 cm at one end of the remaining bias binding. Leaving 12 in/30 cm for the neck tie, pin the bias binding around the neckline with right sides together. When you reach the other side, measure out another 12 in/30 cm for the other neck tie, plus ³⁄₈ in/1 cm for the turn-in, and cut. Turn in the end and press. Turn the folded edge of the bias binding to the wrong side of the neckline and pin, then baste all around, joining the folded edges of the ties together. Stitch from one end of one tie, around the neckline, and to the end of the other tie.

6 Cut two 12³⁄₄ in/32 cm lengths of bias binding for the back ties. Turn in ³⁄₈ in/1 cm at each end and press. Fold the strips in half lengthwise, matching the folded edges, and press. Stitch together along the long edges. Slipstitch both ends of each tie, then slipstitch one tie onto the wrong side of each side of the back opening, 4 in/10 cm below the neck ties.

6

above Use a firm cotton duck or canvas to make this craft apron: anything thinner may not keep all the paint at bay. Alternatively, you could use wipe-clean oilcloth.

left Children's fabrics feature a whole range of quirky characters. Choose their favorite, and then buy just enough so that you can cut out the chosen critter.

opposite Bias binding in the same contrast fabric as the pocket has been applied to all the raw edges for a neat finish.

7 Iron interfacing onto the wrong side of the pocket piece. Turn in and stitch a ½ in/12 mm double hem along the top edge. Turn in and press a single ½ in/12 mm hem on the other three sides. Following the manufacturer's instructions and referring to the instructions on page 178, iron fabric bond onto the wrong side of the animal motif and trim. Peel off the backing paper and position the motif centrally on the front of the pocket piece, and iron to fuse it into position. Using contrast thread, stitch around the outline with close zigzag stitch to secure.

7

8

8 Position the pocket centrally on the front of the craft apron, 4 in/10 cm from the hem. Pin and then baste it in place. Using thread that matches the pocket, stitch along the sides and bottom using zigzag stitch.

TIP
APPLIQUÉ
Although a close satin stitch is traditionally used for machine appliqué, a wider zigzag stitch gives a more contemporary professional finish. Try the zigzag stitch at several settings on a spare piece of fabric to see which you like best.

the perfect finish

DOUBLE-FOLDED HEM

This is the standard way to finish hemlines. The double fold encloses the raw edge, giving a neat, fray-free hem. Although the principle is simple, as with most jobs, preparation is all if you are to get a flat hem that hangs evenly. Whether you plan to hand- or machine-stitch the hem, it is important to work methodically through all the steps; otherwise you could end up with a bulky or puckered hem. The more flared a skirt is, the more this becomes a problem, as you need to accommodate more surplus fabric into the hem. For this reason, keep hems on flared garments to no more than 2 in/5 cm.

1 Turn the garment inside out. Reduce the bulk within the hem by trimming the seams and pressing them flat. Fold the hem along the hemline and pin it in position with the pins at right angles to the hem. Try the garment on to check that it is hanging straight (adjustments may need to be made to accommodate bigger stomachs and bottoms). Baste close to the fold.

2 Make a simple card template of the desired hem width and use this as a straight edge to mark up the hem.

3 Trim off the excess fabric. Turn in the raw edge by ¼ in/6 mm and place a pin at right angles to the hem edge through all the layers of fabric at the seams, making sure they match exactly.

4 You will now be able to see how flat the hem will lie. The straighter the skirt, the flatter it will lie. If the skirt is flared or gored (made from a tapering or triangular piece of fabric), the raw edge will be rippled. These ripples can be managed by easing, whereby the excess fabric is taken up evenly along the hem and won't bunch up as you stitch. Ease the edge, if you need to, by hand- or machine-basting ¼ in/6 mm in from the edge. Pull up the basting and even out the easing along the hem. Baste along the folded edge. If you are machine-topstitching the hem, turn the garment to the right side and stitch around the hem, just inside the basting stitches.

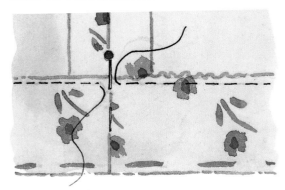

5 Slipstitch is one of the neatest and easiest ways to secure a hem by hand. Thread a short needle, cutting the thread to no longer than the distance from your wrist to your elbow. Knot the end. Working from the right, if you are right-handed, pass the needle through the top of the fold under the seam allowance, so the knot is concealed. Take a tiny stitch through a few threads in the main fabric and then pass the needle into the top fold. Bring the needle up through the top of the fold and take another tiny stitch. Keep the stitches evenly spaced.

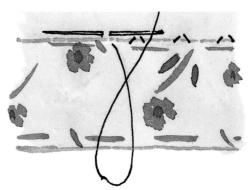

HAND-ROLLED HEM

This pretty edging is used with lightweight fabrics—the classic edging for a silk scarf. You can stitch it by machine, using a special foot that incorporates a scroll to make machine-rolled hems. Zigzag stitch instead of traditional straight stitch creates a more rounded finish. Here's how to do it by hand.

1 Stitch ¼ in/6 mm in from the edge, and then press flat. Weighing down one end of the fabric with a book or other heavy object, so that you can pull the fabric taut as you go, trim along the edge for about 6 in/15 cm close to the stitches.

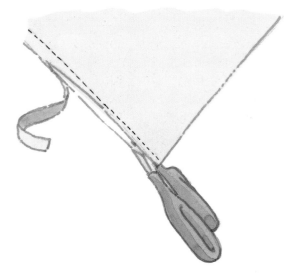

2 Roll the edge between your thumb and forefinger and slipstitch to secure. Trim the next 6 in/15 cm, roll, and slipstitch in the same way. Repeat until the hem is complete.

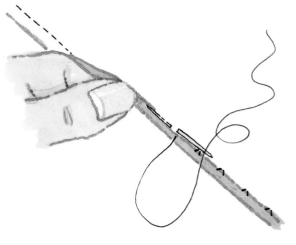

CURVED HEM

Where you have a deeply curved hem, the best option for a neat, flat finish is to make a facing.

1 Add ⅝ in/1.5 cm to the desired finished length. Mark with tailor's chalk, being careful to retain the curve of the hem. Use the pattern to cut pattern pieces for the facings. Do this by marking a line on each of the original pattern pieces that corresponds to the newly cut hem length. Measure 2 in/5 cm up the sides of each piece and draw a line parallel to the hem. Make sure that you include all the seam allowances. Cut out the pattern pieces, and then use these as templates to cut the fabric facings.

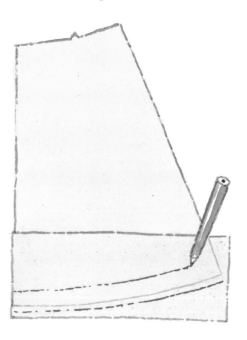

2 With right sides together, join all the facing seams and press them open. With right sides together and raw edges matching, pin the facings to the hem and stitch. Trim, clip, and press the seams open. Press the raw edge under by ¼ in/6 mm.

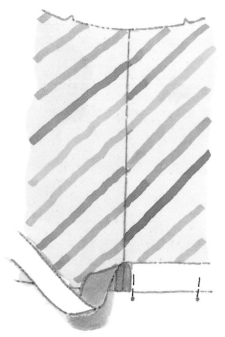

3 Turn the facings to the wrong side and press. Slipstitch the facings into position along the seam lines.

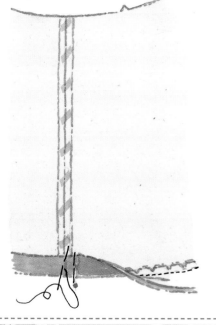

TIP
CURVED HEM
For a really flat hem, it is worth basting the facing to the skirt after pinning at all stages. If you use uneven basting (see page 47), this won't take long and it is well worth investing the time to ensure a neat finish.

4 Pin the hem down, positioning the pins at right angles to the hem. Slipstitch to finish.

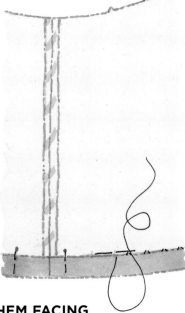

BIAS-HEM FACING

Bias-cut or very flared skirts need a bias-hem facing that will lie flat without producing any bulk. The easiest way to do this is to use ready-made bias binding in a color that is close to that of the garment. Choose a 2½ in/6 cm width.

1 Cut the bias binding to the length of the hem circumference plus 3 in/7.5 cm. Unfold one edge of the bias and turn one end ¼ in/ 6 mm to the wrong side. Starting with the folded end at the skirt seam, with right sides together and raw edges aligned, pin the bias binding to the hem. Stitch along the crease to within 3 in/ 7.5 cm of the start.

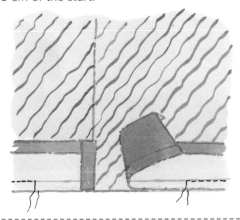

2 Fold the end of the bias binding over at the starting point and trim to ¼ in/6 mm to match the other side. Complete the stitching and continue to stitch for ⅜ in/1 cm. Press the seam open.

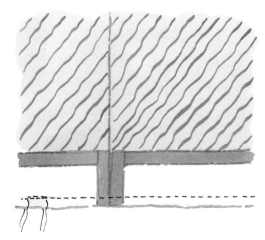

3 Fold the bias binding to the wrong side of the garment so that it can't be seen on the right side of the skirt and slipstitch along the folded edge. Slipstitch the folded ends of the bias binding together where they align on the seam line of the skirt.

TIP
STITCHING BIAS-HEM FACING
As an alternative to slipstitching, you could topstitch along the top folded edge, and then stitch one, two, or more parallel lines below this for a decorative finish.

BIAS-CUT SKIRT

A drawstring skirt cut on the bias is about the easiest garment you could make. The bias cut offers enough stretch to allow it to skim flatteringly over the hips without the need for darts, while the drawstring pulls in the waist, and by wearing the skirt low on the hips, you can avoid unflattering gathers. Drawstring skirts are a fashion classic that can be kept up to date by the choice of material and adapting the length to suit the season.

FIT

To fit size small, hips 34 in/88 cm. Finished garment size at hips 40 in/102 cm. Take in or widen the pattern at both the center front and center back by half the difference between your hip measurement and 34 in/88 cm. To lengthen, extend the side seam lines and draw a hemline parallel to the one on the pattern

MATERIALS

- 1¾ yd/1.5 m fabric 45 in/115 cm wide or 1¼ yd/1.10 m fabric 60 in/153 cm wide
- 4½ yd/4 m narrow braid about ¾ in/ 2 cm wide
- 1¼ yd/1 m wider braid about 1¼ in/3 cm wide
- Matching thread
- Dressmaker's dot-and-cross paper

CUTTING OUT

- Enlarge and make up the pattern piece on page 219 as instructed and cut it out from dot-and-cross paper
- Fold the fabric in half. Pin the pattern on the fabric with the arrow following the straight grain of the fabric. Cut out one skirt front and one skirt back

1 Place the front and back pieces of the skirt with right sides together, and pin and then stitch the side seams. Finish the seams with zigzag stitch and then press them open.

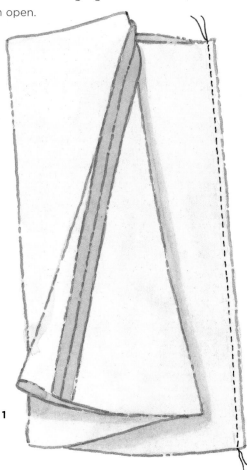

1

2 Allowing for a ⅜ in/ 1 cm turn-in at the waist (see step 5), try on the skirt and cut the hem to a little longer than the desired length. Then fold a ½ in/12 mm single hem at the bottom edge to the right side of the skirt, and press.

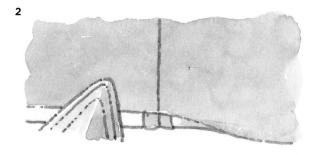

2

3 Starting just beyond one side seam, pin the narrow braid, right side up, to the bottom edge of the skirt, covering the pressed-in hem on the front of the skirt and making sure the edge of the braid aligns with the folded edge of the skirt. When you reach the starting point, cut the braid and turn in the end. Pin the folded end over the other raw end of the braid, aligning it with the side seam of the skirt. Topstitch along the top and bottom edges of the braid to hold it in place.

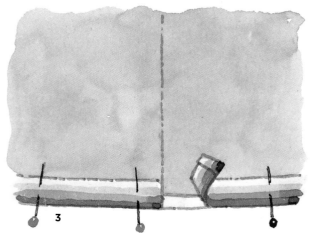

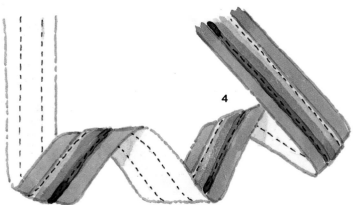

4 Measure out enough of the wide braid to go around the top edge of the skirt to make a waistband, allowing an extra 1 in/2.5 cm at each end. Measure out the same amount from the remaining narrow braid. Center the narrow braid on top of the wide braid and topstitch it in place along both long edges.

5 On the top edge of the skirt, fold a ½ in/12 mm single hem to the right side, and press. Place a pin in the top edge at the center front of the skirt. Turn in the end of the braid by ⅜ in/1 cm and, starting at the center point, pin the braid in position around the top edge of the skirt, aligning the edges. When you reach the starting point, turn in the other end of the braid by ⅜ in/1 cm. Topstitch along the top and bottom edges of the braid to hold it in place.

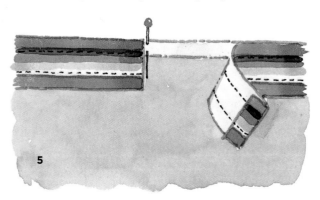

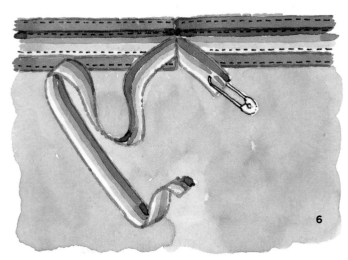

6 Pin a safety pin onto one end of the remaining narrow braid and thread it through the channel. Tie a knot at both ends of the braid.

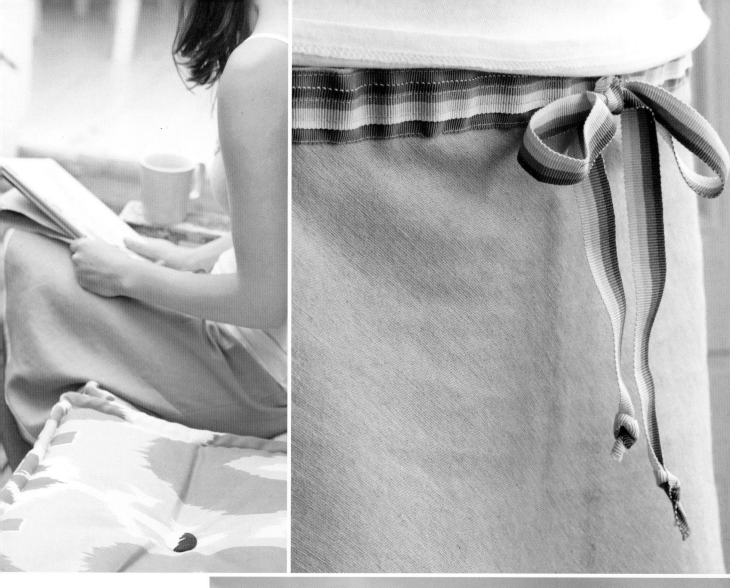

above Just above the knee makes a flattering length for summer; or go romantically long with a maxi skirt in a softer cotton print.

above right Stripy grosgrain ribbon stitched to the top of the skirt creates the drawstring channel while offering classic, preppy design detailing.

right A turquoise linen-and-silk mix offers a cool, summery drape, with a grosgrain-ribbon hemline that matches the drawstring top.

BOX CUSHIONS

Topstitched box cushions make for great garden comfort. The bold design on the heavy-duty cotton fabric used for this one has been centered for greater impact, set off by striped sides. The cushion is made up first, then topstitched by hand using large saddle stitches.

FINISHED SIZE

16¾ x 16¾ in/47 x 47 cm, depth 1½ in/4 cm

MATERIALS

Quantities are for fabric 60 in/150 cm wide:

- ½ yd/50 cm upholstery-weight printed cotton or linen for the top and bottom
- ½ yd/50 cm upholstery-weight striped cotton or linen for the sides (welts)
- 2 coverable buttons, 1½ in/4 cm diameter
- 3¼ yd/3 m batting, 6 oz/170 g weight
- Mattress needle
- White topstitch thread

CUTTING OUT

- Cut two main pieces, 18 x 18 in/50 x 50 cm, for the top and bottom
- Cut four welt pieces, 18 x 5 in/50 x 13 cm
- Enough layers of batting, 18 x 18 in/ 50 x 50 cm, to make a pile 4 in/10 cm deep

1 With right sides together, match the short sides of two welt pieces and pin them together. Stitch, stopping ⅝ in/1.5 cm from the top and bottom of the seam so that the corners will be neat. Repeat with the other welt pieces to make up a square. Press the seams open.

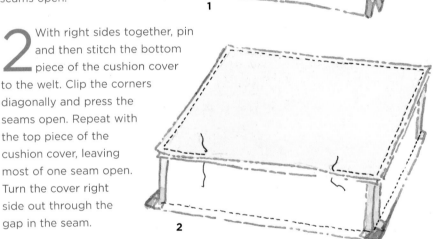

1

2 With right sides together, pin and then stitch the bottom piece of the cushion cover to the welt. Clip the corners diagonally and press the seams open. Repeat with the top piece of the cushion cover, leaving most of one seam open. Turn the cover right side out through the gap in the seam.

2

3 Insert the layers of batting into the cushion cover. Turn in the seam allowance at the gap in the seam and slipstitch to close.

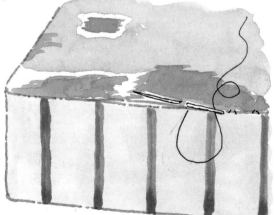

3

4 Work saddle stitch by hand for a decorative finish around the edges of the cushion. Use the mattress needle and strong topstitching thread to make long ½ in/12 mm stitches 1 in/2.5 cm in from the seams around the top and bottom of the cushion, and vertically down each of the four corners.

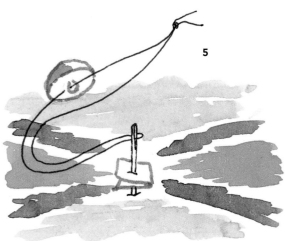

5 Following the manufacturer's instructions, make up the two self-cover buttons. Cut two small rectangles of fabric, 1½ x 3 in/4 x 8 cm and fold them in half, so that they are roughly the same size as the buttons. Thread the mattress needle with strong topstitch thread and then pass one end of the thread through one of the button shanks and knot the ends together. Find and mark the center of the cushion and place one of the small folded rectangles of fabric over this. Pass the mattress needle through the center of the fabric and through to the other side of the cushion.

6 Pass the needle through the other folded rectangle of fabric and then through the shank of the other covered button. Push them both down the thread to the surface of the cushion. Now pass the needle back through the fabric square to the other side of the cushion and through the first button shank. Make about four similar stitches through the cushion and button shanks until both buttons are securely sewn in position. Finish off with several small stitches on top of each other just under one of the buttons.

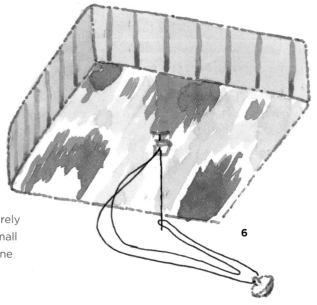

above Hand-worked saddle stitches give the plain box cushion a piecrust edging, quickly lending it a completely different personality.

above right Simple striped welts provide restrained contrast to the extrovert print used for the top and bottom of the cover. This fabric is linen, but it works with the cotton print because both fabrics are of a similar weight.

right It is not difficult to cover buttons in a fabric of your choice using an inexpensive kit available from most notions stores and departments.

mitered corners

One of the neatest ways to deal with corners is to miter them, so that they meet at a perfect diagonal of 45 degrees. If the fabric has been cut straight, this angle is not as difficult to achieve as it might seem, because all you have to do is make an accurate fold. There are many situations where you may need to miter both inward and outward corners. Here is one method for each.

MITERING A TURNED-UP HEM

1 Fold in and press ¼ in/6 mm along the raw edges. Fold in the seam lines on all sides and press firmly using a hot iron. Open out the seam lines and fold up the corner so that the press lines align. Press firmly using a hot iron.

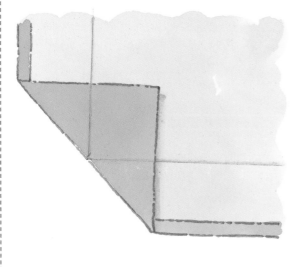

2 Open out the corner and then refold the fabric on the diagonal with right sides together and the pressed-in edges matching. Stitch along the diagonal crease, starting at the fold and sewing down to the pressed-in edge. Trim off the excess fabric at the corner, leaving a ¼ in/6 mm seam allowance.

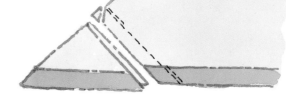

3 Trim the ends of the seam allowance diagonally and press the seam open. Turn the mitered corner right side out and press firmly.

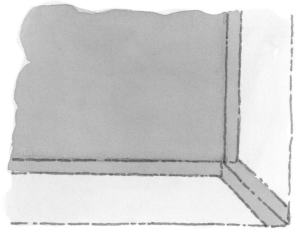

MITERING A FACING ON AN INWARD CORNER

1 Cut enough 2½-in-/6.5-cm-wide facing on the bias (see page 152) to fit the project, plus 1¼ in/ 3 cm for turnings. Turn one long edge ¼ in/ 6 mm to the wrong side and press. Turn in one end of the facing by ⅝ in/1.5 cm and, with right sides together and raw edges meeting, pin the bias to one edge of the main fabric. When you get to the corner, fold the facing back at right angles (so that wrong sides are together). Press firmly with a hot iron to make a crease.

TIP
MITERING
If there is no selvage on the cut-out fabric, pull out a crosswise thread and a lengthwise thread at the cut edges and this will give you straight cutting lines. Then, it is just a case of folding one cut edge to meet the adjacent cut edge.

3 Leaving the corner pin in place to hold the facing right sides together, unpin the bias facing from the main fabric. Stitch along the diagonal press line, and trim off the corner leaving a ¼ in/6 mm seam allowance. Taper the points on the seam allowance and press the diagonal seam open.

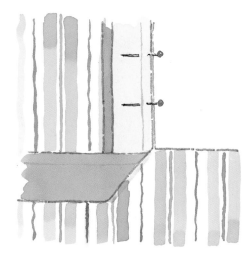

2 At the outer edge of the pinned facing, turn the bias fabric back on itself (so that right sides are now together), so that it can run along the second edge, and press. Place a pin diagonally into the corner, parallel to the diagonal press line.

4 Once all the corners are complete, with right sides together, repin the bias facing to the main fabric and stitch in place with a ¼ in/6 mm seam allowance. Place a pin just inside the stitching, then clip into the corner and trim the seams. Press the seams open. Turn through and machine stitch the turned-in edge of the bias facing.

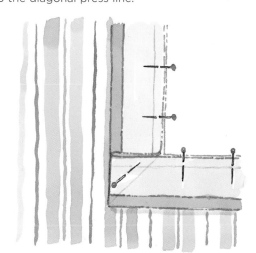

TABLECLOTH AND NAPKINS

Use tiny checked red gingham and toning red-and-white braids to give a simple white linen cloth a fresh country look. The napkins can be coordinated by applying one of the braids around the edges. Careful mitering of the corners lends a professional finish. It has to be said that a strong geometric design, such as gingham, demands extra care with mitering to ensure that the checks match perfectly across the diagonals.

FINISHED SIZE

Tablecloth 5 x 5 ft/
150 x 150 cm, napkins
19 x 19 in/48 x 48 cm

MATERIALS

For one square
tablecloth and
six napkins:

- 2¾ yd/2.5 m linen
  60 in/150 cm wide
- 1 yd/80 cm smallest
  check red gingham
- 7 yd/6 m main braid
- 16¼ yd/14 m detail
  braid
- Thread

CUTTING OUT

- Cut one tablecloth
  5 x 5 ft/150 x 150 cm
- Cut six napkins
  20 x 20 in/50 x 50 cm
- Cut the gingham into
  strips 4½ in/12 cm wide
  and join them end to
  end to make up four
  62-in/155-cm lengths

1 Prepare the miters. Lay the strips of gingham right sides down on the work surface. At both ends of each piece of gingham, fold the short edge diagonally to align with the long edge and press. Trim off the corners of fabric ⅝ in/1.5 cm away from the fold.

2 Take two pieces of gingham and, with right sides together, match the miters and pin. Check the right side to ensure that the miter is correct—this is especially important where patterns, such as this gingham, need to match. Baste and then stitch, starting at the outer corner and stopping ½ in/12 mm from the inner edge. Repeat with the other three corners, then press the seams open.

3 Fold in and press ½ in/12 mm all around the outer and inner edges of the gingham frame. With the right side of the gingham to the wrong side of the cloth, pin the outer edge of the gingham frame to the outer edge of the cloth. Stitch along the press line. Clip the corners and trim the seams. Press the seams open. Turn the border and cloth to the right sides and press flat. Topstitch all around the inner edge of the gingham border.

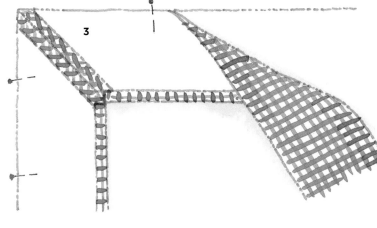

4 Pin the detail braid ⅝ in/1.5 cm in from the gingham border. Pin the main braid ⅝ in/1.5 cm in from detail braid. Depending on the design of the braid, you can either fold it into a miter at the corners or make a square fold. Secure both braids in position by stitching along both edges of each one.

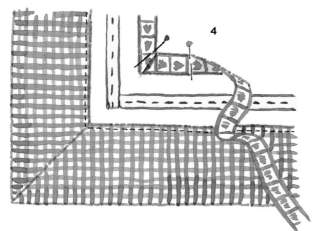

5 For the napkins, fold a hem of ½ in/12 mm to the right side, and press. Trim away the excess fabric at the corners so that they will lie flat. Cut four pieces of the detail braid to length and pin the strips in position on the right side of the napkin to cover the raw turned-in edge. Turn in the overlapping ends of the braid and machine stitch in place along both edges.

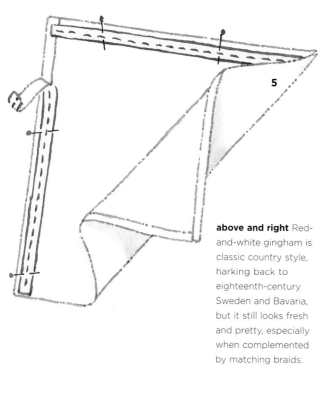

above and right Red-and-white gingham is classic country style, harking back to eighteenth-century Sweden and Bavaria, but it still looks fresh and pretty, especially when complemented by matching braids.

PLACE MATS

Vibrant colors with double borders in brightly patterned cotton and witty pleated bow trims make for fun ethnic-style place mats. Muslin interlining gives the mats a quality heavy drape that also provides plenty of tabletop protection from hot plates. This simple mitering-and-topstitching method make for neat and easy corners.

FINISHED SIZE

18¼ x 14¼ in/46.5 x 36 cm

MATERIALS

Quantities are for fabric 45 in/115 cm wide.

To make six mats:

- 1¾ yd/1.5 m plain fine-weave orange linen
- 1¾ yd/1.5 m pink cotton print fabric
- 1¾ yd/1.5 m green cotton print fabric
- 1¾ yd/1.5 m lightweight iron-on interlining
- Orange thread
- Mulberry stranded embroidery thread (floss)

CUTTING OUT

For each mat cut:

- One rectangle in orange linen and one in printed backing fabric, each 18 x 16 in/ 50 x 45 cm
- Two green strips 18 x 5 in/50 x 12 cm
- Two green strips 16 x 5 in/45 x 12 cm
- Two pink strips 18 x 3 in/50 x 7 cm
- Two pink strips 16 x 3 in/45 x 7 cm
- Interlining for each colored strip and orange rectangle
- 12 rectangles of spare printed fabric 3½ x 1½ in/9 x 4 cm for the bows

1 Following the manufacturer's instructions, bond interlining to the wrong side of all the orange rectangles and the pink and green strips using a warm iron. Fold in and press ½ in/12 mm along one long edge of each of the strips.

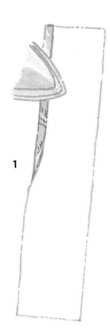

1

2 For each mat, lay one orange piece wrong side down on a flat surface. With raw edges meeting, lay one long green strip wrong side down along each long edge and pin it in position. Using a 1¼ in/3 cm seam allowance, stitch the trim to the mat, starting 1¼ in/ 3 cm from the beginning and finishing 1¼ in/3 cm from the end. Starting and stopping 1¼ in/3 cm in as before, topstitch the turned-in inner edge through all layers.

2

3 With raw edges meeting, place one short green strip along each of the short edges of the mat and pin. Stitch in place in the same way, using a 1¼ in/3 cm seam allowance and starting and stopping 1¼ in/3 cm in from the ends. Baste the inner folded edge in place, starting and stopping where the short strips meets the edge of the long strips.

3

4 Cut off the outer edge of the green trim, cutting close to the 1¼ in/3 cm stitch line all the way around—do not cut the orange layer. Miter the first corner by folding one end of one of the short strips diagonally to the stitch line, aligning the fold with the corners, and press to make a crease. Trim off the corner of fabric to about ⅜ in/ 1 cm from the crease. Turn the raw edge to the wrong side along the crease line and pin then baste the folded edge in place. Repeat with the other three corners.

4

5 Topstitch from the outer corner along the diagonal miter to the inside edge, then along the inside edge, and out to the other corner. Repeat with the other side of the trim.

5

6

6 Repeat steps 2–5 to attach the pink trim, but this time using a ¾ in/2 cm seam allowance and starting and stopping stitching ¾ in/2 cm from the ends.

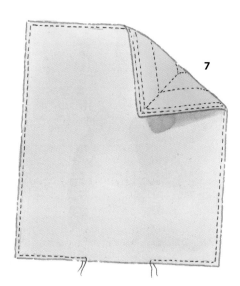

7

7 Lay the mat wrong side down on a flat surface and lay a printed backing piece right side down on top of it. Align the edges and pin the two layers together. Using a 1-in/2.5-cm seam allowance, stitch all around the mat, leaving a 6-in/15-cm gap in the center of one short side. Clip the corners, trim the seams, and press them open. Turn the mat right side out through the gap in the seam and push out the corners. Turn in the seam allowances along the open part and slipstitch to close. Press thoroughly, then topstitch around the outer edge of the mat and re-press.

8 To make the bows, pleat each of the small rectangles of fabric. Wrap embroidery thread several times around the center of each one and tie it tightly to secure, then fan out the ends of the pleated fabric. Hand-stitch six bows at equal intervals along both short edges of each mat.

8

left Little bows, made of pleated fabric tied in the middle with embroidery thread, make a delightful trimming stitched at intervals down the sides of each place mat.

quilting

PATCHWORK AND QUILTING PRIMER

Traditionally, these two skills come together in the making of exquisite, warm bedcovers. The top is made from patchwork pieces that are joined together to make up intricate designs. The backing is often a plain fabric, and sandwiched between the two is some form of batting. To hold all the layers in place, once the bedcover is complete, it is quilted using tiny hand-stitches or by a special long-arm quilting machine.

There are people who spend a lifetime engrossed in patchwork, making exquisite, unique pieces with meticulous care, building their skill as they progress to ever-more complex designs. There isn't the space here to cover—or indeed do justice to—all the complexities, so consider this a taster; just a peep into the world of patchwork to give you an idea of how it works.

Patchwork was born in centuries past, when the cost of cloth was such that it needed to be preserved and recycled at every opportunity. But clothes and linens do, inevitably, wear out, so at this stage, prudent housewives would cut them up into small pieces, discarding the worn bits and using the rest to make patchwork quilt tops. By cleverly juxtaposing the colors, they would make up exquisite designs using a variety of different shapes, developing designs with evocative names describing their lives, such as Log Cabin, Steps to the Altar, Virginia Star. In contrast to the ever-more intricate designs, the quilts of the Amish people were simpler, made of larger patches in stronger colors.

The key to patchwork success lies in the meticulous cutting and piecing together of the patches. Even slight irregularities can result in a misshapen finished patchwork top, and the smaller the pieces, the more this can become a problem. For this reason, if you are a patchwork beginner, it is best to start with fewer larger square pieces and then progress to the more complicated designs as your skills improve.

TOOLS OF THE TRADE

Enthusiastic patchworkers have a whole battery of specialist tools, many of which can be bought at local notions or craft stores. In the past, most patchwork templates were made by hand, using heavy paper or lightweight card, but nowadays transparent plastic templates are available in a variety of sizes in all the classic shapes: square, triangle, hexagon, and diamond. These are both robust and reusable, and mean that you can dispense with the template-making stage.

You can cut the fabric with very sharp scissors, but if you become an enthusiastic patchworker, you will probably want to invest in a rotary cutter and self-healing mat. Using these, you can cut through several layers of fabric at a time and far more accurately than you could using scissors. You would also find a patchwork ruler useful. This is made from transparent plastic and is marked both with a grid and various angle lines, which are a useful aid to cutting accurate shapes.

CALCULATING FABRIC QUANTITIES

For patchwork, allow a ¼ in/5 mm seam allowance on each side of each piece. This will mean you need more fabric for a quilt with small pieces than you would for a quilt of the same size with larger pieces. Keep it simple to start with. If you become an enthusiast, you can hone your calculating skills by following classic designs such as Log Cabin, Le Moyne Star, Windmill, Flower Basket or any number of traditional favorites, using patterns from specialist books or websites.

CUTTING OUT

Templates for machine patchwork should include the seam allowance. If you are cutting simple squares, you can use the gridlines on the patchwork ruler to ensure perfect alignment.

1 Place the fabric on a self-healing cutting mat and line up one horizontal line on the ruler with the selvage, then use the rotary cutter to cut a straight line by rolling the blade firmly up and down the fabric.

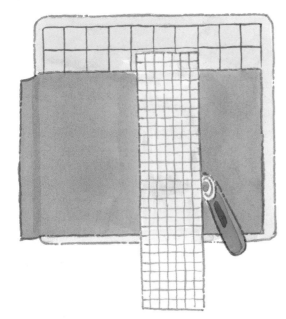

2 Turn the fabric around so the newly cut straight edge is on the left and line this up with one of the verticals to cut the desired square width, allowing an extra ½ in/12 mm for seam allowances. Cut as many strips as you need.

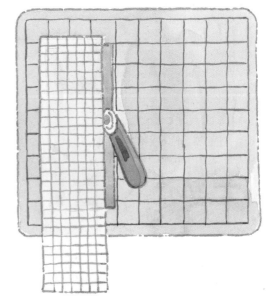

3 Now turn the first strip to the horizontal and align the edge with the same line to cut a square. Repeat until the complete strip is cut into squares. If you are using scissors, it is best to use a template to mark out the shapes on the fabric using a fabric-marker pen before cutting.

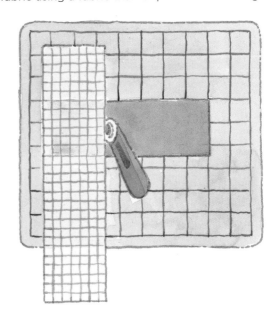

TIP
CUTTING OUT
Quilting enthusiasts favor rotary cutters, as they give a sharp, accurate edge, and several layers of fabric can be cut at once. Roll the cutter backward and forward over the fabric to make a cut. If you don't have a rotary cutter, sharp dressmaker's shears will produce good results, too—but first, you will need to carefully mark out the patches using a straight edge and a fabric-marker pen.

STITCHING

Patchwork is put together in blocks, which are then sewn together. For a simple patchwork of squares, lay out the cut pieces in rows to plan the design. Start with the top row, then the second, and so on. When you are happy with the juxtaposition of colors and patterns, sew all the pieces in the top row together first, then do the same for the second row, and so on. Once all the rows of patches are ready, stitch them together into blocks.

1 Start by making a row of patches. A quick way to do this is to "chain stitch" them. With right sides together, machine stitch two patches together along one edge. At the end of the seam, don't cut the thread, but lift the presser foot when the needle is raised. Put another pair of patches, with right sides together, under the needle, lower the presser foot and stitch the second pair in the same way. When you have stitched several pairs together, just snip the threads between them.

2 Stitch the pairs of patches together end to end, until you have a row of patches the desired length. Press all the seams in one direction.

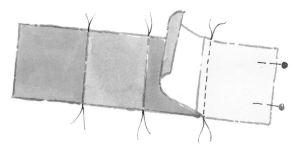

3 Make up the desired number of rows in the same way, but press all the seams of each row in opposite directions. Then stitch the rows together into blocks. Press the seams between the rows open.

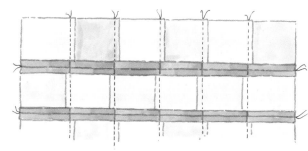

PRESSING

For an accurate and neatly put-together quilt top, you need to press as you stitch to make sure that all the patches are properly flattened out. The seam allowances on each row should be pressed to one side to lend strength to the seams. Using a hot iron, press all the seam allowances on each row in alternating directions. If the patchwork is made up of light and dark patches, the seam allowance should be pressed away from the light patches. Press open the seams joining one row to the next row.

When the whole quilt top has been completed, place it wrong side up on the ironing board, lay a pressing cloth over it, and press thoroughly using plenty of steam. Turn the quilt top over and, using the pressing cloth, press the front well.

TIP
STITCHING
The patches need to be stitched together firmly and accurately, so test the tension first on spare fabric. This is particularly important if you are using fine cotton fabrics, such as shirting, which may need a slightly tighter tension than heavier cottons.

PUTTING IT TOGETHER

Traditionally, the way to put a quilt together was to make a huge sandwich of the back, the batting, and the patchwork top. Then baste lines of stitches down the length and across the width of the whole quilt to keep everything in place while you stitch on the border.

1 The quilt backing should be cut 4 in/10 cm larger than the patchwork top, then laid right side down on a flat surface. Cut the batting a little smaller than this and lay it centrally on top of the backing. Finally, center the patchwork piece on top of the pile, right side up.

2 Make sure all the layers of fabric are flat and smooth. Using quilting pins, pin the three layers together at regular intervals.

3 Sew a line of basting stitches down the center of the quilt from top to bottom, then sew another across the center from side to side. Baste additional lines at 4 in/10 cm intervals across and down the quilt.

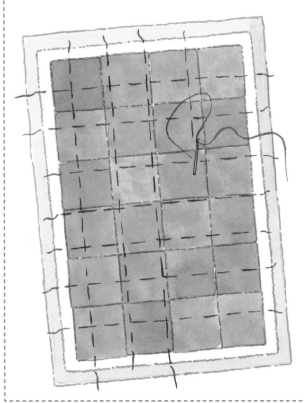

QUILTING

Used to keep the whole piece stable, quilting can be done by hand or by sewing machine. The stitches can be discreet, or they can make up a surface design. At its simplest, quilting is done by rows of tiny parallel running stitches, running across the quilt vertically, horizontally, or diagonally, as below.

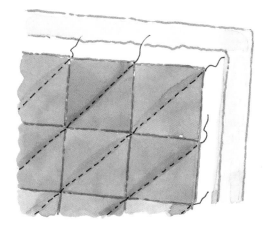

A less noticeable form of quilting is known as "stitch in the ditch," which is worked along the seam lines, as below.

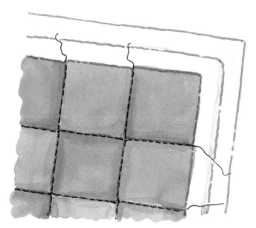

All of these stitch patterns and methods can also be worked by machine. More elaborately, some traditional quilting was worked up into intricate designs, such as flowers, leaves, and trellis, and this can be echoed with machine embroidery. Large quilts are stitched on a long-arm machine.

FINISHING THE EDGES

The edges of quilts can be finished in a variety of ways. Some have a wide border of fabric (known as sashing) around the patchwork, which, depending on the design, may itself be edged with bias binding. Here is a simple alternative.

TO FINISH OFF WITH BINDING

1 Using a pressing cloth to protect the fabric, thoroughly press the quilt from the back, then turn it over and press the front in the same way. The patchwork top and the batting will need to be trimmed back so that the sides are completely straight and the corners make perfect right angles. Measure out from the central lines at several points to the edge and mark with pins, then use a grid ruler or straight edge and tailor's chalk to join these up, marking the cutting lines. Also, use the grid ruler to check the corners. Once marked, use sharp dressmaker's shears to cut along these lines through the top and batting.

2 The backing needs to be cut to 1 in/2.5 cm wider than the top all around. Use the grid ruler and tailor's chalk to mark the line and then cut the backing with dressmaker's shears.

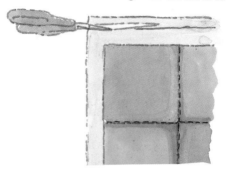

3 Miter one corner by folding in the corner of the backing fabric so that it touches the corner of the patchwork top, and press. Cut along the diagonal pressed line. Repeat with the other three corners.

4 Turn in and press a ¼ in/6 mm hem to the front all around the edge of the backing. Fold the edge of the backing over the batting and onto the edge of the patchwork front, making sure the miters meet neatly. Pin at intervals, placing the pins at right angles to the quilt edge. Slipstitch along the miter diagonals. Using a zipper foot, topstitch close to the edge of the self-binding all the way around.

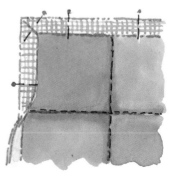

BABY QUILT

Traditionally, quilts have an heirloom quality and are often passed down through generations. In pink and blue, this charming but simple baby quilt can be passed around the family, happily matching nursery décor for both boys and girls. It incorporates all the skills needed for patchwork quilting, with large square pieces that are quick and easy to do, "stitch in the ditch" quilting around the border, and simple hand-worked crosses to secure the main body.

FINISHED SIZE

53½ x 31½ in/136 x 80 cm

MATERIALS

Quantities are for fabric 45 in/115 cm wide.

- 1 yd/1 m blue check brushed cotton for the patchwork
- 1 yd/1 m pink check brushed cotton for the patchwork
- 1¾ yd/1.5 m printed brushed cotton for the quilt backing and border
- 1¾ yd/1.5 m batting, 4 oz/113 g weight
- Thread
- Blue stranded embroidery thread (floss)

CUTTING OUT

- Cut 23 blue squares 6¼ x 6¼ in/16 x 16 cm
- Cut 22 pink squares 6¼ x 6¼ in/16 x 16 cm
- Cut one piece of batting 33½ x 57 in/ 85 x 145 cm
- From the printed fabric, cut one rectangle 33½ x 57 in/ 85 x 145 cm for the quilt back
- Cut two strips 33½ x 4 in/85 x 10 cm for the short edges of the border and two strips 57 x 4 in/145 x 10 cm for the long edges of the border

1 Use ½-in/1-cm seam allowances throughout. Referring to page 206, with right sides together, pin and stitch a total of nine rows of five squares, alternating colors. Make five rows starting with a blue square and four rows starting with a pink square. Press all the seams on the rows starting with a blue square in one direction, and all the seams on the rows starting with a pink square in the opposite direction.

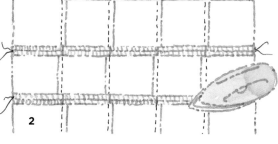

2 With right sides together, pin and stitch the rows of squares together. Press the seams open along the rows.

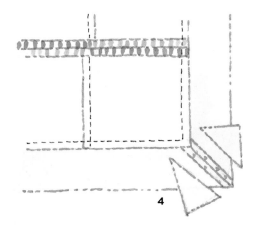

3 With right sides together, pin one long border strip to each long edge of the patchwork, making sure the strips overlap the patchwork by the same amount at each end. Stitch in place, starting and stopping ½ in/1 cm in from the ends. In the same way, attach the shorter border strips to the top and bottom edges of the patchwork.

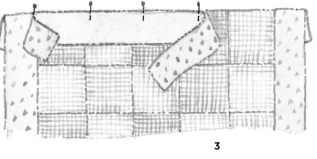

4 Lay the quilt top right side down on a flat surface to miter the corners. At each corner, fold the end of one border strip diagonally to the outer edge and press. Cut away the excess fabric to exactly ½ in/1 cm from the fold. Do the same with the end of the adjacent border strip. Pin the cut edges with right sides together and stitch along the fold line. Repeat with the other three corners. Press the seams open. Press the quilt top thoroughly.

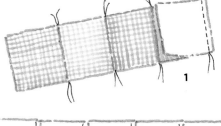

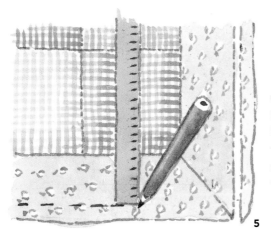

5 Lay the quilt on a flat surface to trim around the whole top. You need to be very accurate about this, cutting the border to precisely 2½ in/6 cm wide all around. Do this using a ruler, measuring out and marking 2½ in/6 cm at regular intervals. Using your ruler, join up the marks to form a cutting line. Cut all around the edge of the quilt. Now lay the backing fabric on a flat surface. Lay the quilt top on top of it and make sure both layers are completely flat and smooth. Cut the backing fabric so it is precisely the same size as the quilt top.

5

6

6 Pin the quilt top and backing fabric with right sides together and raw edges meeting. Using a ½-in/1-cm seam allowance, stitch all around the edge, leaving a gap of three squares along the bottom edge. Clip the corners and press the seams open. Turn the quilt cover right side out through the gap in the bottom seam. Press the cover.

7 Lay the batting on a flat surface and lay the quilt cover on top of it. Trim the batting to precisely the size of the cover and then trim a further ¼ in/6 mm off each side of the batting. Now, insert the batting into the quilt cover as if you were putting a duvet into a cover, making sure the corners are properly located in the corners. Hold the top corners and shake the quilt to make sure it is smooth inside. Turn in the seam allowance at the gap in the bottom edge and slipstitch to close.

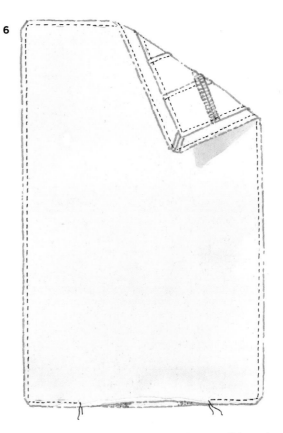

7

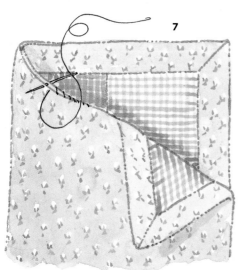

8 Lay the quilt on a flat surface and use quilting pins at the corner of each square to secure the batting inside the quilt. Using a zipper foot, stitch along the join between the border and the patchwork. This is called "stitch in the ditch." Finally, using embroidery thread (floss), make a neat cross-stitch at the corner of each patch, also creating a cross on the underside (see opposite).

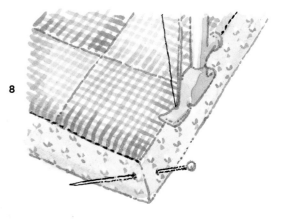

8

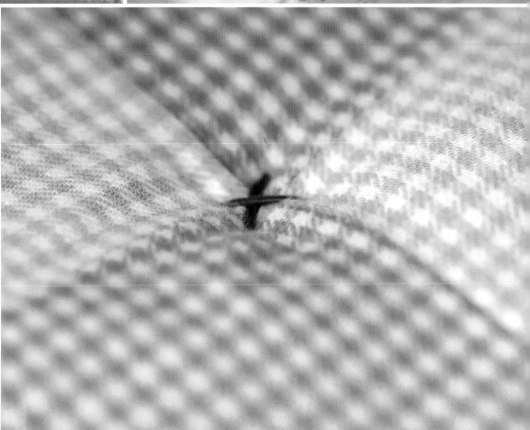

above This pretty pink and blue patchwork quilt will work equally well in a baby boy's or a baby girl's nursery.

above right The quilt is made from a trio of coordinating fabrics in soft brushed cotton that is gentle on the baby's skin.

right A simple embroidered cross at each corner of the patches is enough to anchor the batting, adding interest to the finished quilt.

PATTERNS AND TEMPLATES

cut here for lining

cut here for bag

place on fold

TOTE BAG SIDE

cut 2 shorter pieces in main fabric
cut 2 longer pieces in lining fabric

TOTE BAG

See page 104

Have the templates enlarged by 270 percent at a photocopy shop, then fold a piece of dot-and-cross paper or newspaper in half and place the dotted line of the template on the fold. Cut out and unfold for full-sized pattern pieces.

place on fold

**TOTE BAG
TOP BAND**

cut 2 in lining/contrast fabric

cut 1 larger oval in main fabric
cut 1 larger oval in lining fabric
cut 1 smaller oval in buckram

TOTE BAG BASE

PAJAMA PANTS (opposite)
See page 110

Have the top part of the pattern pieces enlarged by 400 percent in sections onto pieces of tabloid size paper at a photocopy shop. Tape the sections together, then cut out the whole of both pattern pieces in dot-and-cross paper or newspaper.

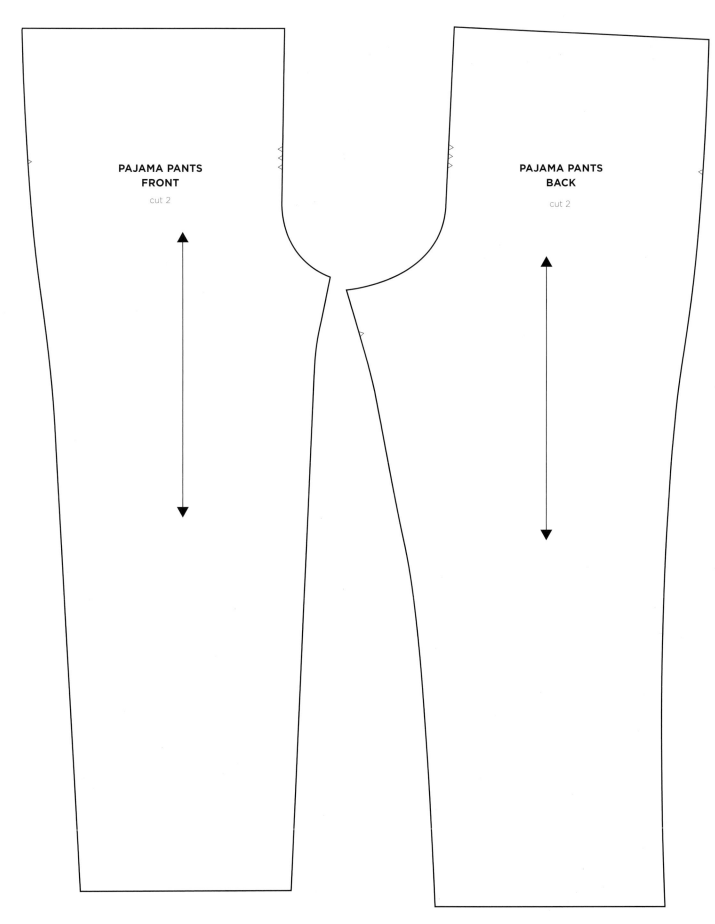

PAJAMA PANTS
FRONT
cut 2

PAJAMA PANTS
BACK
cut 2

CAMISOLE

See page 116

Have the templates
enlarged by 400 percent
at a photocopy shop,
then cut out the pattern
pieces in dot-and-cross
paper or newspaper.

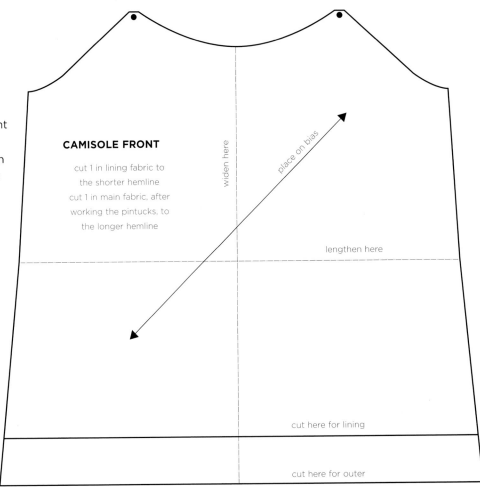

CAMISOLE FRONT

cut 1 in lining fabric to
the shorter hemline
cut 1 in main fabric, after
working the pintucks, to
the longer hemline

widen here

place on bias

lengthen here

cut here for lining

cut here for outer

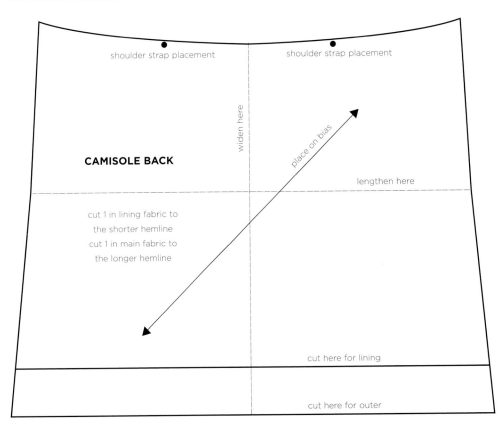

shoulder strap placement   shoulder strap placement

widen here

place on bias

lengthen here

CAMISOLE BACK

cut 1 in lining fabric to
the shorter hemline
cut 1 in main fabric to
the longer hemline

cut here for lining

cut here for outer

SWEETEST SUNDRESS

See page 123

Have the front and back bodice templates enlarged by 200 percent at a photocopy shop. Trace them onto dot-and-cross paper or newspaper and cut out the pattern pieces.

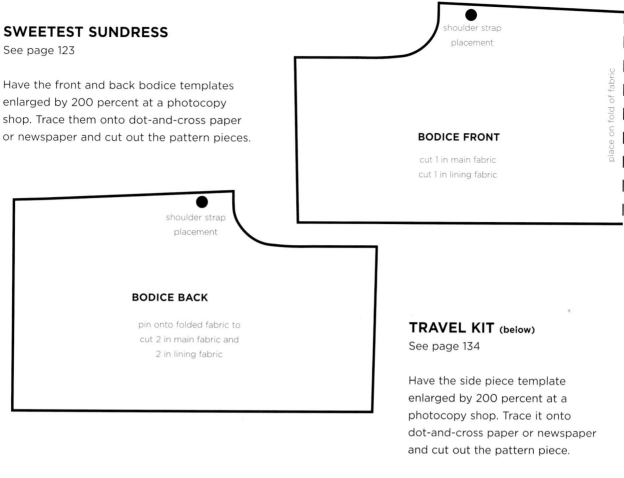

shoulder strap
placement

BODICE FRONT

cut 1 in main fabric

cut 1 in lining fabric

place on fold of fabric

shoulder strap
placement

BODICE BACK

pin onto folded fabric to
cut 2 in main fabric and
2 in lining fabric

TRAVEL KIT (below)

See page 134

Have the side piece template enlarged by 200 percent at a photocopy shop. Trace it onto dot-and-cross paper or newspaper and cut out the pattern piece.

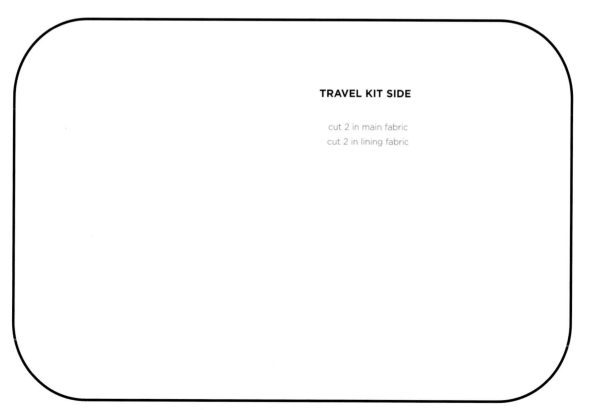

TRAVEL KIT SIDE

cut 2 in main fabric
cut 2 in lining fabric

DRAWSTRING BAG

See page 149

The shoe and shoe detail templates are shown at 100 percent. Trace them onto dot-and-cross paper or newspaper and cut them out.

Fuse fabric bond onto the wrong side of your chosen appliqué fabrics before cutting out the shapes.

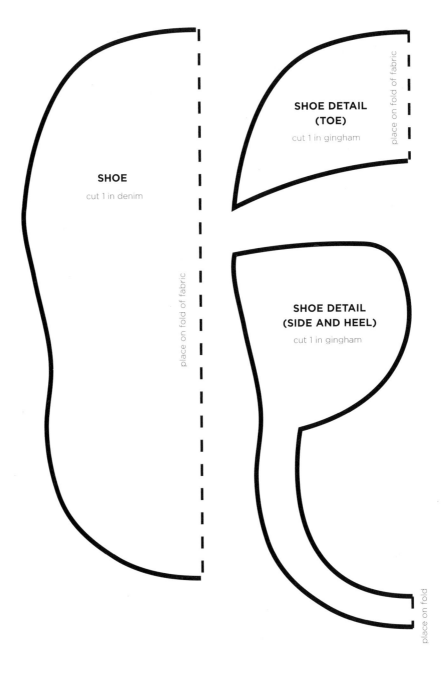

SHOE

cut 1 in denim

place on fold of fabric

SHOE DETAIL (TOE)

cut 1 in gingham

place on fold of fabric

SHOE DETAIL (SIDE AND HEEL)

cut 1 in gingham

place on fold

CUSTOMIZED T-SHIRT
See page 163

Have the master frill template enlarged by 340 percent at a photocopy shop and then cut out a separate template for each of the three frills from dot-and-cross paper or newspaper.

To draw your own master frill template, fold a large piece of paper (at least 15-in/45-cm square) in half to find the center, then open it out again. Using a thumb tack, fix one end of a piece of string to this center point. Measure 3½ in/9 cm along the string and attach a pencil at this point. Use this as a compass to draw a semicircle with a diameter of 7 in/18 cm. Repeat in the same way to draw three more semicircles with the pencil attached 8 in/20 cm,

10¾ in/27 cm and 13¼ in/33 cm from the center point. Cut out the largest curve, which is 9½ in/24 cm deep. Draw a wedge measuring 1½ in/3.5 cm from one straight edge along the inner edge and 3¾ in/ 9.5 cm along the outer edge, and trim the paper along this line. This is the master template from which you will cut a paper pattern for each of the frills. First, recut the master on a separate piece of paper to make a pattern for the largest frill. Now, trim the master template back along the 10¾-in/27-cm line and use it to make a pattern for the middle frill, which is 7 in/18 cm deep. Finally, trim the master template back along the 8-in/20-cm line and use it to make a pattern for the smallest frill, which is 4¼ in/11 cm deep.

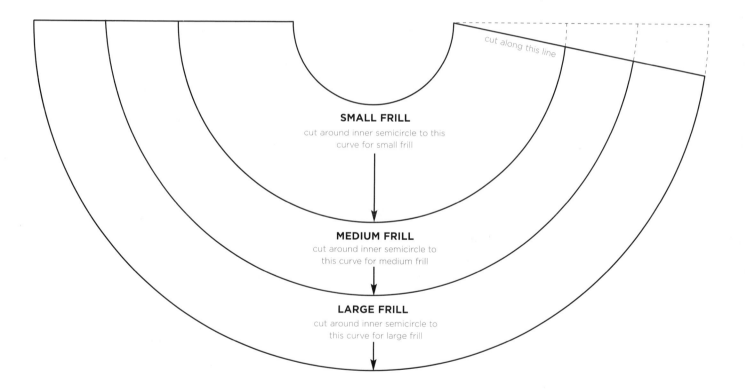

cut along this line

SMALL FRILL
cut around inner semicircle to this
curve for small frill

MEDIUM FRILL
cut around inner semicircle to
this curve for medium frill

LARGE FRILL
cut around inner semicircle to
this curve for large frill

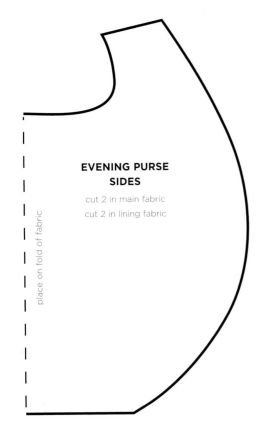

place on fold of fabric

**EVENING PURSE
SIDES**

cut 2 in main fabric
cut 2 in lining fabric

place on fold of fabric

place on fold of fabric

**EVENING PURSE
GUSSET**

cut 1 in main fabric
cut 1 in lining fabric

EVENING PURSE
See page 175

Have the purse side piece and gusset piece enlarged by 200 percent at a photocopy shop. Trace them onto dot-and-cross paper or newspaper and then cut out the pattern pieces.

BIAS-CUT DRAWSTRING SKIRT

See page 188

Have the skirt template enlarged by 400 percent in sections onto pieces of tabloid size paper at a photocopy shop. Tape the sections together to make up the full-size template, trace it onto dot-and-cross paper or newspaper, and cut out the pattern piece.

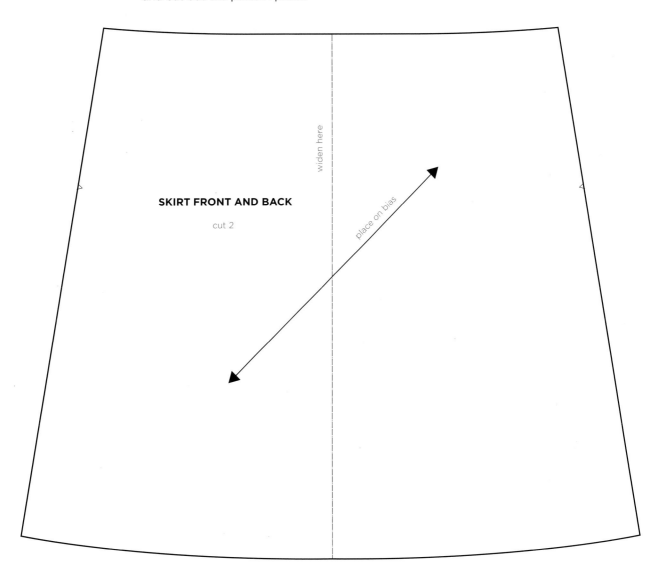

SKIRT FRONT AND BACK

cut 2

widen here

place on bias

CHILD'S CRAFT APRON

See page 179

Have the templates enlarged by 270 percent in sections onto pieces of tabloid size paper at a photocopy shop. Tape the sections together to make up the full templates, then cut out the whole of each pattern piece from dot-and-cross paper or newspaper. For the front, fold a piece of dot-and-cross paper in half and place the dotted line of the template on the fold, then cut it out to create the whole pattern piece.

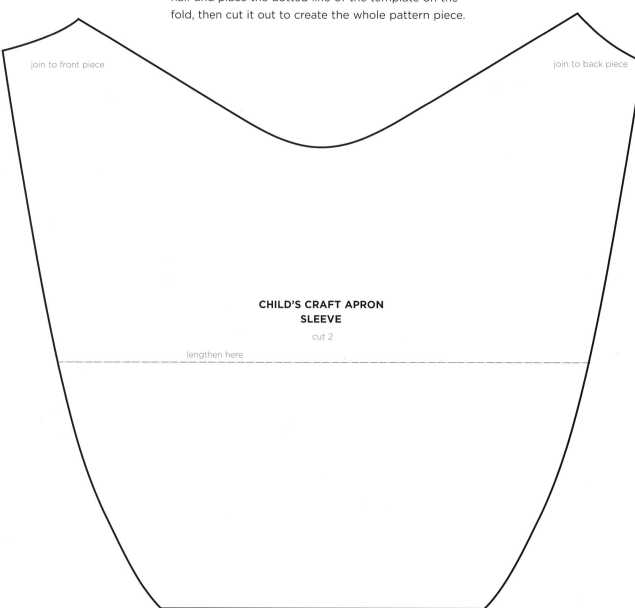

join to front piece

join to back piece

**CHILD'S CRAFT APRON
SLEEVE**

cut 2

lengthen here

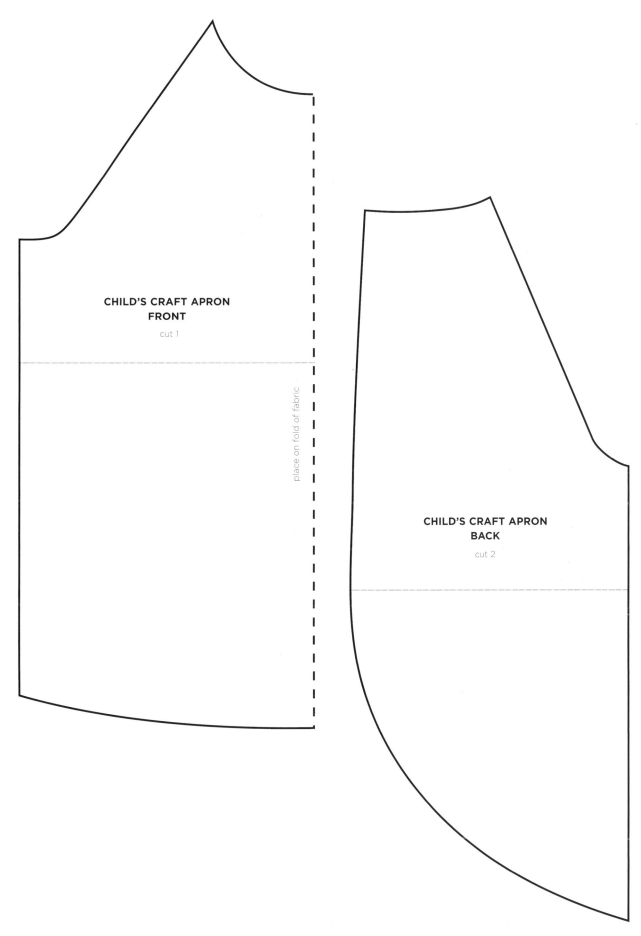

CHILD'S CRAFT APRON
FRONT

cut 1

place on fold of fabric

CHILD'S CRAFT APRON
BACK

cut 2

INDEX

A
acetate 82, 84
acrylic 82
adapting patterns 58–59
air-soluble pens 18
alpaca 84
Angora wool 84
appliqué 177–83
aprons
    child's craft apron 179–83
    vintage apron 164–67

B
baby cord 74
baby quilt 208–11
backstitches 48
bags
    drawstring bag 149–51
    tote bag 104–06
ballpoint needles 14
basting 47
batik 72, 84
batiste 84
batting 68
beading needles 14
beads 34, 172
    beaded fringing 30
    beaded trim 30
betweens (needles) 14
bias binding 96–97, 152–53, 182
bias-cut 11, 56, 187
    skirts 188–91
bias-hem facing 187
blanket stitch 48–49
bodices, gathering 123–25
bolsters 156–58
bouclé 84
box cushions 192–95
braid 30
    applying 168–71
    golden-toned braid 30
    sari braid 33
brocade 70, 72, 84
broderie anglaise 84
broderie perse 178
buckles 34
buckram 68, 84
bugles 34
bulk, reducing in seams 94
bust measurements 54
button elastic 22
buttonholes 138–39
buttons
    covering 195
    as embellishment 172, 173
    evening purse 175–76
    sewing on 137
    types of 25

C
cambric 84
camisole 116–19
canvas 84
carbon paper, dressmaker's 18, 62
care of fabrics 68
cashmere 84
casings 148–51
cavalry twill 84
chalk, tailor's 18
challis 84
chambray 74, 84
chenille 84
chiffon 84
    chiffon roses 30

child's craft apron 179–83
chintz 84–85
collars 99
contouring garments 113–15
cording 154–58
corduroy 85
corners
    mitered corners 196–202
    trimming to reduce bulk 94
cotton
    cotton union 75, 103
    in mixed-fiber fabrics 82
    ribbon 33
    types of 66, 74–75
cotton thread 21
crepe 85
crepe de chine 85
crewel needles 14
crotch measurements 54
cuffs 99
curved hems 186–87
curved needles 14
curved seams
    pressing 99
    reducing bulk 94
    stitching 93–94
cutting mat, self-healing 18, 203, 204
cutting out patterns 61

D
damask 70, 72, 78, 85
    cotton damask 75
    drapes fabric 82
    wool damask 81
darning needles 14
darts 113–15
    contoured darts 115
    single-pointed darts 114
denim 85
devoré 85
dimity 85
discharge printing 72
dobbies 72
dobby loom 70, 78, 85
double-folded hems 184–85
doupion 85
drape 68
drapes 11
    classic drapes 126–28
    fabric 66
drawstrings 148–51
    drawstring bag 149–51
dresses
    ruffles on 160, 163
    sundress 123–25
dressmaker's carbon paper 18
dressmaker's pins 14
dressmaker's shears 17
drill 85
duck 85
dyeing fabrics 163

E
easing 122
Elastane 82, 87
elastic 22
embellishment 172–83
embroidery
    embroidered patterns 72
    embroidered silk 79
    needles 14
    scissors 17
    sewing machines 38
    stitches 48

enclosed seams 107–09
evening purse 174–76
eyelets 29, 147

F
fabric 66–87
    batting 68
    care of 68
    choosing 11, 66–68
    construction 70–71
    cotton 74–75
    cutting out 61
    drape 68
    dyeing 163
    fabric pencils and pens 18, 62
    fashion fabrics 66
    furnishing 66
    grain 56
    interlining 68, 200
    lining 68
    linen 76–77
    patterned 72
    pile fabrics 98
    pinning 61
    preparing 56
    pressing 98–99
    quantities for patchwork 203
    silk 78–79
    striped 56
    synthetic fibers 82
    weave 81
    with naps 60
    wool 80–81
facings
    mitered corners 197
fashion fabrics 66–68
fastenings 22–29, 129–51
    buttons 24, 137
    buttonholes 138–42
    drawstring bag 148–51
    elastics 22
    eyelets 147
    hooks and eyes 29, 144
    jeans buttons 25, 147
    no-sew fasteners 147
    press studs 29, 143
    secret fastenings 22
    snaps 29, 146, 147
    studs 29, 143
    tape fasteners 144–46
    zippers 26, 129–34
feather trims 30
felt 70
fibers, synthetic 82
finishing 184–202
    bias-hem facing 187–91
    curved hem 186–87
    double-folded hem 184–85
    hand-rolled hem 185
    finishing stitches 48–49
    mitered corners 196–202
flannel 85
flannelette 85
flat-fell seams 108
French seams 107, 112
frills 159–67
fringes 30
furnishing fabrics 66

G
gabardine 85
gathers and gathering 120–25
    easing 122

gathering into a waistband or
    bodice 121, 123–25
    hand gathering 120
    machine gathering 120
    pressing 99
gauge, sewing 18
georgette 85
gingham 72, 75, 85
gingham ribbon 33
goblet heading tape 126, 128
golden-toned braid 30
grading 94
grain, fabric 56
grosgrain ribbon 33, 85, 191

H
hand sewing
    hand appliqué 178
    hand gathering 120
    hand-rolled hems 185
    stitches 46–49
heading tape 126, 128
hems and hemming
    curved hems 186–87
    double-folded 184–85
    hand-rolled 185
    hand stitches 48
    invisible hem stitches 49
    machine stitches 49
    mitered corners 196–202
    stitching 185
herringbone 70, 77, 80
hip measurements 54
Hong Kong finish 97
hook-and-loop tape 22, 145
hooks and eyes 29, 144
    hook-and-eye tape 22, 144–45
houndstooth check 72, 85
household pins 14

I
ikat 72, 85
interlining 68, 200
interlock 85
ironing fabrics 98–99

J
jacquard fabrics 85–86
    jacquard looms 70, 85, 86
    jacquard weaves 72
    preparing 56
    silk jacquard 78
    woven wool 81
jacquard ribbon 33
jeans buttons 25, 147
jersey 70, 86

K
knit 70, 71, 81
knots, tying in thread 46

L
lawn 86
linen 76–77, 82
lingerie 107
linings 68
Lycra 82, 87

M
machines 36–43
    accessories 40
    appliqué 177
    basic stitches 49
    buttonholes 138–39